Jenny Hartley read English and American Literature at the University of Kent, and gained her M.A. and Ph. D. from the University of Essex. She currently lectures at the Roehampton Institute of Higher Education, where she teaches courses on women writers, images of women and the literature of war. Virago also publishes her anthology, *Hearts Undefeated: Women's Writing of the Second World War* (1994). Jenny Hartley lives in London with her husband and two sons.

MILLIONS LIKE US

British Women's Fiction of the Second
World War

Jenny Hartley

A Special Edition for **PAST TIMES**®, Oxford, England

A *Virago* Book

Published by Virago Press 1997

A CIP catalogue record for this book is available from the British Library

ISBN 1 86049 080 8

Typeset by Solidus (Bristol) Limited
Printed and bound in Great Britain by Clays Ltd, St Ives plc

Virago
A Division of
Little, Brown and Company (UK)
Brettenham House
Lancaster Place
London WC2E 7EN

FOR NICK

CONTENTS

and intensities of emotion in Mollie Panter-Downes and Elizabeth Taylor; Elizabeth Bowen's stories of invasion and menace; historical fiction and the uses of other wars, Daphne du Maurier; the shame of the months of Munich camouflaged and rewritten in Virginia Woolf's *Between the Acts*.

Whatever you are these days, you are rather more so. That's one thing I've discovered about this war.

Elizabeth Bowen, 'Pink May', *Collected Stories*, 1980

INTRODUCTION

Their time sat in the third place at their table.
Elizabeth Bowen, *The Heat of the Day*, 1949

During the present war women have contributed more than ever
before to the life of the nation.
Elizabeth Dunn, 'Women's Minds', *Spectator*, 1943

Millions Like Us is the title of a film made in 1943 to encourage women
into the war factories. The film emphasised women's new and vital roles
in the collective enterprise of wartime Britain. The Second World War
brought hardship into women's lives at work and home, but it also invited
them into the public arena and gave them value, status and pay. Contemporary observers were in no doubt about what J.B. Priestley called the
'tremendous social and economic upheaval' taking place in women's
lives.[1] The fiction of the time bears its unmistakable imprint. Whether a
woman was writing about a fourteenth-century convent or a seventeenth-century prostitute, the war inevitably added its own particular accent.
The result is a startling and intense legacy, a body of work which offers an
alternative literature of war, as women responded to their new world with
a literature of citizenship.

Barbara Cartland called her wartime autobiography *The Years of
Opportunity*: 'opportunity' might seem to be an unusual word for war,
especially from a woman. To appreciate its significance we need to see what

lay behind the Second World War. The huge loss of life in the First World War meant that few were exempt from mourning, and the historian David Cannadine sees inter-war Britain as a nation obsessed with death.[2] The great public institutions and ceremonies of grief – Armistice Day with its poppies and two minutes silence, the Cenotaph and the Tomb of the Unknown Warrior – all date from the period immediately after the First World War. Through public grief the nation could be united: 'the great multitude bowed its head,' reported *The Times* on the effect of the Armistice Day service in 1920; 'we were made one people, participants in one act of remembrance.'[3] The other inheritance from the First World War was a powerful collection of war literature, most of it anti-war, certainly in its cumulative effect. These were two liabilities for a nation entering another war. In order to fight effectively a country must be united, but being 'made one people' (as *The Times* put it) by bereavement, would not be helpful. Sacrifice had been at the heart of First World War rhetoric, and had been taken to task in the ensuing literature. Class had also had a strong presence, sometimes persisting even beyond death: on some First World War memorials officers are listed above other ranks.

Second World War rhetoric needed new quarters and new flags. Work replaced sacrifice as the rallying call, or rather 'toil' as it was transformed in Churchill's ennobling poetry. His vocabulary of heroic labour also embraced sweat, struggle, exertion and hard roads; he liked to refer to war as 'our task' and 'the job'.[4] The communion of grief and the divisiveness of the class system are to be replaced, countered and healed by a new togetherness, the collectivity of the People's War. The war will unite all in communal effort: men, women and children, old and young, combatants and non-combatants. All are enlisted in the fight against fascism and women are more directly involved than in the previous war. This shift in attitudes is apparent from a comparison between two posters: the First World War's 'Women of Britain Say – "GO!" ' uses women as images to mobilise men; the Second World War's 'Women of Britain Come into the Factories' speaks directly to women in an open-armed invitation to join the war effort. Women's fiction was also going to have to change. In 1945 the novelist Winifred Peck characterised the fiction of the inter-war years as a middle-class 'fiction of self-pity', and self-pity, even if 'more or less humorous' and confined to 'minor trials',[5] is not attractive in wartime. In adjusting to their times, women wrote an exciting new chapter in literary history.

The historian Peter Hennessy points out that 'The Second World War and Britain's part in it is one of the most heavily ploughed patches of our history',[6] but little attention has been given until recently to women's fiction from the period.[7] It is generally acknowledged, however, that reading and writing occupied central roles in wartime life. 'The demand for books seems to be unlimited', observed the Archbishop of York in 1945,[8] and as early as November 1939 *Good Housekeeping* was telling its readers, 'You need books more than ever now'. By September 1940 the magazine was inviting its readers to 'Enjoy the permitted luxury of a good book', suggesting that fiction was one of the few luxuries left to the conscientious good housekeeper of the day. Domestic fiction could have a quasi-maternal role in easing the more tractable problems of wartime life: reviewing Helen Ashton's *Tadpole Hall* in 1941, Myfanwy Piper welcomed it as 'another of those comforting library books . . . about nice people dealing with problems we can all appreciate'.[9] More urgently, books could help to order a shifting world. People needed to make sense and shape of a world which was suddenly losing both as the bombs fell. 'Everyone here, as is known,' wrote Elizabeth Bowen to her American audience in 1945,

> read more: and what was sought in books – old books, new books – was the communicative touch of personal life. To survive, not only physically but spiritually, was essential. People whose homes had been blown up went to infinite lengths to assemble bits of themselves – broken ornaments, odd shoes, torn scraps of the curtains that had hung in a room – from the wreckage. In the same way, they assembled themselves from stories and poems, from their memories, from one another's talk.[10]

Readers attempting to assemble their scattered selves could turn to the ordered ways of the past. *War and Peace* was understandably popular – although not always with women, as a librarian reported in 1943:

> One educated woman asked me the other day if 'a woman could read' *War and Peace*, . . . so widespread is the alarm with which women regard such a novel.[11]

Trollope, the British classic most often mentioned, may also have been more popular with men than women, as a *Times* Leader in the autumn of 1939 suggests in its casting of the novel as paterfamilias:

> Now is the time for the head of the family to set about reading aloud in the grand manner. What is required is a good long novel which shall continue, if not 'for the duration,' at any rate for many and many an evening. Without presuming to dictate it may be said that TROLLOPE is excellent for the purpose.[12]

Women often mentioned Jane Austen (the second favourite of the war), with more affection. 'I've re-read her three times since the war began,' says Rose Fairlaw in Winifred Peck's 1942 novel *House-Bound*. For Janet Teissier du Cros, living in Occupied France, 'it was Jane Austen who saved my soul'. She explained why:

> Jane Austen lives, and makes you live, in a luminous world whose characters are never evil and where even the vulgar are civilised . . . You had only to establish a link at any point between Jane Austen's England and the world Hitler was forging to know that Hitler's world was a nightmare which could never last. My favourite link was to imagine Miss Bates being roused from bed at five in the morning by the Gestapo.[13]

Charlotte Yonge also had a devoted following;[14] and the *Times Literary Supplement* Novel of the Week on 10 August 1940 was a new edition of Elizabeth Gaskell's *Cranford*, beautifully illustrated by Joan Hassall. A woman reading *Wuthering Heights* during a 'very bad blitz' wrote to her husband:

> I enjoy it as much as ever before. This is strange, for though I still think it one of the world's greatest novels, it is wild and formless and unrealistic. But perhaps that is why I enjoy it now – because it echoes my state of mind.[15]

For other readers the past brought no solace: Rosamond Lehmann reacted to the 'broad, romantic, expanding scene' of nineteenth-century fiction with more pain than pleasure.[16] Writing in 1941, Lehmann remarked, 'It's queer how one's tastes have altered during this last year: at least mine have.' She had two young children at the time, and the book she recommended was Sylvia Anthony's *The Child's Discovery of Death*. So war could urge the reader to the page, and it could determine what the reader chose, but it could also intervene between the reader and the page. Diana Hopkinson, whose husband was serving overseas, noticed the pressures of war on her reading habits:

> I *rush* through books now, particularly novels, and try to seize the contents quickly. I think this is because I am so impatient to know about the next development of the war – and the end of the story – *our* story, that, symbolically, I hurry on to the conclusion of a book.[17]

Reading about the present war could use fiction more directly to give shape and meaning to fractured wartime lives, and books set in the war were popular. Our village in wartime, complete with Home Guard, rations and evacuees, was a popular theme, as was the refugee novel.[18] But readers also wanted to look beyond the village, as the list of books taken out of the lending library in Stella Gibbons' *The Rich House* (1941, 66) suggests:

> All that day people came into the library and went away again with their choice: Miss Gaye with *Italy and the New Europe*; Colonel Bracebridge with *Europe – Whither?*; Mrs Ullathorne with *Fallen Bastions*, and Mr Cannondale with *Disgrace Abounding*; Miss Robinson with *Europe: Can it Survive?* and Miss Brown with *Can America Stay Out?*; Mr Hapgood with *Insanity Fair*, and Major Morrison with *Africa: Unity or Collapse?*
>
> The Island Race, indeed.

Opinion among reviewers was divided about whether they wanted war in their fiction or not. By 1942 some had had enough:

> The evacuee theme has, by this time, been worn almost to shreds, and the very words on the jackets of our lighter novels has been enough to depress the war-sick reader.[19]

Others rebuked novelists for ignoring the war:

> This is a story of the year 1940, . . . it is faintly irritating to find these young men and women pursuing the intricate round of their love affairs entirely unaffected by what was going on around them until they were actually hit by a bomb.[20]

Reviewers were quick to catch the spirit of the People's War: in 1940 Margery Allingham found Rachel Ferguson's snobbish *A Footman for the Peacock* 'curiously insensitive',[21] and the *Times Literary Supplement*'s reviewers warmed to novels about 'ordinary' English families.

Much was read during the war, much was written, and much of it has disappeared: the unpublished all too easily, and the published too. Appearing in short print-runs and unattractive war-economy editions, these books were the first candidates for salvage and jumble. The figures for the decline in new editions are well known,[22] but even the leanest of the war years saw the publication of over a thousand new adult fiction titles a year, and the *Times Literary Supplement* found plenty of new novels to review each week.[23] On February 6 1943, for example, twelve new novels and six new detective stories were reviewed, and publishers were advertising many others. This compares with similar figures for 1937: ten new novels and five detective stories on February 6 in that year. Stevie Smith was reviewing as many as fourteen new books a month for *Modern Woman* during the war;[24] so new fiction was being published, but always in short print-runs. The ensuing famine drove readers to their local libraries. By 1942 to 1943, according to the cultural historian Steve Chibnall, 'library borrowing figures were increasing, particularly for novels'.[25] This demand must have come from women, since 'men . . . rarely take the trouble to look at ordinary fiction', as Elizabeth Dunn explained when she transferred *War and Peace* to the non-fiction shelves in her library, where she thought it would have more chance of being read.[26] Women, then, were reading more, and they were writing as much as they had before. Although many grumbled that the war made novel-writing impossible, some writers thrived. Agatha Christie noted the increase in her 'wartime output':

> I produced an *incredible* amount of stuff during those years. I suppose it was because there were no distractions of a social nature; one practically never went out in the evenings.[27]

From the outset literature was conscripted into the war effort. By 1940, the art historian David Mellor notes, 'poetry, literature and the landscape are presented as the values and the very identity which Britain is fighting for,' through 'Ministry of Information propaganda exhibitions such as "Books and Freedom" '.[28] This sort of propaganda helped to ensure the freedom of the press from censorship: the only fixed prohibition on fiction was against passing information to the enemy. Fiction was also freer than either films or women's magazines from the pressures of propaganda. The cinema was, the media historian Keith Williams observes, 'inextricably linked with MOI bureaucracy',[29] and skirted round such subjects as illegitimate motherhood and the unpopularity of factory work,[30] topics which were tackled frankly by women's novels of the period. Women's magazines were also directly harnessed into the war-machine, through a committee of editors and government officials, 'to ensure that official "lines" on matters related to women were put over as powerfully as possible'.[31] Nobody at the MOI was responsible for novels; they had, according to the historian of the People's War, Angus Calder, 'a Scrutiny Division which aimed to read through everything published in Britain; but the censorship itself, under this wary eye, remained voluntary'.[32]

With the importance of a free literature enshrined as a democratic principle, the novel's freedom was secure: Nazi book-burning was a potent image. It was a paradox that this was a time when the novels which were being produced were consistently undervalued and denigrated. The impetus for such criticism came from the premature hoisting of the First World War standard, with inevitable consequences. As soon as war broke out in 1939 critics were enquiring as to the whereabouts of the war poets; unsurprisingly they were disappointed. Although some critics later became more enthusiastic – E.M. Forster found 'the 1941 lists are much better than could be expected'[33] – the consensus was that 'war is peculiarly destructive to the novelist',[34] and that this was not fiction's finest hour. By December 1941 Tom Harrisson, co-founder of the Mass-Observation social survey organisation, was dismissing 95 per cent of the fiction he had read for his *Horizon* review of 'War Books' as a 'cataract of tripe'. Much of this fiction was by women, and Harrisson was particularly exercised by the 'right-wing' attitudes which he saw gathering strength. Novelists had, Harrisson thought, chosen the wrong side in the People's War. Three years later, on the other side of the Atlantic, the critic Diana Trilling also took exception to the conservative nature of contemporary fiction, as 'novels put themselves at the service of established institutions' and endlessly celebrated ideals of 'domestic strength'.[35] Perhaps Harrisson's expectations were too high in asking novelists to toe such a narrow political line. The war would manifest itself in diverse ways, and it would take some time to do so. Harrisson also chose easy targets – he despatched 'lady novelists' *en bloc*. He omitted from his review *Between the Acts*, which was published in July 1941 and into its third impression by September of that year, and other lesser known but interesting novels, such as *Farewell Leicester Square* (1941), Betty Miller's sensitive study of anti-semitism. It was unfortunate, too, that Harrisson's brief did not extend to the short story, acknowledged by critics to be in strong form during the war, as he could have then included work by Rosamond Lehmann and Elizabeth Bowen.

Diana Trilling's negative critique addressed different material from Harrisson's: she concentrated upon American rather than British fiction. It is important to remember that the differences between American and British war experiences and culture were much more visible at the time than they may seem now.[36] But Harrisson and Trilling were not alone; and women's writing suffered in particular from denigration. It was disparaged by Ethel Mannin ('We seem to be a little short of distinction on the feminine side'[37]), and almost completely ignored by John Lehmann in his 1940 survey, *New Writing in Europe*. Some of this undervaluation of women's writing can be attributed to the prevailing attitudes of mid-twentieth-century literary criticism, attitudes aggravated by a more specific hostility to women writers in the manly zones of war. War is seen as men's stuff, in the field and on the page. Women should keep out, and Robert Graves voiced his resentment at their intrusion in an article on 'War Poetry in this War'. He regretted that in total war the soldier did not have exclusive rights to the romance of military danger. Now that he is no longer the lone soldier in the trench, 'he cannot even feel that his rendezvous with death is more certain than that of his Aunt Fanny, the firewatcher'.[38] What Aunt Fanny might write could be of little interest to Graves. In terms of what was considered appropriate war writing by men and by women, it is useful to compare two writers who were well-regarded at the time.

Richard Hillary's *The Last Enemy* (1942) was an instant bestseller, its Spitfire pilot author the perfect new warrior image for the Second World War. Hillary tells the story of his training, accident and recovery with assurance; he is happy to place himself centre-stage, solo and confident as he is in his Spitfire. The book ends on a note of heightened rhetoric: Hillary addresses 'Humanity', secure in the knowledge that he has earned the right to be taken seriously, as indeed he was. Writers such as Arthur Koestler reviewed and discussed his book.[39] Women could not hope to occupy this position; and when women writers did achieve literary recognition it was because they conformed to criteria established by a male elite. Inez Holden was one of the few women to be published by *Horizon*, the most esteemed and influential literary journal of the war.[40] Holden wrote stories and documentary novels about her war work, for which she achieved considerable acclaim. *Night Shift* was praised by J.B. Priestley as 'the most truthful and most exciting account of wartime industrial Britain',[41] and there were plans for her to collaborate on a war diary with George Orwell.[42] Holden's work is detached and dislocated, it adopts the alienated stance which Hewison and Piette identify in the male writers of the time:[43] this is why the *Horizon* set admired her, she was the man's woman writer. Fashions change. The 1980s and 1990s have preferred versions of the women's war which are upper class or glowing with sex, or both.[44] This has pushed the work published by women at the time still further into the background.

How did women writers see their role? Some of them clearly identified with the State at war, in the work they did for the Ministry of Information. Phyllis Bentley, E. Arnot Robertson, Kate O'Brien, Theodora Benson, and P.L. Travers (the creator of Mary Poppins) all worked for the Ministry; E.M. Delafield, Sylvia Thompson and Naomi Jacob were among the many writers the MOI used as speakers round the country.[45] Lettice Cooper worked for the Ministry of Health, Rebecca West worked for the BBC, and even Agatha Christie, who declined Graham Greene's invitation to do propaganda work at the beginning of the war, wrote an essay, as requested by the MOI, on detective writers for a Moscow journal.[46] Daphne du Maurier's uplifting stories of wartime courage on behalf of the Moral Rearmament Movement appeared in the press during the hard months of 1940 and sold over half a million in booklet form.[47] Most women writers seem to have had a strong sense of all their writing as war work, however unmartial the literature itself might appear. Although Helena Normanton exhorted her *Good Housekeeping* readers in September 1940 to 'boldly face the matter. Ought not every girl learn to use a rifle accurately and well?', direct physical engagement with the enemy was not a realistic option for women. Writing, however, was and Virginia Woolf was not alone in seeing hers as a 'whiff of shot in the cause of freedom'.[48] In times of war, writing is a politicised act; and Elizabeth Bowen spoke for many women when she described 'all wartime writing' as 'resistance writing'.[49] More positively, women responded to being one of 'millions like us' with a willingness to join the collective enterprise.

This reading of women's wartime fiction as a fiction of affirmation might seem to be only one half of the story which Adam Piette tells in his account of primarily male British Second World War literature: 'The public stories stressed vital resistance, public heroism, stoic good humour; the private stories are stories about broken minds, anaesthetized feelings, deep depression and loss of any sense of value.'[50] Piette's 'private stories' confirm Robert Hewison's description of the 'inner emigration' practised by alienated and disillusioned writers, again mostly male.[51] But women writers were moving in the opposite direction to their male contemporaries. Part of the 'public version' perhaps for the first time, these women were pleased to be participants and co-workers.

Some novelists saw their function quite straightforwardly as historians of the scene. Noel Streatfeild's wartime diary records 'an interesting argument about the place of the novelist in the world. I stood up for their value as historians of the age'.[52] Streatfeild went into top gear during the war; Storm Jameson thought it 'brought to life in her a spirit she may not have known was hidden in her'.[53] Her voluntary (and unpaid) work included being an air-raid warden, setting up and running a canteen service in London's East End, and speaking extensively for the Women's Voluntary Service.[54] She also published nine novels under her pseudonym of Susan Scarlett and eight in her own name, alternating between novels for children and novels for adult readers. These novels for adults recorded the downside of war on the home front: evacuation, bombing and the break-up of the family.[55] The role of historian of the age seems to have inspired Streatfeild. The war could have its benefits, as a reviewer remarked:

> It is arguable that since nearly everyone is engaged in war service of one kind or another, practically all our novelists have had experiences thrust upon them which they can no more help turning into fiction than a cow can help turning the surrounding herbage into milk.[56]

War service of many kinds penetrated the world of women's fiction, as we shall see, as did the consciousness of writing history. One of the most common characteristics of the wartime novel is its obsession with precise chronology. The date of completion is logged at the end of the novel; events set in wartime are carefully tied to a particular moment. Dates are not just background, they are the story and give the novel its meaning and identity as a text-in-history.[57]

The political responsibility of the writer in wartime was, of course, very much a live issue. Storm Jameson, who was President of the English branch of PEN, had no doubt about the necessity of the writer's engagement in war, although it need not be through writing. His first responsibility was to fight: 'If he is needed as a soldier he has no right, for the sake of preserving his special skill, to run away.'[58] As a writer, he was 'not born to express himself', but should rather 'insist on the value and equality of human life' and attempt to instil confidence in the future. War was not the time for the articulation of disillusion or inner doubt. In stressing these serious responsibilities Jameson's personification of the writer was emphatically male – only in men's clothing could the image of the writer carry sufficient *gravitas*. Rebecca West, on the other hand, who also contributed to the 1941 PEN Symposium on the 'Duty of the Writer', felt that writers 'must turn away from political work'; she believed the duty of the writer was rather to the truths of the imagination.[59] Phyllis Bentley succinctly summed up the double-bind in her piece on 'Propaganda and the Temptations of the Writer': 'It appears that we are false to life if we don't write political propaganda, and false to art if we do'.[60] She argued that the objectivity of the writer was a dangerous illusion; a writer could not but be implicated, even if he or she tried to remain aloof: 'Not to choose is, after all, a rejection' (56).

Virginia Woolf also had the responsibility of the writer in mind when she addressed the Workers Education Association in Brighton in May 1940, but she was setting her sights further into the future, towards the post-war creation of a classless society. It was with this end in mind that she radically proposed the writings of 'millions like us' as a political weapon. The 'new order in Europe', a world of 'equal opportunities', which politicians were currently heralding as the goal of the war, provided Woolf's utopian framework.[61] She urged her WEA audience, the 'we' who are not the male public-school elite, to become more critical readers and to appropriate the culture of the nation:

> in future we are not going to leave writing to be done for us by a small class
> of well-to-do young men who have only a pinch, a thimbleful of experience
> to give us. We are going to add our own experience, to make our own
> contribution. (124)

'Reading omnivorously' as well as writing – Woolf encouraged her audience to 'write daily; write freely' – would help bring down class barriers. 'Commoners and outsiders like ourselves,' she told her audience, must make literature 'our own country'. 'We need not wait till the end of the war. We can begin now' (124). Two years earlier, in *Three Guineas*, Woolf had imagined a Society of Outsiders, formed to prevent war, and to work 'by their own methods for liberty, equality and peace'.[62] With the advent of war Woolf's political sensibilities drew her from the outside to the inside; and in 'The Leaning Tower' she identified herself with the 'we' of the People's War.[63]

While women writers felt part of wartime Britain, their co-option into the war-machine had two inescapable qualifications. War, although potentially emancipatory for women, could never be their congenial habitat. It brought separation, suffering and death; and its values and codes of behaviour were inimical to many women. Secondly, women's place in the public ranks of war was always seen as temporary – 'for the duration' – as feminist historians have emphasised.[64] This could prove a bar to total commitment, and some of the fiction does hold back. While contemporary observers celebrated female competence, novelists were less whole-hearted. Women in novels work hard, but their work is conducted slightly off-stage; they have a career on the side. Pamela

Frankau's Caroline Seward is complimented for ' "making good in the Army" ' in *The Willow Cabin* (1949, 255); she progresses from private to corporal and officer, but her love affair is much more engrossing. Elizabeth Bowen tells us that Stella Rodney is employed in 'exacting, not unimportant work' in *The Heat of the Day* (1949, 26), but it is secret so we never hear about it, and Stella seems to have no work colleagues. The demanding life of a single mother in wartime is downplayed by Rosamond Lehmann in her story 'Wonderful Holidays' (1944–1945) in which Mrs Ritchie's slightly absent-minded efficiency is portrayed as the normal stuff of wartime life, what women must do in order to keep that life going.

'For the duration': women's fiction has often conformed to this paradigm, whereby the heroine is allotted a limited space for ordeal or pleasure before the doors of marriage close. This temporary period is marked by its relative freedom, and this holds true for the wartime novel too. Women's war literature is a literature of diversity and plurality. It comes out of a culture which developed practices of multiple female imagery, as cultural historians Pat Kirkham and Antonia Lant have shown,[65] encouraging women to be more than one thing at once, both worker and home-maker, mother and tool-maker. But this was to be understood as a strictly temporary phenomenon. When a writer suggested otherwise she tended to be misunderstood. Daphne du Maurier's play *The Years Between* (1944) shows a woman developing in independence when her MP husband is presumed killed on active service. She is elected MP in his place, and successfully manages both her home and career. When her husband returns from his secret mission he resents the new woman he finds.[66] Du Maurier admitted the play was autobiographical and clearly felt for the wife who finally opts for self-sacrifice. Audiences, however, found the wife unsympathetic and chose to admire the husband instead.[67]

The woman writer in wartime made her appearance early in the fiction of the period. Martha Gellhorn's novel, *A Stricken Field*, was written during 1939 and published in 1940. The novel tells the story of the accomplished American journalist, Mary Douglas, whose experiences in Prague follow Gellhorn's own in October 1938.[68] The Nazis are consolidating their power in the city, and Mary fails in her attempts to help her refugee friend Rita. In the book's most agonising scene Rita hears her lover being tortured to death in the room above her; at the end of the book Rita herself faces persecution and death. Mary also fails on a larger scale, when the meeting she has set up between the Czech Prime Minister, a British diplomat and a French general fails to secure a short period of grace for thousands of persecuted refugees in Prague. The atmosphere of tension, apprehension and fear is brilliantly evoked in this 'dark story' as Gellhorn called it,[69] as is the helplessness of the journalist. Rita says that the refugees' only chance is ' "pressure from England and France and America" ', and she implores Mary and her colleagues to write and ' "make an opinion in your countries" '. Mary agrees without enthusiasm, ' "you had better not count too much on the moral indignation of the world" ' (56). Some of the stories Mary is told she knows she cannot use, and some she cannot process properly:

> She wanted to place her knowledge in paragraphs (a good opening sentence? she thought), so that it would be easy to handle when she came to write it. But it did not fit in paragraphs and she could not see it, plain and informative, colourful but unimpassioned, on a page. There was no beginning, no middle, no end. (118–119)

As she witnesses the persecuted refugees and the all-pervading fear, Mary finds herself getting too involved. Her 'bright and dispassionate' journalist's armour slips (84), and to no purpose. She cannot help: 'I'm not Joan of Arc, I'm only a journalist' (177).

But – and this is what saves *A Stricken Field* from being unremittingly dark – Mary manages to bring some hope out of Prague. Although she cannot help Rita, she does help another woman, an anonymous visitor to her hotel room, by smuggling some documents out for her. Mary is pessimistic about the impact of these typewritten histories of the victims of Nazi persecution:

> I can't use it. We wouldn't be believed. We'd be accused of propaganda, the way we always are. She thought: safe people will not believe this and who will dare publish it? (286–287)

But Mary is impressed by what the nameless woman represents: the faith in the written word. This woman explains to Mary:

> 'We are still fighting, each one, and here a few of us together, and we do the only thing we can do. To tell the truth, so that it shall not disappear and be forgotten, is our fighting. In the end, we must win with such papers, in the long end, perhaps, but someday.' (284)

Mary realises that the 'bundle of papers' she agrees to smuggle is 'proof that everyone is not beaten yet', it is a tangible proof of faith in the power of the written word, of the witnessed truth. Furthermore, the form taken by the nameless woman's 'truth' is particularly appropriate for Mary, who has difficulties with cold, impersonal facts:

> Statistics were only black marks on paper to her, and if she learned that an unpronounceable Czech manufacturing town had become German it meant nothing, until she thought of the people who worked in the factories, and where would they go now: you would see them on the roads, with bulging sacks over their shoulders, walking from place to place, looking for jobs that had disappeared forever behind an unreasonable line of barbed wire: the expanding Nazi frontier. (21)

Mary, like Gellhorn herself in her unsurpassable war reporting, writes history through the individual story: this, for both of them, is where the meaning of history is to be found. So it is fitting that the documents Mary successfully smuggles out consist not of statistics and cold facts, but rather the histories of ordinary people, the three-page lives of postmen, policemen's wives and children. A journalist may not be Joan of Arc, and novels may not 'accomplish' anything, as Gellhorn agreed with one of her book's reviewers in her 1985 Afterword. But it is clear from *A Stricken Field* that the writer does have a political function in wartime: both journalist and novelist have responsibilities as messengers. Novels, as Gellhorn memorably wrote,

> don't decide the course of history or change it but they can show what history is like for people who have no choice except to live through it or die from it. (313)

Most British women writers were messengers from a war far less dramatic than Gellhorn's. They were none the less aware of their appointment with history, and keen to honour it.

British women's fiction from the Second World War is a fiction of diversity and plurality. It tells many stories, and sometimes more than one story at once. Women novelists do not immediately shed their habits of analysis and criticism, of standing at an angle to society, even when they find themselves more in tune with society, as they did during the war. And they could never be fully in tune with war. In their fiction we find a range of investigations into the meanings and implications of war, even while its necessity is accepted. For example, between the words of Virginia Woolf's *Between the Acts* we can read the shame and dishonour of the Munich months; in Elizabeth Taylor's *At Mrs Lippincote's* we can gauge the emotional suppressions necessary in wartime. Rosamond Lehmann explores the effects of illicit charisma in *The Ballad and the Source*, and Elizabeth Bowen meditates on questions of allegiance and complicity in *The Heat of the Day*. Betty Miller's *On the Side of the Angels* analyses the effects of war on the individual, and Rose Macaulay's *The World My Wilderness* takes stock of the unhappiness and devastation caused by war. Even when it is critical, this is a literature of commitment and citizenship, and this may be why it has received comparatively little attention. Feminist criticism has favoured fictions of subversion, opposition and negotiation. The heroine of the People's War does not start fires in attics; she is more likely to stay up all night fire-watching in a cold garage.[70]

In the chapters which follow I have tried to cover some of the many aspects of women's fiction from the Second World War. With a few exceptions I have confined my commentary to British women writers; other countries and cultures would need other books. Each country's experience of war is distinctive, and to bring too much together risks eliding their differences. Even so, there are large gaps; British women wrote prolifically during the war, and it is impossible to do justice to everything. There is, however, one characteristic common to almost all British women's wartime fiction, and this is the quality of intensity. What Elizabeth Bowen called the 'high-voltage current'[71] of the times has infused the literature with its electricity. 'Daylight Alert',[72] the title of E.J. Scovell's blitz poem, describes well the state of these wartime writers. The heightened awareness with which they responded to their times is still palpable today.[73]

1

BLITZ AND THE MOTHERS OF ENGLAND

War moved from the horizon to the map.
Elizabeth Bowen, *The Heat of the Day*, 1949

'Blitz makes people *better*' is how Angus Calder characterises the Myth of the Blitz,[1] and on the whole women's fiction rose to the occasion. Novels about the blitz, or with blitz episodes, appeared almost as soon as the bombs did. They often sold very well; Doris Leslie's *House in the Dust*, for example, was published and reprinted five times in 1942. In giving readers a fictional version of the blitz these novels offered models of behaviour, patterns of interpretation and sources of comfort. Common to much of the fiction is an emphasis on community, a supportive group wider than the family. This community is stabilised by the figure of the mother, anchor of England. At the same time these novels directly tackled, as women themselves had to, the realities of intensive bombing. Death and injury, pain and suffering, fear and grief are all part of women's representations of the blitz. Thus, these blitz-time novels show both history as it happens and history turning into myth.

Women were well placed as witnesses to the realities of the blitz: they worked in the front line, in shelters and First Aid posts, driving ambulances, fire-engines and mobile canteens, nursing and helping to identify victims. Women went where the police, who would not touch corpses or bits of bodies, refused to go. Frances Favell worked at a First Aid post and recalled having to reassemble bodies for burial: 'I myself thought butchers should have done it'.[2] Novels of the time such as Jane Oliver's *The Hour of the Angel* (1942), Lorna Lewis's *Tea and Hot Bombs* (1943) and Richmal Crompton's *Weatherley Parade* (1944) show women working steadily through the blitz in the roughest conditions. Writers were anxious to insist on the truth of their fictions, and vouched for their authenticity on the grounds of personal experience. Lorna Lewis's prefatory note to *Tea and Hot Bombs* assures the reader that 'These descriptions of the London Blitz are drawn from my own experiences while serving with one of the voluntary canteen services'. Writers such as Bryher wanted to convey the specificity of blitz sensations, in her case the smell:

> The air began to fill with the smell of wet dust and burnt brick that was peculiar to a badly bombed district. It was a new smell for London, unlike either the musty odour of the plague pits or the charcoal rawness of a fire.[3]

Inez Holden used her documentary skills to itemise in minute detail the different sounds which made up the blitz:

> I thought of the way in which we lived by sounds and in my mind I began to go through the sounds of the evening. The penny whistle, the siren wail, airplane hum, gunfire, penny whistle again, howling of dogs, a tear-sheet sound of bomb, crackling sound of fire, running feet, dragging of a stirrup pump along a floor, human voice giving out directions, water jetting against burning rafters, the stones of a house falling in quickly, talk, ambulance bells, fire-engine bells, breaking glass, patter of shell splinter like fine rain, boots brave-walking along a street, machine-gun fire in the air, shell splinter on the ground – a noise like a barbed wire rug being rolled up, wardens' whistles, firewatchers' whistles, auxiliary fire-engine wheels and shouted orders. And so these same sounds again in two-sound, three-sound time, altogether or separately.[4]

The narrator in Part II of Lettice Cooper's *Black Bethlehem* (1947) wants to record the different stages of reaction from the moment when a bomb drops and 'the whole room seemed to come up through my stomach' (194). Exhilaration is followed by the determination to pretend that all is normal:

> I was determined on two things. I was going to the Ministry on time, and I was going to sleep in my own flat that night. Lots of people had been

bombed out and all their things really destroyed, and had turned up to work as usual in the morning. It was the fashion and I have always liked to be in the fashion . . . I cleaned my bedroom and sitting-room feverishly as the light came . . . I had breakfast. I have never been so hungry. I have never before been so absolutely aware of the taste of bread and coffee. I made up my face rather carefully and put on my fur coat and a hat. I don't often wear one nowadays. Then I went off to the Ministry and signed that beastly book with a flourish as the clock struck nine. I was frightfully pleased with myself. (196–197)

Lucy bustles into work, 'enjoying the feeling of being gallant'; later she collapses, weepy and exhausted. She reflects on her blitz behaviour:

I was busy putting on an act. It's an act that we've had to put on to get through this winter, but it is an act all the same. To start clearing up and make yourself look nice and pretend you don't care, when people are killed three doors away! (199)

Later in the war, as the V1 'buzz bombs' fall around her, Pamela Frankau's Caroline Seward candidly admits her fear: ' "I still don't know why these things appear to have shattered my morale. I never minded the quaint, old-fashioned blitz" ' (*The Willow Cabin*, 1949, 263). Caroline fortifies herself with beer and cigarettes, and Frankau gives an authentic glimpse of London during a V1 attack:

She hurried along, walking close to the houses; when she came into Tottenham Court Road, she saw a man standing on a refuge look up and then begin to run. Overhead the bomb had cut off and was sailing down, in a long diagonal; a small black aeroplane, a toy. ('And it looks gay and conceited, as if it were shouting, "Here I come." ')

It struck, a few hundred yards south of where she stood. The explosion was thunderous and a thick bonfire-column of grey smoke billowed up. It was curious to feel more frightened after it had fallen; to be dumb with fear while all around her people were chattering. 'I *saw* it,' a woman was repeating indignantly, 'a *tiny* little thing; *tiny*.' She sounded as though she had a genuine grievance against it for its not being larger.

'Come on now,' Caroline said to herself. 'Get this knotted feeling inside you straight. Stand up and settle for it. Walk with your shoulders back.' . . .

Wherever she looked in her mind there was a thought that she did not want to think. There was the ruin of the Brookfield Galleries, as she had seen it yesterday; there were the crowds with frightened, up-turned faces, swaying back and forward across Brompton Road; there was the woman ticket-collector in the Tube, screaming angrily at a white-faced boy, 'Be a man and get up them stairs!' (265–268)

In Anthony Burgess's opinion the novel which most successfully evoked 'the very feel and smell of London in the 1940s' was Elizabeth Bowen's *The Heat of the Day*. Angus Wilson agreed: 'there will be only two English writers who convey what life in blitzed London was like – Elizabeth Bowen and Henry Green'.[5] Bowen's essay 'London 1940', a handful of stories,[6] and *The Heat of the Day* re-create the surreal intensities of the blitz. *The Heat of the Day* is set in 1942, but looks back to the 'heady autumn of the first London air-raids' as a time of violence and arousal. 'Never had any season been more felt; one bought the poetic sense of it with the sense of death.' Her descriptions of London burn off the page: the 'singed dust', the 'acridity on the tongue and nostrils', the 'arch of strain'. In Bowen's extraordinary portrait the bombed city represents a force of nature; London's 'organic power' is a fount of energy and resistance:

somewhere here was a source from which heavy motion boiled, surged and, not to be damned up, forced for itself new channels.
   The very soil of the city at this time seemed to generate more strength: in parks the outsize dahlias, velvet and wine, and the trees on which each vein in each yellow leaf stretched out perfect against the sun blazoned out the idea of the finest hour. (91)

In this world of heightened awareness the sense of sight becomes an X-ray vision through which, 'in that September transparency people became transparent, only to be located by the just darker flicker of their hearts' (92). It is the 'other realm' described in E.J. Scovell's blitz poem, 'where silence is so loud'.[7] For Bowen too, reality has shifted. Traffic becomes 'phantas-magoric', silence and absence are sensible presences: the lakes in the park are 'dazzlingly silent', people admire the 'sunny emptiness' of bombsites. In this strange world of present absences, the newly dead are still alive:

Uncounted, they continued to move in shoals through the city day, pervading everything to be seen or heard or felt with their torn-off senses, drawing on this tomorrow they had expected – for death cannot be so sudden as all that. (91)

The falling city brings down other walls with it: 'The wall between the living and the living became less solid as the wall between the living and the dead thinned' (92). Bowen implies that this is partly the light-headedly over-sensitive state of the over-tired, in which 'fatigue was the one reality'. But there is also that 'exalted' sensibility which the proximity of violent death gives to the living. A time of fear, of arousal, of illicit excitement: this is the birthdate of Stella Rodney's affair with the traitor Robert Kelway, and her complicity with war.[8]

The Heat of the Day glances back to the blitz from the standpoint of 1942; but even novels which take place during the blitz present the air raid as a short interlude. It interrupts the flow of domestic fiction suddenly and violently, much as the blitz itself impacted on women's lives. This juxtaposition, the eruption of the extraordinary into the ordinary, the shift from real to surreal, is a hallmark of blitz fiction.[9] ' "What's odd," ' according to a suburban housewife in Barbara Noble's *The House Opposite* (1943, 9),

> 'is that it will seem so far away tomorrow morning. If anyone had told me
> five years ago . . . I wouldn't have been so surprised about the air raids, but
> I should never have believed that life could be so normal in between.'

Since more bombs fell on towns than villages, blitz stories and novels tend to be about the urban and the suburban, and to celebrate London in particular, often featuring it in their titles.

Inez Holden was one of the very few women writers determined to dwell on the negative side of the blitz. Her story of an air raid, 'Exiles in Conversation', is a bad-tempered tale of tiresome misfits.[10] The disputatious narrator watches from the window with Miss Mallins, who lives in the flat above, as the siren sounds. ' "Like a lot of ants, aren't they?" ' comments Miss Mallins. The narrator instantly rejects the idea:

> There came into my mind the various ways in which the street passers-by
> were not like ants; they were not organized, did not build anything and
> often bumped into each other. In all these ways they were not like ants. (82)

The misanthropic narrator craves solitude and silence, but these are out of the question during a raid and she joins the company sheltering in a ground-floor flat. Miss Mallins has been giving a dinner party for a friend just released from internment; the group is cosmopolitan and could be a ' "happy little gathering" ', as the clergyman's widow suggests. Instead all is 'secret obsession and melancholy'. The idea of coming together in adversity is shown to be a cliché: Holden's shelterers are miserable and argumentative; Miss Mallins' ex-internee friend collapses and is taken to hospital, and the narrator never enquires after him. She ends the story: 'Miss Mallins . . . walked very slowly and I passed her without a word' (92).

Such disaffection was neither generally shared nor popular; most writers preferred a more positive approach. Jane Nicholson's *Shelter* (1941), which was highly praised by the *TLS* reviewer – 'nothing more vivid . . . a place among the historic documents of 1940–1941'[11] – seems to convey the dominant mood of the time, and to exhibit some typical blitz-fiction characteristics. Nicholson opts, as other blitz novelists do, for London in close focus: *Shelter* is set in the area around Piccadilly Circus in September and October 1940. Nicholson's protagonist, Louise Mason, is hard-pressed: she is simultaneously looking for a job, trying to accept her husband's infidelity, deciding whether to terminate her pregnancy and coping with the nightly air raids. *Shelter* is about meeting a different set of values. To her surprise, Louise is sustained by the community of her air-raid shelter, an orderly, quietly respectable world where 'a little buzz of artificial chatter from the rest covered any unseemly sounds' from the boarded-off latrines (135). This is middle England under fire, a slightly comical but absolutely steady and dependable world. Louise's attempts to arrange an abortion fail (the abortionist's house has been bombed), and in deprecating self-mockery she comes to acknowledge her wartime role: 'You're old Mother Nature's creative element, up against the forces of destruction' (128). Louise, as mother-to-be, is set in opposition to the death-bringing blitz, and ends the book with a strange new alliance: her husband is killed fire-fighting and she befriends his mistress. The blitz kills but it is also the scene of fresh life, new friendship and above all community. 'You' is a pronoun frequently used as Nicholson reaches out to involve her readers in the world of London under fire. She gets the blitz on to her pages graphically by the fragmentation of the text. Each chapter ends with a 'West End Newsreel': a disjointed collage of cheery newsreels, chilling pieces of war news, voices from the bombed streets and snapshots of society London. Breaks and omission marks labelled '[Not Passed by Censor]' remind us that the full story could not yet be told.[12]

Writers did not close their eyes to the destruction, but they often gave it a positive spin. Doris Leslie's bombed *House in the Dust* (1942) was once the home of a tyrannical Victorian paterfamilias and his unhappy daughter.

The child buried by the bomb is a metaphor for the suppressed child of the past; some houses and institutions, Leslie implies, are better off in the dust. In Noel Streatfeild's *I Ordered a Table for Six* (1942), set like Nicholson's *Shelter* in fashionable London, the blitz brings enlightenment. We follow the fortunes of the six characters who are dining together in a smart restaurant when it is bombed (as the Café de Paris was in March 1941). With mythic symmetry the three most worthy people die, and the three who wished for death all survive. In accordance with Calder's maxim that 'Blitz makes people *better*', the survivors come to ponder life's larger meanings. The young war widow muses:

> 'It does look as if someone, or something said; "Not you. Death is not just an easy way out." . . . That's as far as I've got. It's a hell of a way considering where I was.' (256)

The title of Lettice Cooper's *Black Bethlehem* also invites readers to consider the blitz as a spiritual experience, with bombed London the site of Christ's second coming. Enlightenment is one of the most common blitz by-products, offered to characters and readers by authors such as Barbara Noble in her 1943 novel *The House Opposite*. This is an honest and detailed record of the war in a solidly middle-class and much-bombed South London suburb. Noble is concerned with presenting Saffron Park as the repository of the normal; she wants to record how average, comfortably-off people respond to being bombed. If 'next door' suggests friendship and neighbourliness, 'opposite' suggests opposition. Noble's singular title suggests the closed, oppositional life of the middle-class suburb which the blitz helped both to prise open and to bring together.

Our native guide to suburbia is Elizabeth Simpson, a secretary in her mid-twenties who commutes daily to central London. Elizabeth diligently documents the behaviour of people 'hurrying home to their little burrows'. She notices the smell of stale urine in the Underground in the mornings, and on her homeward journey she gives a new version of a picture familiar to readers fifty years later. Elizabeth's account suggests that we might want to make some readjustments:

> She sat facing the sliding doors of the train and at every station, until the line moved out into the open, a peculiar section of other people's lives presented itself to her. Three-tiered sleeping bunks with wire mattresses which stretched between steel uprights had been erected along the length of the platforms and by now some of the ticket-holding occupiers had retired to

bed. From modesty, or to shut out the glare of the lights overhead, a few of them had hung makeshift curtains round their bunks. Others lay with their backs turned to curious eyes, their heads almost covered by nondescript bedding, with curl-papers or a hairnet adding an occasional touch of oddly intimate domesticity. There was something rather touchingly dependent in these sleeping ones, for they were mostly young and had, Elizabeth imagined, hard work behind them and an early rising ahead. But the middle-aged and the old, women who had gossiped, arms akimbo, on their doorsteps, walrus-moustached men who had collected at street corners for companionship, these sat or stood in groups of two or three, eating, drinking and talking, unaggressively but consciously a community of their own. The passengers stared out at them, but the shelterers ignored their curiosity. It . was the passengers who were intruders . . . Like many Londoners who had habitually and defiantly slept in their own beds throughout the air raids, Elizabeth had a slight contempt for the Tube shelterers and needed to remind herself that many of them were homeless or had suffered damage to their nerves in proportion to the damage to their backgrounds. (161–162)

Living through the blitz requires continual adjustments of body and mind: working-class life is exposed to middle-class view, and the classes involved in the People's War start to make one another's acquaintance. It is characteristic of Noble's novel that Elizabeth should look carefully, pause and reluctantly reassess.

Elizabeth's family exhibit the responses of middle-class suburbia: her middle-aged solicitor father feels guilty 'for the deaths of young men in the sky, for the suffocation of women and children trapped under the smouldering refuse of their homes' (16). Her mother's main sensation is fear, and her solace the bottle. Elizabeth goes to wake her during a night raid and 'realised that her mother was drunk. It was one of the most unpleasant moments of her life' (134). Her own work (unpaid but compulsory) as a nursing auxiliary exposes her to gruelling sights and experiences. Noble is intent on reminding us that this is the primary meaning of the blitz: she gives us the details of the smell of burnt flesh and the fragments of white brain poking out of a woman's skull (183). Summoned to her hospital after a raid, Elizabeth nurses a little girl who dies after two days of vividly described suffering. Elizabeth feels wretched about her inability to help, and she recognises it is not only the directly hit who suffer. She learns that a 'shelter case' who has contracted pneumonia through lying in water in the shelters is 'as much a raid casualty as if he'd been bombed' (58).

Noble appreciates the national significance of her cast of suburb dwellers. During a raid Elizabeth argues with her neighbours in the house opposite, when one of them comments: ' "Well I'm afraid nothing we decide in this room will make a ha'p'orth of difference to the result either way." ' Elizabeth's reply expresses the spirit of the age:

> 'I don't agree with you. I think that what people like us decide in suburban sitting rooms with Jerry chug-chugging overhead is going to make all the difference in the world.' (166)

So what do they decide? Elizabeth, motivated by her experience with the dying child, decides to train as a nurse. She will be a more active member of England's army. This move is characteristic of many of these novels: out of the blitz experience comes some practical action, a broader outlook, an involvement in the life outside the self. In terms of attitude too, a shift is under way, both in what characters think and in how they are presented by their authors. Liberalism is on the march, most evident in attitudes to sexual behaviour. Noble treats the three-year affair between Elizabeth and her boss matter-of-factly: it is irritating rather than immoral. Elizabeth has her own lesson in broad-mindedness which nudges her towards tolerance. At the beginning of the book she offends the adolescent Owen in the house opposite when he overhears her referring to him as a 'pansy boy'. The book charts the initial tension between the two, and their growing friendship. Forced to fire-watch together, they become acquainted through the long hours spent playing picquet in a cold garage. This unusual friendship between an awkward teenage boy and a girl in her mid-twenties is a blitz bonus: the blitz has loosened up closed houses and attitudes. Together Owen and Elizabeth end the book with a summary of the effects of the blitz:

> 'Have you noticed how much encouraged everybody is by a really heavy raid?' she asked.
>
> 'Yes, odd isn't it? Particularly after a spell of bad news on other fronts, such as we've had lately [about North Africa]. I suppose it's because one feels like a participant again. It's always more alarming to be a helpless onlooker. You get an idea that you're contributing something by surviving and not letting yourself be demoralised.' (236)

The theme of the participative and supportive community recurs in many blitz novels. The physical absence of the enemy (except in the form of bombs), meant that the aggression needed to fight a war was inappropriate. Instead, the qualities called for were the peaceful ones of collective co-operation and assistance (important components of the Myth, according to Calder, 196). It was an often noted paradox that it takes a war to make people live more harmoniously with one another. An air-raid warden in Cooper's *Black Bethlehem* observes: ' "when you were in battle you loved your companions more than you hated the enemy" ' (18). The drama of personal choice, often centre-stage in women's novels, gives way to issues of a more collective nature, though qualities traditionally associated with female behaviour – co-operation rather than competition and caring for others – are valued most highly. Working women are deemed more admirable than leisured women. The exploited secretary, Letty Smithson, earns Noel Streatfeild's admiration in *I Ordered a Table for Six* for her fortitude and good humour. ' "Nice way with her, hasn't she?" ' comments the barmaid at her local. ' "She makes me think of a glass of stout. You know, kind of strengthening" ' (54). Letty is a junior member of the team; the strengthening properties of the women of England are usually to be found in the figurehead of the mother.

The working-class matriarch presides over women's blitz fiction, as its guiding spirit and *genius loci*. She is the representative on the written page of the figures in Henry Moore's shelter drawings of 1941 where, according to David Mellor, 'a great maternal body emerges in the darkest of spaces'.[13] Mellor associates this maternal figure in the art and photography of the time with nurturing, 'a master metaphor in the imagination of some national humanism of the time' (22). She also appears in the contemporary writings of the psychoanalyst Melanie Klein as 'the good breast mother'. (Klein's bad breast mother also had a strong war presence, as we shall see in Chapter 6.[14]) The vulnerability felt by many during the war made the mother's function correspondingly important. Her primary attributes are her nurturing, home-making roles. Sometimes she operates from off-stage; Bill the canteen-driver in Streatfeild's *I Ordered a Table for Six* is inspired by his memories of his widowed mother, 'a grand manager'. Through her he appreciates the re-creations of home effected by housewives in the shelters, the 'effort to carry on the tradition' with what lies to hand in damaged and inhospitable surroundings (105). At other times the maternal home-maker must learn to sacrifice her home to the greater good; this is the story of Phyllis Bottome's *London Pride*, an early and popular novel of the blitz (published in 1941 and reprinted six times before the end of the war).

London Pride celebrates the Docklands, the area hardest hit by the raids on London. The high infant fatality rate is a source of moral dilemma for Bottome: should she join in the praise of the resourceful cockneys for 'taking it', when children's deaths could be avoided through the official policy of evacuation? (By the time the blitz started in September 1940 many London children had returned from the country.[15]) Bottome's uncertainty is reflected in the literary styles which compete in the portrayal of Mrs Barton's house the day after an air raid:

> She had been minding all day, for love, a sick baby of a few weeks old, shaken and un-nerved by having swallowed more dust and plaster than at his early age he could appreciate. The baby had lived – in a blue and shaken manner in Mrs Barton's arms on and off all day, while its mother, part of whose roof had been ripped off, went with three other children to make her report to the claims office; standing in an endless queue, to get what help she could for the night to come. The baby died at twilight. Its mother had returned just in time to hold it, till the end; and when Ben came back she was still in the kitchen, drinking a cup of tea. (67–68)

Documentary reporting about claims offices, sentimental infant deaths at twilight and the Dickensian phrasing of the baby 'having swallowed more dust and plaster than at his early age he could appreciate', all suggest Bottome's mixed responses to an unnecessary death. The uncertainty about what terms to use to describe the blitz – by turns black comedy, enjoyable melodrama and rightful retribution – finally sets towards morality. The book follows the exploits of Ben and Em'ly, urchin warriors, who have a high old time: for them the blitz means freedom from school and authority, treasures for looting and adventures in the ruins.[16] But then the moral enters the story. The children are buried alive in an empty bombed house, and suffer days of harrowing pain and suffocation before they are rescued, whereupon the emphasis shifts to Ben's mother. Mrs Barton is faced, as is her author, with the dilemma of childcare. In contrast to the heroine's usual choice – whom to marry? – this middle-aged, working-class mother of five must choose which of her children to protect. Should she leave for the country with one-year-old Mabel (too young to be evacuated without her mother), or should she stay for her barely adult children who must work in London and still need her care? Mrs Barton ponders these questions in Bottome's chronic cockney:

' "You ought to think of your children!", that's wot they say ter me,' Mrs
Barton told herself grimly, 'but which children – or wot yer got ter think
abaht them – *that* they carn't tell yer – nor the Govern-mint neither! When
all's said an' done, yer 'ave ter find that aht fer yerself!' (173)

Mrs Barton's decision about her children determines the meaning of
London Pride. Like other working-class matriarchs in blitz novels, she
speaks for England. (As a charwoman, hers must have been one of the few
working-class women's voices heard by middle-class writers at the time.)
As 'the home was Mrs Barton' (138) so the home (now one only in name
after its destruction by bombs), can be disbanded by her decision alone.
Mrs Barton comes to recognise that in the interests of the larger
community, her smaller, domestic community must be sacrificed. The
officials in charge of Air Raid Precautions and evacuation schemes who
tell Mrs Barton that ' "Docklands just now is no place in which to bring
up the young!" ' (94) are backed up by their author: one child is sent for by
a gruff Yorkshire uncle and the other joins an older brother and sister in
Cornwall.

This solution might look like dissolution, the death of the family; but
Bottome has taken pains to celebrate London as the wider family, and
London Pride ends with a vision of the city spiritualised. The novel
abounds with diverse images of London. Bombed, burned and looted, it is
also the haven of the shelter, where families are mutually supportive, and
where cats, dogs and canaries lie down together in peace. The citizens of
London are temporarily transformed: policemen are kind, foremen give
away coal and feeding centres dispense delicious food – 'moral miracles',
observes the author in mythic mood (69). But in her more realistic
moments Bottome knows that in 1941 London is no place for children. It
has always been violent – 'a well-aimed blow from Mrs Barton deprived
Mrs Corrigan of a rather badly decayed front tooth' (102) – and immoral
too – neither parents nor children can say who God is. Nevertheless, it
has always possessed a strong sense of itself as a community; and rather
than abandoning London as the children leave it, Bottome punctuates the
closing pages with tableaux of London transposed. When Mrs Barton
visits Ben, who has been evacuated with his hospital to Gloucestershire,
rural charms are not for her:

What Ben found his mother enjoyed most, was London itself spread out
over the park. Huts had been put up, and rows of tents; and here were men,
women and children who'd been bombed out, or blasted across streets, or

just buried and dug out again, but not too badly hurt to be up and about. Mrs Barton never got tired of sitting down near them on a bench or a fallen tree, and listening to their stories. (189)

London can recuperate in a pastoral haven, and the book ends with Ben in Cornwall, where he has a vision:

Suddenly he could no longer see the golden light across the waves. It was as if he saw instead, his own river Thames, flowing between two measureless darknesses of sea and sky. Above the river's silver floor, shot up the towers of Westminster. These were the palaces of freedom . . . He had only to listen, to hear within his heart the long reverberating strokes of Big Ben.

London had been made for people – and by people – like Ma and Dad, Flossie and Bert; and even Em'ly. For Em'ly had the courage of those ancient towers. (207–208)

Just as the seagulls can 'ride out a gale and often make good use of it' (208), the Londoners who survive will be able to return and rebuild Jerusalem, as the book's epigraph promises, in 'England's green and pleasant land'.[17]

Working-class matriarchy presides again in Eileen Marsh's *We Lived in London* (1942). In this novel we are again invited to see London as maker and sustainer of its people who, in turn, carry London's meaning when its buildings are destroyed. Marsh's London is suburban – Penham, like Noble's Saffron Park, is in the much-bombed South East. Marsh dedicates her novel 'To the People of the London Suburbs'; she presents her suburb as the backbone of England, and the Smith family at 47 Jessamine Grove as the family of England. The Smiths have much to bear: the death rate is high among young and old alike. Anxiety for their sons overseas colours the atmosphere, and the fatigue of blitz life is a permanent presence. In these circumstances watching dog-fights becomes a legitimate pleasure:

Ma went on strike.

'I just can't go down that shelter in the day time. It's more than I can do, Dad. There's the house to see to and the cooking to be done, and there's Ginger shouting to me to look every five minutes.'

'I don't blame you,' said Dad. 'There was one brought down over Hayes Common this morning. I could no more have stopped shouting and waving my arms like a fool than I could fly. Makes up a bit for the nights, don't it?'

'You're right there,' agreed Ma . . .

'What's that little black speck behind?' asked Nellie.

'That's a Spitter, that is. Watch him. See him creeping up? Now – look – he's underneath – he's – oh boy! He's got him!' . . . the delight of watching the downfall of an enemy is more than most people can bear to forgo. (122–123)

Marsh's novel revolves round Ma – she never has any other name – and is mostly narrated from her perspective. Ma is the matriarch as provider, anchor and defender of the hearth. In the interests of peace she moves towards militancy; this war must be fought actively rather than merely endured passively.

Ma went to the kitchen window. The house across the road had its roof tilted drunkenly forwards. A little farther on up the Grove was a crater where a house had stood. One could not look very far nowadays without seeing some evidence of devastation.

'We got to finish it off.'

'That's right, old girl.'

'We can't let this happen again. Once we build all these places up again and planted our gardens, we can't let it happen again.'

'That's a fact, we can't.'

'So we got to finish it off proper this time.'

All over London, all over England, this opinion was crystallizing, hardening, that it must be finished off properly this time so that it should never happen again. Future generations must be able to go to their work without the pendant gas-mask. Gardens must be planted without reference to the shelter. Children must be allowed to grow up in their own homes, not evacuated to however wonderful and pleasant spots. And to this end the job must be finished off once and for all, the menace must be stamped out, the evil thing driven out of the earth. Tolerant is the Londoner, and easy-going, but there is a limit, and the limit was fast being reached. (159)

The family of England over which Ma reigns is the extended family as closed tribe. The Smiths register little outside themselves, they rarely read newspapers or listen to the radio. They have few friends beyond the family: neighbours feature only as potentially hostile critics. When someone marries into the family or has a steady relationship with one of its members, he or she is enrolled as one of the tribe. Daughters are indistinguishable from daughters-in-law, sons from sons-in-law. Ranks are opened to admit a soldier with nowhere to go who is convalescing after Dunkirk, and all the members of the tribe are assured of protection. Resourceful and self-sufficient, this group is mainly adult, since the children have been evacuated; England's family is England's army.

Even within this enclosed world attitudes are changing; and the blitz as a force for broadening the mind works powerfully in Ma. The episode which best illustrates this comes near the end of the book. Ma's daughter Doris, a hard-working, upright WAAF officer, sleeps once with her fiancé, the socialist Arthur. He is a Spitfire pilot (coming from the working class, he readjusts popular perceptions of the boys in blue), and is shot down and killed. Doris has to tell her mother she is pregnant.

'Oh dear!' Ma sat down heavily. 'However did you come to be so silly, dear?'

Doris did not answer, and Ma leaned her head on her hand. This was disaster. This was disgrace. Nellie [her daughter-in-law], the honourable matron, was licensed to produce unlimited infants if she wished, but not Doris. What would everyone say? What would everyone think? All these years they had held their heads up in Jessamine Grove. But now–

Ma got up and went on silently with the washing-up. As she worked, her mind, having rid itself of the conventional things that it was bound to think first, began to range with the new freedom with which nights in shelters seemed to have endowed it. After a while she spoke.

'I suppose you had a right to take what you could, dear. Things being as they were.'

Doris was astounded. She had been prepared for tears or even for anger. Now she put down the tea-cloth and fumbled for her handkerchief.

'It wasn't that, quite, Ma. But he was so nervy and upset, and trying hard not to let me see–' (174)

In the 'new freedom' of her blitz philosophy Ma offers Doris her whole-hearted support. She begins 'to think of practicalities', by which she means homes for unmarried mothers and adoption schemes. Her emergent liberalism takes another step in accepting Doris's plans for keeping the baby. She becomes Doris's champion, warning off Dad:

'I'm not going to have her bothered, see?'

Dad did not reply immediately. Perhaps the apparition of Ma fighting a rearguard action startled him into silence. (177)

Dad finds his militant and free-thinking wife more shocking than Doris's 'misdemeanour', as Ma makes good her words by agreeing to look after the baby, so Doris can return to her WAAF job. Ma's new spirit of broad-mindedness extends still further, to inform her views on extra-marital philandering. Ginger, the convalescent soldier, has been 'carrying on' with Ma's daughter Irene. After Irene's death in a raid, Ma discovers that Ginger is married, but none the less she approves of the way he 'cheered up' Irene's last weeks.

In addition to all this tolerance, Ma is forced to register the physical blows of war. Her home, like Mrs Barton's in *London Pride*, constitutes her identity, and like Mrs Barton she must face its destruction. Ma is wounded by the raid on number 47 and she nearly dies, but not from bomb-inflicted injuries. Without her home – her only setting until the end of the book – she loses the will to live. 'The shock had been, of course, not the bomb that had wounded her but the knowledge that her home had gone' (212). Sent to the country, with Nellie's baby to look after and the promise of Doris's to come, Ma gradually recovers. The book's final words are those of its title: a kind enquirer asks Ma whether she will be settling in the country now, and Ma rejects the idea with the self-evident explanation, ' "We lived in London!" ' Thus the book closes, as *London Pride* does, with a celebration of London outside itself, with an image of Ma as the city elsewhere. Ma's recovery and her determination to return home make bearable the destruction of the fabric of London; its spirit survives in its displaced citizens.

These versions of the blitz put mothers at the centre of the stage and identify their role with the survival of the city. Realistic documentation goes hand-in-hand with stories of enlightenment and powerful matriarchy. But by 1946 some novelists were tempted to transform devastation into idyll. Stella Gibbons begins *Westwood* with a eulogy for early blitz life:

> London was beautiful that summer. In the poor streets the people made an open-air life for themselves under the blue sky as if they were living in a warmer climate. Old men sat on the fallen masonry and smoked their pipes and talked about the War, while the women stood patiently in the shops or round the stalls selling large fresh vegetables, ceaselessly talking. (5)

The ways writers found to create an enabling fiction of purpose and identity are no longer needed; by 1946 blitzed London has been transformed into Arcadia, 'a city in a dream'.

2

FROM CLASS TO COMMUNITY IN FORTRESS ENGLAND

Class is everywhere in English fiction before the Second World War.
  John Lehmann in Gillian Tindall, *Rosamond Lehmann*, 1985

A phrase . . . in one of the regional summaries: 'home-made socialism'.
  Paul Addison, *The Road to 1945*, 1975

Then there comes too the community feeling: all England thinking the
same thing – this horror of war – at the same moment. Never felt it so
strong before.
  Virginia Woolf, *Diary*, 1939

The Second World War was a great 'leveller of classes' according to
historians,[1] but class, which had played such a dominant part in pre-war
English fiction, would not suddenly vanish from the novel. In women's war
writing we find a double story: we have a record of the dying of the elite, a
story told sometimes with pleasure, sometimes with regret, and we also find
stories about the revised communities of wartime England, versions of the
new societies forming inside the fortress of England at war.

Historians of the People's War take their cue from Churchill's wartime
speeches, whose appeal to the whole nation involved 'not only soldiers
but the entire population, men, women and children. The fronts are
everywhere'.[2] 'This was a people's war', wrote A.J.P. Taylor,[3] a description
vividly fleshed out by Angus Calder and others. The historian Paul

Addison has persuasively described the 'new consensus of the war years' as 'positive and purposeful'.[4] According to Addison,

> From 1940 egalitarianism and community feeling became, to a great extent, the pervasive ideals of social life: whether or not people lived up to them, they knew they *ought* to. The political influence of the ration book seems to me to have been greater than that of all the left-wing propaganda of the war years put together. The slogan of 'fair shares', sometimes thought to have been invented by Labour propagandists in 1945, originated in fact in the publicity campaign devised by the Board of Trade to popularise clothes rationing in 1941. (18–19)

Subsequent redrawings of the map qualify 'the idea that the war straightforwardly boosted social solidarity'.[5] The literature of the period has been similarly reassessed: Adam Piette suggests that 'public stories' of togetherness are challenged by 'the private voice' speaking of 'deep fissures and rifts in the society'.[6] Despite these qualifications, the moral imperative was still the most important feature. As Addison says, 'whether or not people lived up to them [the ideals of social life], they knew they *ought* to' (18). This 'ought' carries extra weight in wartime: 'The moral code of a society at war demanded that no one should benefit unduly from a collective effort in which men were getting killed' (131). The 'collective effort' accordingly mobilised itself towards the future altruistic goals of winning the war and building a better society, inspired by what Addison brilliantly characterises as 'the passion for modest progress'.[7]

Did women writers join this orchestra of togetherness and commitment to progress? The war was clearly an integrative pressure. Elizabeth Bowen in the ARP, Rose Macaulay in her ambulance, Noel Streatfeild in her mobile canteen, Rebecca West and Virginia Woolf at their local Women's Institutes: war work gave these and other women writers an invigorating sense of community. 'Marylebone is my village', wrote Elizabeth Bowen in a blitz-time eulogy of the 'village communes' of London.[8] But at the end of the war Bowen deserted her commune for Ireland and the decaying grandeur of Bowen's Court, declaring, 'I can't stick all those little middle-class Labour wets'[9], so perhaps she had only been playing at villages. Evadne Price accurately nailed one version of the wartime mood in *Jane at War*:

> It was all delightfully democratic. Jane's sister, Marjorie, was learning to drive an ambulance in a uniform, and Vilet the cook was talking about joining the ATS once the Army claimed Arnie, her husband.[10]

Jane's parents, meanwhile, sack gardener Arnie as 'a needless expense': not much community feeling there. Women novelists were not of course a homogenous group – they numbered among them some of the most entrenched diehards[11] – but we can map in them a shift from about 1941 to 1942. There is unease with traditional hierarchies and rigid codes, welcome for more democratic ways, and a trajectory of dysfunction and slow decease for the ruling class. Nevertheless, old attitudes lingered on to flavour stories of the advent of war in England's pleasant shires.

Rachel Ferguson's *A Footman for the Peacock* (1940) tracks the approach of war to Delaye, a country house detained, as its name suggests, in an enchanted timewarp, where there is no car, radio or adequate telephone and the newspaper always arrives late. Ferguson sees being cut off and out of touch as rather wonderful. The Roundelays have proudly chosen their exclusion: 'Delaye is not officially a show place, mainly because the family recoils from exposing portions of their home for gain, love or charity, to that mythical trio, Tom, Dick or Harry' (12). War is a bore, and the Roundelays reject evacuees and refugees alike. Nannie is eccentric enough to frighten off the billeting officer, and when Margaret mentions a letter from a German schoolfriend, 'Lady Roundelay smote the table with her fist. "No! No she doesn't! My heart bleeds for the German Jews as much as anybody's but I *cannot* face a pale fugitive running tear-stained in what she stands up in down *this* avenue" ' (151). Fortunately, Sir Edmund's ultimatum – ' "If she comes, I go" ' – is not put to the test. The schoolfriend is not Jewish and has ' "joined the Youth Movement and her brother's in the army and he's got a commission" ', much to the relief of the Roundelay family, who seem blithely unaware of Fascism. Delaye is an idyll blessed by God. The curate says he ' "can see Him liking Delaye for its space and mannerly air" ' (87), and its owners behave like God: 'You merely said to the staff let there be light, and there was light' (65). If there is satire, it is very mild; Ferguson seems to endorse the Roundelay view of class as a matter of 'caste' which 'permeates nearly everything' (52). In such a world prejudice and snobbery are the charming prerogatives of the upper class. Lady Roundelay worries about the spread of education: 'Wouldn't it perhaps tend toward keeping the masses from knowing their place?' (33) How prescient she is, as the sun gently sets on this snobbish paradise, well-tended by cooks, maids and butlers, a feudal 'fortress' (17) which has no sense of obligation beyond its own self-perpetuation. The curate expounds his theory that ' "Eldest and only sons ought to be exempted entirely except for Home Defence, particularly in the case of the old name and historic house. Too much is at stake; it's race suicide of the worst type" ', to which Lady Roundelay wisely replies, ' "I know" ' (180).

Then came the Battle of Britain and the onslaught of the blitz, and the world of Delaye could no longer be so easily tolerated. Beautiful, well-connected and wealthy, Esther Daleson in Helen Beauclerk's *Shadows on a Wall* (1941) is indeed the 'luxury object' (30) she describes herself as, in a country which is no longer able to afford such things. ' "I can't thank you enough," ' says one of her sycophants, ' "for looking so lovely. For reminding one, in all this squalor, that there are still lovely women wearing lovely clothes. You must keep it up. It is very important" ' (86). Beauclerk's satirical view of England in 1939 would be purely light-hearted, were it not for the more sinister half of the novel which is set in a France overrun with corruption and about to fall. Esther takes sleeping pills to escape from the present, accidentally overdoses and dies; the leisured class she represents is shown to be ineffectual, selfish and self-destructive. Nor was the aristocratic Lord Peter Wimsey, popular from Dorothy L. Sayers's detective novels of the 1920s and 1930s, the right man for the times. Sayers concocted a few ill-judged 'Wimsey Papers' for the *Spectator* at the end of 1939 and the beginning of 1940,[12] after which Lord Peter was withdrawn. 'Tallboys', a story written in 1942 about Wimsey family life, where discipline is kind but firm, and Wimsey 'thwacks' his young son for stealing a peach from the garden wall – ' "You will find the cane behind the dressing-table" ' – but then colludes with him to introduce a snake into the bed of an unpleasant middle-class female guest, was not published until 1972.[13]

By 1941 Stella Gibbons's *The Rich House* is in terminal decay:

> All the furnishings of the Rich House – the clocks and sofas and sideboards, the occasional tables and vases and fenders, the cushions and beds and books – were trembling upon the edge of becoming rubbish. When they were new, they had been solid and handsome and the best of their kind to be bought, but that was long ago; and for years now they had not been cleaned or repaired, the clocks had stopped and never been rewound, stuffing was coming out of the cushions and leaves out of the books, the springs of the beds were broken, the vases were chipped, the fenders were scratched and dented. (261)

This world nearing its end is the home of an elderly actor who 'liked the rooms to be as brightly lit as *Act I: Lord Mountmallion's Flat in Clarges*

Street; he liked them to look as if, at any moment, the play might begin' (48). But the play is long over, and the Rich House is now a defunct stage-set, its owner stranded among his old theatre programmes.

With the progress of the war, women's novels show bridges being built between the classes. In the drab world of 1942 the trappings of upper-class life are too attractive to ditch altogether, and dances must still go on in 'Park Lane mansions', but now they are Red Cross Balls. And as for the 'couple of footmen with tin hats hanging on gilded brackets beside them': ' "Did you see? They're stretcher-party men off duty, doing a bit extra. I hope they're not too uncomfortable in that livery" '.[14] Writers are inclined to promote harmony and communication, to suggest a coming together of the classes. The *Family Pattern* which Pamela Hansford Johnson traces in her saga of 1942 is a pattern of family ties crossing class boundaries. One middle-class sister marries into the titled gentry, the other into the working class. Each woman identifies strongly with the class she has married into without forfeiting the close relationship with her sister. Hansford Johnson's story stretches from the 1890s until the 1940s, and ends in the Second World War with the institution of the family as a force for cohesion in the nation at war.

Society, however, would not shed its prejudices overnight. In 1944 a respectable character in one of Patricia Wentworth's 'Miss Silver' novels succumbs to blackmail in order to conceal his 'guilty secret' which finally emerges: ' "I'm a pork butcher." There was an electric silence'.[15] The incumbent of Trollope's Barsetshire terrain, Angela Thirkell, resolutely holds the pass, even though – perhaps especially because – the owners of Harefield Park have been dislodged from their ancestral home by a girls' school in *The Headmistress* (1944). Ousted from their 'plain-faced Palladian' house, the Beltons still enjoy some vestiges of power: 'The keys [to the park] remained the property of the reigning Belton and were not lightly bestowed' (36). The grand plot of the novel is, even in 1944, class in all its various ramifications. Is the headmistress, Miss Sparling, a lady? Investigative work includes an inspection of the fly-leaves of her books to establish the identity of her grandfather. The evidence confirms Dr Perry's guess that there's ' "breeding somewhere all right" ' (48), and Thirkell comments:

It may be snobbishness to think the better of a person because your Vicar had known her grandfather who was a Canon; but it lies deep at the roots of social life, and there is good reason for it. (134)

But this 'good reason' is not forthcoming; instead Thirkell sounds the bugle of defiance from the embattled landed gentry of 1944, after five years of war. Reviewers on the other side of the Atlantic were unable to understand Thirkell's popularity. A Canadian critic asked: 'If England is to be completely changed, as we are assured it will be, why do so many people want to read about an aspect of English life which would not survive a revolution?'[16] The critic Diana Trilling spotted Thirkell's hostility to all threats (such as Jews, intellectuals and Irish girls) to her closed world, and she concluded that although 'advertised as a pleasant bundle of froth, Angela Thirkell is in fact quite a grim little person'.[17] All is not always harmonious inside the fortress of England at war.

Novels written immediately after the war look back at the changes wrought on the social fabric, sometimes with regret, sometimes with satisfaction. Mollie Panter-Downes's *One Fine Day* (1947) logs the damage that has been done. Wealding, for so long the 'perfect village in aspic, at the sight of which motorists applied their brakes, artists happily set up easels' (8) has subtly changed. It has been 'invaded': 'Uncertainty floated on the air with the voice of the wireless which had brought the worm of the world into the tight bud of Wealding' (8). The novel's tone is pastoral–elegiac; England is still a beautiful garden but an unweeded one, the gardeners cost too much. The book's title suggests optimism for the future (good things will happen 'one fine day'), but the optimism is illusory. Panter-Downes's title yields meanings both literal – the action occurs over one fine summer's day – and reversed: it is the fine day of England's past rather than her future. The metaphor of the house controls the book. Laura Marshall's actual house is beloved but tyrannical, exhausting Laura in her efforts to maintain pre-war ways. The Cramners, 'the family up at the Manor', are 'giving up' their house to the National Trust. Sad but inevitable seems to be the attitude of the novel. Old Mrs Cramner still inspires respect, 'standing reassuring as a rock or a tower in the frightening uncertainty of everything' (126). Panter-Downes introduces her novel with a parallel image of 'the big house' of England; it is 'empty and shuttered' but indestructible, 'the house said I will stand when you are dust' (8–9). But this mythical house is positioned on top of Barrow Down, the hill with its ancient history of human habitation to which Laura escapes for the last third of the book. In this book comfort comes not from the houses of the present or the future, but from the geography of the past, the prehistory of Barrow Down.

Marghanita Laski's *The Village* (1952) examines the class shifts as England readjusts after the war. 'The night the war ended,' the book begins, 'both Mrs Trevor and Mrs Wilson went on duty at the Red Cross Post as usual.' Mrs Wilson was Mrs Trevor's cleaner before the war; during the war they have worked together, and now they both leave the Red Cross post with regret:

> 'There's a lot of us will miss it,' Edith [Wilson] said. 'We've all of us felt at times, you know, how nice it was, like you and me being able to be together and friendly, just as if we were the same sort, if you know what I mean.'
>
> 'I'll miss it a lot too,' Wendy [Trevor] said. There was no point in her saying it could go on now, the friendliness and the companionship and the simple human liking of one woman for another. Both knew that this breaking down of social barriers was just one of the things you got out of the war, but it couldn't go on. (27–28)

Class divisions provide the plot, with the end of the war situating the 'gentry' world of the Trevors as bankrupt and played out. ' "Now the chicken-farm's gone down the drain the Major's almost an invalid and can't do anything but potter about in the open air" ' (15). The Trevors and their kind are characterised as mean-minded, desperate to keep up appearances and unkind to their children. ' "A pathetic bunch," ' decides a brisk American observer, ' "they give you the impression all the time that they're scared stiff of anything happening that's the least bit different" ' (116). The working-class Wilsons, on the other hand, are flourishing. While the jobs Margaret Trevor aims for (cooking, nannying) are rejected as unsuitable by her parents, Roy Wilson is earning good money as a trained compositor. Roy and Margaret's courtship finally overcomes her family's opposition, but they pay the price of emigration to Australia. Laski presents the Trevors as a dying breed with little regret: who can feel sorry at the failure of snobbery and a dilapidated chicken-farm?

Laura Talbot's *The Gentlewomen* (1952) uses the *Concise Oxford Dictionary*'s definition of a snob as its epigraph, which suggests that she will target those with what the Dictionary calls 'exaggerated respect for social position or wealth'. But although this evocation of the great house in wartime is hard on the snobbery of those low on the social ladder, Talbot is more restrained when it comes to the prejudices of the aristocracy. In her eyes the great house of England belongs in the hands of its traditional owners, who are currently handicapped by the pressures of war – the head of the house is absent on service overseas for more than half the book.

The Gentlewomen's principal snob is Roona Bolby, and Talbot's achievement is to elicit our sympathy for this unpleasant woman. Roona is an ageing beauty, a well-connected woman who is forced to earn her living by governessing, thus employed and exploited by her own class. The novel opens as Roona joyfully abandons her dingy Birmingham boarding-house for a new post at Lord Rushford's country seat. In her obsession with class, Roona hunts out and insinuates social connections (' "You know the Atherton-Broadleighs, I expect, Lady Archie?" ' (41)), bridles at suspected insults (the invitation to sing with the Italian POWs), and makes sure that she rather than the new secretary gets the bedroom that Edward VII slept in. Her plots all backfire: Edward VII's State Room is uncomfortable, she deprives herself of pleasure by refusing to sing, and the social connections she unearths rebound to her disadvantage. The many mirrors she looks into tell sad stories to the dependent woman:

> The furrows were furrows, not the mirror's fault – a disturbing reflection. The furrows had deepened with the war. War was a lonely battle for the lonely, for those not urgently connected with it, and in her case a lonely battle for what? That she might continue to be a governess – she had not ceased to shudder inwardly at the word – in houses such as Rushford, continually reminded she was the governess, and there were few houses such as Rushford left. She must at all costs stay at Rushford, whatever the disadvantages; it would be better than giving daily lessons from Hillstone House in the draughty dining-rooms of Birmingham's suburbia. (56)

Roona can be a moving figure, and a courageous one: ' "Roona," she said, looking sternly at the reflection, "where is your patriotism? . . . even if you are no longer beautiful, *stick it*, you are brave" ' (56–57). But her insecurity makes her unkind. She exercises what little power she has autocratically, refusing until the last moment to let her charges go to the much-anticipated Gymkhana. She bullies the timid, deaf Miss Pickford, and her snobbery repels us. Even poetry is not immune – ' "One moment Louisa, please; it should be Alfred *Lord* Tennyson" ' (116) – and nor is respect for the dead: Roona hears Miss Pickford's funeral bell as the wedding chimes for herself and Lord Corwen.

Roona's fault is not just that she is a snob, but that she is not upper class enough. Her parents' house in Worthing and her mother's social pretensions – ' "Just get me the Peerage again, Roona; somehow I must find Lady Alice" ' (21) – are good game for Talbot, as are some upper-class attitudes. Lady Rushford's comfortable exploitation of her position does not go unnoticed:

> She herself had been fortunate enough not to have had to wait in queues; it was possible to sail in ahead of them because the order had been given by telephone: 'Oh, and by the way, Mr Simkins, if you've *got* any biscuits ...' Yes, there *were* advantages after all, even in war, in being, well, who one was ... (26)

Lady Rushford is condemned by her elderly neighbour Lady Archie as ' "well, not *absolutely* out of the *topmost* drawer" ' (268); Lady Archie deplores the ostentatious coronet on the cuff of the dressing-gown Lady Rushford lends her (46, 65). Is Lady Archie in her turn convicted of snobbery? At this social peak Talbot seems finally to cede approval. She admires Lady Archie's relaxed freedom of speech and Lord Rushford's vow to ' "hang on to Rushford ... until my dying day, if I can" ' (201). Talbot appears not to notice that the only relationship her aristocrats conduct with anyone outside their peer group is a master/servant one. In this last stronghold of feudalism there are ' "plenty of servants and no evacuees and two delightful prisoners and some land girls" ' (40). Talbot's wartime aristocrats stand at bay, their beautiful world under threat; they are the home-front breed of the 'Unicorns, almost,' described in Keith Douglas's poem 'Aristocrats'.[18] The war's presence is registered indirectly, as atmosphere rather than event. We sense it constantly as waves of violent noise – the low-flying bombers from the nearby aerodrome – and as fog, oppressive and unavoidable. In this atmosphere of Midlands blight Rushford is vulnerable and all the more valuable; Roona's all too visible and self-lacerating snobbery has its counterpart in the invisible stance of her creator, Laura Talbot, born with the title Lady Ursula Chetwynd-Talbot.

Class survived the war then as a preoccupation and motivation, its story nearly always told from a middle or upper-class perspective. In 1944 Ethel Mannin commented:

> It is very significant that, with the exception of myself, if I may be allowed to say so, we have no proletarian women writers – women writers of proletarian origins, that is to say, identifying themselves with their class and writing of it.[19]

The voice of the working-class woman writer was not established, though at least its absence had been noted. Occasionally we find critiques of the community of wartime England; to some women society could present an extremely hostile face. The sailor's wife searching for lodgings in Ann Chadwick's story 'The Sailor's Wife' (1945)[20] meets rejection in a town where hotel beds are cold and egg-laying ducks get more care than babies. The sailor's wife – she has no other name, her identity is submerged beneath this label – has her plea well-rehearsed:

> And is it just yourself you want for?
> My husband comes home on leave occasionally for a day or so, and we've a baby. But he's too young to run about and break things, and I've got his cot with me, said the sailor's wife. She thought – that's my family, I'm talking about, brushing over. My own family – the only thing.

Exhausted, she falls under a lorry, to find herself at last an object of interest. This is her opportunity: 'She had their attention. Well, quick'. Protesting that she 'did it on purpose' because she had nowhere to live, she manages to turn her painful accident to her advantage. It is the only weapon she has. She refuses to sign the paper absolving the lorry driver of responsibility until he finds her lodgings and she can finally relax: 'I've got a place. She fell asleep half smiling'.

Revenge is at hand, if only the small revenges available to women like the downtrodden secretary of Sylvia Townsend Warner's story, 'A Speaker from London'.[21] Mrs Benton is the Speaker from London who patronisingly arranges for her secretary, Miss Tomlinson, to wait in the rectory kitchen during the meeting. Miss Tomlinson's persistent coughing has paid off and she now has time to write to her fiancé. As she writes, lamenting 'this everlasting war', her voice counters that of the official 'Speaker'. Miss Tomlinson's voice is critical: she loathes 'the Organiser's kitchen. It's just the sort of kitchen you'd expect, with one of these posh cookers like a family vault, and everything so neat and hungry-looking it's enough to give one the creeps.' In particular, she loathes her employer:

> Sometimes I feel so blue, darling. I don't know what to do with myself. And then I hear Mrs B doing her bloody piece about how after all one has only to remember our brave men and our own small troubles seem such small things, don't they? And then she gives one of her wistful grins, and bears up even if her tea is late. The war means simply nothing to these people, simply a wonderful opportunity to be paid six hundred a year by the

Government for going round telling kids what splendid fun they'll have being killed. Only now it's going down mines and scrubbing floors. I look at her and think of you.

When a man selling stationery comes to the back door with what he 'dismissingly' calls ' "just another hard-luck story . . . I was a Desert Rat all right, believe it or not" ', Miss Tomlinson steals extravagantly for him from the rectory store-cupboard. 'She took tins of salmon, of meat, of treacle, of peaches, cartons of tea, slabs of chocolate, and packed them in a carrying-bag and remembered to add a tin-opener.' For her all war-talk is bogus, and she tells the man to go ' "before I begin to believe in you" ': stealing for this impostor is her revenge on the impostors in charge.

Antagonism was, however, only a minority sport. On the whole what we see is the community superseding class as the big interest for women writers, and taking centre-stage as a benevolent protagonist. Not without faults, society becomes a hero in the sense of being an active force in women's novels, a figure with characteristics to be analysed and progress to be charted. It is tempting to relate this shift of interest to the changes in women's lives. At a time when war work increasingly took women outside the home, we find in women's novels versions of the community revitalised and revalued. Most wartime novels approve of this wider group which sustains rather than constrains; its major assets are openness and the ability to improvise. To fall in step with the times, these societies may be all-female like the convent in Kate O'Brien's *The Land of Spices* (1941); all-female worlds are also well-represented in wartime thrillers, such as Gladys Mitchell's *Laurels are Poison* (1942) and Josephine Tey's *Miss Pym Disposes* (1946). Also in line with the times is the way in which the values of the group approximate to those of the home. England at war is portrayed as a close-knit family which shares, supports and co-operates. Helen Ashton's *Yeoman's Hospital* (1944) presents the hard-working hospital as a version of this family; Bryher's *Beowulf* (1956) offers the Warming Pan tea-room and boarding-house as another. A 'home from home', a peaceful haven in the middle of the blitz, this is the face of the community hospital:

A few feet away the buses stopped on their way to and from the City, the Underground was beneath them, but here, as Angelina said, they had a 'corner of an English garden flowering in our great Metropolis'. (133)

Beowulf, a huge and hideous plaster dog, presides over the tea-room, the spirit of an ancient British past blessing the improvised societies of wartime England.

Bryher's Beowulf in the 'garden' of the Warming Pan, and the creation of the good microcosm of England in other novels, show that women writers played their part in the invocation of the 'Nation as Pastoral' which the critic Simon Featherstone has located in British wartime writing. According to Featherstone, the depiction of England as rural and organic softened the heavy hand of government control by recasting the state as a village.[22] Women novelists sometimes embraced this version of national pastoral: it fitted contemporary notions of 'home-made socialism' and the sense that Spender and others had of England as a New Jerusalem.[23] Paul Fussell balks at the 'new self-congratulatory mode' in which 'Goodness became the all-but universal theme,'[24] but he is looking back with hindsight – or rather hindtaste – and principally concerned with American experience. British readers were more receptive to the virtues of community-mindedness; and 'Joanna's earnest good will', suggested a *TLS* reviewer in 1942, 'will be found to match that of many a wartime mood'.[25] More interesting to us fifty years later is the analysis of the society of the fortress to be found in two novels by Pamela Hansford Johnson and Sylvia Townsend Warner.

Pamela Hansford Johnson's *Winter Quarters* (1943) is unusual for a women's novel insofar as it focuses on an all-male community, an army Battery stationed in an English country village in the autumn of 1942.[26] Time and place make meaning, as Hansford Johnson explains in her prefatory note: 'My aim has simply been to explore the reactions of "ordinary" men to an "extra-ordinary" way of living ... The action of *Winter Quarters* takes place during the anxious lull that preceded the offensive of the Eighth Army in Egypt.' Precisely dated January 21, 1943 at its close, the novel documents a particular moment in the progress of the war – or rather its non-progress: the novel is an anatomy of the 'anxious lull'. Hansford Johnson reports on the 'small brief worlds newly created all over the land' (77), and in order to bring this temporary world on to the page she mobilises a large cast of characters (forty-three in all), and a daring opening tactic. She does not draw each character forward in turn for our attention, but plunges us into the already existing group, and we have to find our feet just as we do when we arrive late to any group. This manoeuvre effectively gives the group precedence over the individual. Claud Pickering, the narrator-hero of the trilogy Hansford Johnson was writing between 1940 and 1948, appears again in this novel but here he is just one among many, and is seen from the same perspective as the others. Instead of a single hero, Hansford Johnson gives us an ensemble piece; some of the group we get to know well, others we stay on nodding terms with. They are not all likeable, but even the most unpleasant – Bert Lilley is a Mosleyite bully – have some redeeming features on closer acquaintance. More importantly, we see the group growing and taking shape as the hero of the novel and the war. A motif which threads through the book is the question of what makes a hero. One character asks:

> 'Well, after all, what is a hero? They aren't born. We talk about "our brave boys" when war comes, but they're just the same boys we knew when they were in shops and offices. Ordinary men.' (210)

Heroes, the 'colourless' Madge is saying, are not born but made; it is the job of this community to turn the ' "thousands of men [who] don't want to be soldiers" ' into fighting men.

Gunner Tom Berry's one-line poem 'Suddenly there was no news' (153) pleases him immensely in its summary of the current war situation. Hansford Johnson characterises the lull not as the absence of fighting, but as the presence of its substitutes: the 'little frets' which germinate while the soldiers fill their lives with lectures, cross-country runs, gunnery practice and endless waiting, ' "rotting here while the Russians get murdered, poor beggars, yelling 'Good old Joe' and able to do damn all" ' (203). ' "This hanging-about drives me nuts" ' (95): the frustration of smothered aggression inevitably leads to small dramas of jealousy and violence. ' "The lull in the war. Anyone might do anything to make a diversion" ' (96), remarks a member of the group, astutely quoting *Othello*, another tale of wartime frets. Hansford Johnson's Battery is a society shot through with complicated currents and tensions, a family who gossip, intrigue and support.

This is not a world of men without women, in contrast to Anthony Powell's portrayal of wartime army life, in his *Dance to the Music of Time* sequence, where women inhabit a separate space, barely visible and of little account. Powell's narrator is so out of touch with his wife, even though geographically close, that he wonders if 'Isobel hasn't had the baby yet without anyone telling me?' (*The Valley of Bones*, 1964, 146). Hansford Johnson's women, by comparison, impinge forcefully on the Battery. They can endanger its well-being: Gillie, the publican's bored wife, wreaks havoc with her flirtations, and the simple-minded fourteen-year-old Eily, ' "that pathetic skivvy with the yellow sausage curls" ' (19), pursues soldiers round the village with relentless avidity. Eily is protected from herself by the older members of the group: the avuncular Gunner Mangan tells her, ' "You're only a silly little bit, Eily, and you're no beauty. All you'll do, hanging around the lads, is get yourself into trouble. You're just a joke here, see? –but all the lads ain't so nice as me" ' (132). Eily escapes the seemingly inevitable consequences, and by the end of the book she has reformed: ' "I'm not going about with men any more" ' (283). Even the selfish Gillie can sometimes act for the good of the group: she extricates a soldier from being blackmailed by Eily's mother, and helps to put Eily straight on the facts of life. On balance women bring benefit to the society at war, and this includes a broad-minded generosity with their affections. Phyllis, whose 'grandeur' is praised by Hansford Johnson, scorns the idea of valuing herself ' "just as if you were a gold watch or a canteen of cutlery. You just want to take love when it's held out to you. I want yours" ' (203). Other women's generosity can be more surprising. Despite her previous infidelity Bert Lilley's wife unexpectedly stands by him after his arrest for hitting another officer. At the centre of the book stands the figure of the happily married Strutt, the most balanced and sympathetic man in the Battery. Some of the book's most effective scenes follow Strutt and his wife during the weekend they have together, as they make all the necessary minute adjustments to each other. We see them testing the ground and sending out feelers; we see the small rebuffs, the flares of temper and jealousy, and then the reconciliations and the joy as Stacey announces her pregnancy.

News of mobilisation comes at last in the form of a posting overseas. 'All the bother of establishing a temporary world' (77) pays off as the Battery pulls together in anticipation of their move. Within itself the group acknowledges and handles fear of different sorts, such as Dakin's physical cowardice and Tawney's dread of public disgrace. While some men paint 'a future of desert glory' (287), others long for peace, but even they recognise that ' "I wouldn't take a Peace at any Price" ' (287). Hansford Johnson's community at war has effectively conditioned its members for war. Not bloodthirsty, their balanced attitude is exemplified by Strutt's careful response to the news of their draft: ' "Yes and no. Yes, I'll be glad to get to see some movement at last. No, I've got a family" ' (233). This is how the 'fortress of England' (288) is constituted in the middle years of the war.

Sylvia Townsend Warner's *The Corner That Held Them* (1948) is an investigation of community life which has both nothing and everything to do with the war. Written between 1942 and 1947, Townsend Warner's novel follows the fortunes of a small East Anglian nunnery over nearly forty years, between 1345 and 1382. As a succession of prioresses and bishops come and go, the convent declines slowly in prosperity amid a profusion of minor events and intrigues. The unfolding of what the critic Gillian Beer has called this 'strange epic'[27] reveals Townsend Warner's inspired choice of analogue for the fortress of wartime England. Her biographer Claire Harman has commented on the contemporary relevance of the convent to 'wartime Dorset, simmering as it was with provincial womanhood';[28] what the convent also does is to illuminate aspects of the wartime community which are physical, social and spiritual. The novel of Townsend Warner's which pleased her most,[29] *The Corner That Held Them* is an odd and fascinating book which grows increasingly on the reader; and that is part of its meaning.

The most obvious correlation between the fourteenth-century convent and wartime England is fear – the emotion controlling the novel. 'Sometimes I am blue with fear,' wrote Townsend Warner at the beginning of June 1940;[30] on 19 February 1942 her diary reads 'We are losing the war', and two days later: 'It gets colder and colder. Our pipes freeze, and I begin to write a story about a medieval nunnery'.[31] This is the climate for the novel's birth. Its epigraph, 'For neither might the corner that held them keep them from fear', is taken from a passage in the Apocryphal 'Wisdom of Solomon' which elaborates an extended metaphor of fear as the prison of 'unnurtured souls . . . fettered within the bonds of a long night'.

The nuns of Oby live in all kinds of fear. Some nuns are afraid of thunder, some of owls hooting in daylight, some of being raped. Fear of financial insecurity is a constant refrain: Oby hovers on the brink of insolvency and its nuns hear nervously of other convents forced to dissolve or retrench. Fears of labour shortages, bad weather and unfriendly bishops pattern the forty-year span of life in this unstable world, where even the landscape shifts uncertainly, with the river Waxle 'constantly revising its course' (5). There are also the particular fears of the moment: at the beginning of the book the Black Death is devastating England; later the Peasants' Revolt threatens insurrection and unrest. The critic Wendy Mulford has drawn convincing parallels between the kinds of 'transition and rapid social change' which both the fourteenth century and the mid-twentieth century were experiencing;[32] the peasants of 1940s England were not in revolt, but the time for more 'fair shares' had arrived. Townsend Warner herself made the Black Death analogy explicit, commenting in June 1940:

> people here would be much more frightened if the Germans were the Black Death. Then the news – The Black Death is in Rouen, in the Channel Ports, has appeared in Paris – would set people to thinking: soon I may catch it, and die.[33]

Even 'the corner that held them' cannot keep fear at bay; Oby is dedicated to Saint Leonard, patron of prisoners (the fearful, according to Solomon, are 'shut up in a prison without iron bars'). Corners can be places of punishment or safe havens. Oby, the 'threatened community' (289), represents the beleaguered fortress of England in war, simultaneously sanctuary and prison.

Oby is a convent, dedicated to the life of the spirit. Townsend Warner's choice of setting illuminates another aspect of her own time, what Stephen Spender referred to as 'the religious mood of the war'.[34] The nuns of Oby squabble and struggle but they belong to a group which is committed to something beyond itself. The parallel with wartime England is suggestive. Early in the war the notion of 'something bigger than yourself' was recognised by the MOI as an aid to morale.[35] Although England was not a particularly religious country in the 1940s, it did move to an exalted mood – the whiff still comes off Churchill's speeches – which spurred people to hard work in the common causes of winning the war and building a better society. Townsend Warner's interest in the part played by the spiritual in the life of the community finds an appropriate setting in Oby. The convent gives her scope to explore the relationship between the life of the spirit and the life of the body, the interface between the spiritual and material. At first glance the spiritual seems to be nowhere, in keeping with Townsend Warner's claim that she began the novel

> on the purest Marxian principles, because I was convinced that if you were going to give an accurate picture of the monastic life, you'd have to put in all their finances; how they made their money, how they dodged about from one thing to another and how very precarious it all was.[36]

This impetus informs the novel, but it is only part of the story. The first impression of *The Corner That Held Them* is that material considerations continually elbow out the spiritual. The nuns themselves grumble:

How could a nun contemplate when within earshot there was a dispute about whether or no William Scole would yield his ox on Thursday to bring in a load of firing, whether or no the family of Noot should pay a fine for the loss of their son to the manor? (52)

The Prioress Alicia longs 'to be freed from beef and mutton and misunderstandings; to sit silent in chapter' (95), but the world of mutton and misunderstandings continually intervenes. When the nuns are bid to a meeting by the Prioress they expect to

hear an admonition on the narrow space of time left them on an earth where, as in the time of Noah's deluge, the waters were rising, and of how that space should be filled with prayers and final meditations. They were surprised to hear themselves urged to be more economical: to darn little holes before they became big ones, to be sparing of fuel, to keep a sharp lookout for moths. (33)

Even on a death-bed, spiritual fervour is qualified by the ambiguous 'vocabulary of the body'. As Dame Joan lies dying, Sir Ralph anoints her feet and

she had suddenly quivered, making an intense effort to come out of her stupor, and the hand which had been clawing the pallet was extended, blindly caressing the air. The tremor, and that enamoured gesture of the hand, had revealed such an intensity of love that he had stayed by her, thinking that if she recovered her senses it would please her to be god-speeded towards the God she loved so fervently. Or was it that she was ticklish? (24–25)

In what looks like a campaign of ironic diminishment Townsend Warner seems to show the material world obstreperously asserting itself at the expense of the spiritual. To this end she brings the material world of the fourteenth century powerfully on to the page; never was a novel fuller of the physical specificity of its time, the profusion of its objects, and the density of its very air, with 'the peat-smoke . . . which was spoiling Dame Beatrix's eyesight' and 'the chips of dried cod that flew under the mallet' (65, 49). But, having brought the material so pressingly to our attention, the novel then insidiously and persistently resists any polarisation into an opposition between the material and the spiritual. Instead it draws us towards a vision of their relationship which has more to do with infiltration, inherence and immanence, as the salt of the Viking past gets into the grain of the Church timbers and the 'taint of the supernatural' mixes with 'the healthy odour of drying shallots' (83, 86).

' "What you eat's vocation" ' pronounces a worldly character during a sociable christening (101), thereby anchoring spiritual considerations firmly to the body and the needs of the flesh. But this apparent deflation of the spirit can also be read as an invitation to see the soul immanent in the flesh, the material imbued with the spiritual. Townsend Warner transposes the philosophy of Browning's 'Fra Lippo Lippi' from Florence to East Anglia, and repeatedly reminds us of the mixed origins of the beautiful and the spiritual in the world of the flesh. The fact that the convent owes its existence to an act of carnality is strikingly emphasised in the book's first scene of adultery and murder. Out of the belated remorse of the cuckolded widower comes the convent. Its buildings proclaim its mixed genesis, the chapel is a 'reach-me-down conversion of what had been the dungeon and cattle-hold of the original manor house' (7). Likewise, the intensely beautiful singing, 'concords so sweet that they seemed to melt the flesh off his bones' (203), originates from an ill-kept leper house where the convent overseer breaks his journey. 'Such music, and such squalor! . . . never had he seen a house so dirty, or slept in a more tattered bed. But out came the music as the kingfisher flashes from its nest of stinking fishbones' (205). Townsend Warner likes to remind us both of the force of beauty and of its material source, how it is produced. Sweet music comes from the lepers, and the rich altar-hanging skilfully embroidered by the nuns is created by grimy hands which need wiping (259).

The Corner That Held Them tells us that complete severance from this world is not possible; it is only through and with the body that we can experience the life of the spirit. The spire which Prioress Alicia vowed to build to the glory of God – although born in a spurt of ambition as she watches the previous prioress choke on a plumstone – is finally completed, but leaves her with a sense of anticlimax. The spire necessarily disappoints in its failure to remove her from the sphere of the material world. Even the deathbeds of the devout filter the hereafter through the here, as prayer mingles with sweat:

> The lulling of prayers and the buzzing of insects were broken by shooings, scratching, and slaps at the flies which settled on cheeks and foreheads. (66)

Spiritual experiences come from and through the most vividly felt physical and tactile experiences. Townsend Warner excels at describing the sensation of touch: she shows how the spiritual spark is engendered through the body's direct encounter with the contingent world. Touch gives Sir Ralph such an experience with his first hawk: 'When he felt her hard feet fidget on his hand Sir Ralph experienced an authentic happiness' (81). The larger perspective is also to be apprehended through the senses, and again the idea is one of permeation. From her vantage-point in the 1940s Townsend Warner looks back to the earlier invasion of the Danes:

> Their boat was all that was left of them, and some of its timber was built into the roof of Lintoft church. If you licked on a wet day you could still taste the salt water in it. (83)

The wood impregnated with salt promotes a startlingly intimate sensation of invasion – taken into the building and on to the tongue.

Permeation and a blurring of boundaries characterise *The Corner That Held Them*. Sir Ralph weathers into the Oby landscape (91) and the names of individual characters sometimes elude us (a prioress but which one?). The narrator's individual voice blurs with the choric voice which peppers the commentary with proverbial sayings, and what persists is the life of the community. The convent's beautiful artefacts are lost or stolen (the silver-plate and the altar-hanging are never found); but the achievement lies in the process of their making. Townsend Warner is less interested in what the nuns produce than in what happens while they are producing it: 'During the months they had worked on it [the altar-hanging] together the nuns of Oby had become a community' (268). It is through the life of its stories that Townsend Warner conveys most powerfully the vitality and cohesion of the group. 'A clatter of dishes and a steady rattle of narrative' (245) run through the book: characters tell and relish stories on almost every page. One character 'brought what to the bulk of the convent was almost as good as a dowry: a narrative' (195). Stories – often untrue, always passed on – sustain Oby, and in Townsend Warner's analogue it is our commitment to the story which keeps this world alive. Although it lacks conventional enticements (there are no central characters, little suspense, no love interest or unifying plot), the reader wants to be inside the world of Oby with its gossip and its stories. When Sir Ralph is racked with curiosity as to why Prioress Alicia has resigned, we are racked too. Such impatience is a mark of the reader's commitment both to this community and to the power of story.

The novel contains an image of itself in the 'Lay of Mamillion', the 'wandering' narrative. Sir Ralph discovers the poem by chance while he is in search of a hawk. Described by the poet's widow as ' "an English epic" ' (118), the poem has more in common with romance than epic, with its enchanters, chivalric trappings and rambling adventures. The poem is unfinished, its end unknown. Sir Ralph resists it at first but converts to affectionate loyalty, a model for our own relationship to Townsend Warner's odd novel. Appropriately enough in a novel which plays across boundaries, Mamillion's own status is blurred. Sometimes he is the hero of the poem and sometimes he is a character in his own right. Sir Ralph imagines him journeying to London to gain an audience in 'a new series of wanderings, taking the track to Lintoft and westward' (273). The novel is likewise a 'wandering' text which grows on acquaintance, and inspires in the reader an unexpected loyalty to its vagaries. It too is a disguised epic, taking the shape of a rambling romance peopled not by huge heroes but by fearful nuns exhilarating themselves with tales of small cata-strophes (7).

Townsend Warner herself appreciated only too well the value of books and stories, particularly in times of threat and unrest. In the pre-Caxton world of Oby books are precious objects, a status they achieved again in Townsend Warner's wartime world of austerity and paper shortages. She considered that 'perhaps the only significant result of our war-working careers' was the work she did sorting through books collected for pulping: she rescued rarities and books of use to the Blitzed Libraries Scheme.[37] She was also a kind of story-teller:

> She embarked on an extraordinary career as a lecturer, first for the WEA, then for the Labour Party and eventually for the forces. The range of subjects she covered was quite phenomenal . . . 'I haven't repeated myself yet, though we are getting wilder and wilder'.[38]

It is fitting that the final story of the novel, which has no reason to stop at any point, should be about the nun who deserts Oby. By reading about Oby we have kept it alive as Sir Ralph did with his beloved 'Lay of Mamillion'. When we leave the novel at the end it feels as if we are deserting Oby and its nuns. In this way Townsend Warner reinforces her point that stories are what keep communities alive and together. Ulti-mately, the best community to dedicate oneself to in wartime, Townsend Warner tells us, is the community of the story; she called *The Corner That Held Them* 'my most personal book probably.'[39]

Although we might be disappointed by the lack of working-class women's fiction which emerged from the People's War, the shift this chapter has tried to show is significant. With the progress of the war, class diminished as a structuring principle and an over-riding concern in women's fiction. Some novelists reacted with nostalgic regret, others with relief as tired old hierarchies dissolved. As the tide turned towards collectivity, writers such as Hansford Johnson and Townsend Warner cast the societies in their novels into shapes to match the new patterns of wartime Britain. To look in more detail at how the war affected the inner workings of the community in its most vital constituent part, the home, we shall need another chapter.

3

OPEN HOUSE AND CLOSED DOORS

Canon Palfrey walked up the vicarage drive and looked in through his drawing room window, hardly knowing what he might see there. He had learned to expect anything on a Monday evening between the hours of six and eight when the ladies of the parish had their Red Cross lectures. He remembered the first occasion very vividly and his shock at seeing a skeleton dangling in front of the large still life painting of the Dutch school, which had been given to them by an aunt of his wife.
Barbara Pym, 'Home Front Novel', 1939

One got a feeling of functional anarchy, of loose plumbing, of fittings shocked from their place.
Elizabeth Bowen, 'In the Square', 1941

The war was a great opener of homes. Bombs blew them apart, and official policy forced them to open their doors to strangers. The war disrupted domesticity and brought new habits into the kitchens, living rooms and bedrooms of the nation. Women's fiction, always alert to alterations in the domestic terrain, was quick to respond. Novelists showed that the opened home could be a more hospitable and tolerant place, with new patterns for living and a refreshing frankness. But they also questioned the merits of some of these restructured households, as well as the sincerity and success with which doors were being opened to evacuees and refugees. While new ways with food were applauded, new ways with sex were greeted with more ambivalence: some boundaries were still essential and not all doors could be flung open with impunity.

One of the first effects of the war on the home was to make it more visible. The very word forced itself on to the public consciousness in September 1939: 'On the night of Friday, 1st September 1939, you heard for the first time the now familiar words "This is the BBC Home Service" '.[1] By the end of September the BBC was giving the home a public presence, with the start of 'The Home Front', a radio programme 'describing aspects of wartime life in Britain'.[2] Radio helped to open up the workings of the home, to make it both a more accessible place and a more self-aware one. The home quickly became the headquarters of the People's War, and of the nation itself as Churchill conceived of 'our island home'. An icon of the war, the home represented what must be defended and protected; but at the same time it was changing its constituent elements and altering its behaviour patterns. At the very least, it demanded to be seen from a different perspective. In the epigraph to this chapter Canon Palfry stands at an unaccustomed angle to his home, looking in from the outside and superimposing a skeleton, a *memento belli*. Most women writers seemed to welcome the changes, albeit with some obligatory circumspection. ' "Oh God," ' prays Connie on the night of the Red Cross lecture in Canon Palfrey's drawing room, ' "don't let there be a war." But at the back of her mind was the thought that a war might be rather exciting. It would certainly make a difference to the days that were so monotonously the same.'[3]

The motif of the open house expresses the prevalent mood, as novels kept pace with the ideals of 'home-made socialism'. The open house is the emblem of the nation's adaptation to war: the values it exemplifies are those of hospitality, tolerance and community. Novels often locate themselves in large houses run by competent women (the men are away at the war, or if they are still in charge they are inadequate or bogus[4]). These large houses have opened their doors: Mrs Anstruther's house in Susan Ertz's *Anger in the Sky* (1943) is filled to capacity with a motley collection of fifty or sixty evacuees, poor relations, bombed-out friends and hangers-on, all held together by Mrs Anstruther's home-making talents. These new domestic groupings can be an improvement when a dysfunctional family is replaced by better versions: the aunt in Dorothy Whipple's *They Were Sisters* (1943) makes a good home for the daughters of her two sisters. Women novelists usually responded positively to revisions of the domestic; 'loose plumbing', to use Bowen's phrase, could be a trial, but it could also be exciting.

Writers used the image of the broken home to chart changes to the fabric of buildings and society alike. Bowen's story 'In the Square' (1941) measures the present against the past, as a man returns to a house he used to visit before the war. The beautiful London square has been damaged by bombs; it is a fractured world, broken but brighter than before, and the 'breach' is 'dazzling'. The extra-bright double summer time evening light let into the Square by a bomb-created gap brings 'illicit gold' to the treetops, and the self-contained square of domestic life 'exposes' itself like the wallpapers of bombed houses, 'exaggerated into viridians, yellows and corals that they had probably never been'. As for the breach in the house Rupert visits, its head is absent and the ill-kempt rooms are occupied by his mistress and his wife, an 'independent' caretaker couple and their children, and a transitory schoolboy. ' "The house seems to belong to everyone now" ' says the wife, Magdela. In this louche and 'functional anarchy' Magdela seems to be having an affair; the mistress now loves 'someone else in a big way' and wants to leave. She has no sense of the past in the Square:

> The perspective of useless dining-room through the archway, the light fading from it through the bombed gap, did not affect her. She had not enough imagination to be surprised by the past – still less by its end.

So the past is over, the elegant Square breached, but the future has yet to take shape: 'As to her plans tonight – she never knew'. Magdela also resists the future, evading Rupert's offer of dinner and insisting, ' "Of course, I have no plans. This is no time to make plans, now." ' The schoolboy Bennet sees no future for the Square: ' "You think this place will patch up? I suppose it depends who wants it. Anybody can have it as far as I'm concerned. You can't get to anywhere from here." ' Bennet, a strangely regressive figure, is the only character in the story with a plan, and that only for food. 'Bennet, going out to hunt food, kept close along under the fronts of the houses with a primitive secretiveness.' Things ending, coming apart, and a sense of primitive energy infuse Bowen's broken Square with their 'illicit' light, as this inconsequential moment reveals: 'this singular summer evening – parched, freshening and a little acrid with ruins'.

As the homes of Britain were opened up and remade, novelists moved in to explore the new domestic arrangements – usually women living without men. Sylvia Townsend Warner shows the People's War county-style in her story 'Sweethearts and Wives',[5] which pitches the reader into confusion from the start:

> Sometimes Justina and Midge discussed what would happen if all their husbands came on leave together. Lettice could go to her grandmother's – but then William would not see her, and really she was now a nice, displayable baby. The Sheridans might find a double bed at the farm – but that would not take away Roy and the twins, and if Mrs Sheridan slept out, one could not expect her to be back to get breakfast.

'All their husbands' – what is going on? Townsend Warner blurs our sense of who is who in this 'compound household', where indirect speech is sometimes unattributed and a visiting husband has the 'disquieting impression of having four children at Badger Cottage, and two, or possibly three, wives'. Although the amused narrative voice evades overt judgment, the bad faith of the landed gentry obtrudes. Midge and Justina's mothers assume that their daughters 'should stay on at home, keeping their spirits up, poor little things, by giving a helping hand in country houses suddenly denuded of servants'. These mothers pave the way for their daughters who 'decided to set up house together', a game which can be played successfully only with the help of Mrs Sheridan, 'the king-pin and glory of the establishment; she cooked'. Ambiguity haloes Mrs Sheridan; is she exploited or in control? In the first paragraph much depends on her preparing the breakfast. Justina and Midge rely on her, but uneasily: ' "She had better have the sole and we'll have toasted cheese" '. Midge's husband William loathes Mrs Sheridan, but he does ride her horse and use her as a baby-sitter. The relaxed freedoms of Badger Cottage may be a noble goal, but they result in chaos, bad food, and marital rows between the women: 'Midge lit another cigarette. She was still looking like a guilty wife and spoke savagely. "What else could I do, Justina?".'

As the men were leaving the homes of Britain, the evacuees and refugees were arriving. It was 'ordeal by evacuee' which first challenged the home's status as the Hearth Virtuous. Would it be open enough to cope with its new family? The ability to deal well with these new arrivals was an important mark of grace. Evacuation became a moralised issue, as the social historian Margaret Cole recognised:

> What the evacuation scheme did was to make the countryside and the comfortable classes suddenly and painfully aware, in their own persons, of

the deep and shameful poverty which exists today in the rich cities of England.[6]

Novelists fought shy of Cole's vision of sudden enlightenment, but knew they should be on the side of the evacuee angels. The potential for plot and sentiment offered by evacuees was too good to miss, though novelists needed tact with their perhaps evacuee-stressed readership. Reluctance to open one's arms and one's house at the outbreak of war earned instant disapproval. Aubrey who says he would ' "rather be *dead* than share the cottage with a slum family" ' is an easy target for Margaret Lane in *Where Helen Lies* (1944); and many novels contrasted disagreeable middle-class coldness with welcoming working-class hospitality. If this was a convenient excuse for avoiding responsibility, it did carry some condemnation of middle-class attitudes. The rural community of Margaret Iles's *Nobody's Darlings* (1942) may squabble over the cash opportunities the evacuees provide, but this is a friendly world in comparison with the widespread hostility elsewhere. Betty, the homesick evacuee from Kentish Town in Ruth Adam's *Murder in the Home Guard* (1942) is shunted round six billets and spends two interludes in hospital when no one else will have her. Adam describes how middle-class enthusiasm for sweeping away class barriers collapses within minutes, as Betty and her head-lice are shown the door. Betty runs away, and is rescued by a kindly policeman who takes her back to his home. Adam scorns the sentimental resolution where 'the pathetic wistfulness of the little waif melts the heart of the hard housewife', but she none the less endows the working-class kitchen with the attributes of heaven for Betty:

> The crowded room, the food, the wailing baby . . . filled her with a sense of rapturous fulfilment, like a pilgrim who, on seeing the pearly gates at last, realises that the Evangelists have not fooled him. (251)

And what of the evacuees themselves? Here women writers seem to have held their fire. Criticism could be tantamount to treason, a lapse of faith in the powers of the open house to take in and heal. Their evacuees are rarely as repellent as the Connolly children in Evelyn Waugh's *Put Out More Flags* (1942), but adults were fairer game. Sylvia Townsend Warner's baleful Evie, 'a tremendous blonde girl with a heavy jaw . . . a sense of something resentful in a bedroom', has a dire effect on the house in 'The Proper Circumstances' (1944).[7] Cisterns overflow, plaster drops, bluebottles and clothes moths swarm. Many years ago, the narrator remembers,

> I read a book called *Wild Talents*, a book about vampires, werewolves, and poltergeists. All of us, so the author implied, are potentially one or another of these things. It is just a matter of circumstances being right for us to develop that way. The proper circumstances to develop poltergeistism include being adolescent, preferably female, far from home, dull-witted, oppressed, and resentful.

The narrator begins her story with her grandfather's record for buying dud horses, 'My grandmother said it was destiny'; she ends awaiting the effect of the 'Conscription of Labour (Female) Act' on the malingering Evie. Destiny in this story is the curse of the evacuee.

Towards evacuee children, however, Townsend Warner is much more sympathetic. The children in 'Noah's Ark'[8] have witnessed terrible scenes in the Plymouth blitz before being evacuated to the country; their imaginative refuge is the zoo of exotic, destructive wild animals which their shepherd host encourages them to draw. Quoting Blake's poem 'The Tyger' – 'What dread hand? and what dread feet?' – the little girl tries to make the violence of her habitat consonant with the violence of nature. The story ends with the shepherd's wife reading the children a newspaper article, and their adjustment to 'ordinary' responses to warfare:

> 'Owing to the continuance of blitz bombing the authorities of Plymouth Zoo have caused all the dangerous animals to be destroyed.'
>
> The girl stared in front of her and the boy, with desperate solicitude, stared at the girl. *O God*, he prayed, *O God, don't let her cry*! She did not cry.
>
> Their Ark, so brightly painted, so gloriously companied, had foundered under them. They swam on the waste of waters and for a little it seemed that a few small harmless beasts swam with them; but presently these disappeared, and nothing broke the surface except a distant unpeopled Ararat. As Mrs Purefoy remarked, you could see with one eye what a weight had lifted off their minds. By the time the school re-opened they were drawing bombers and stoning water-rats like any other children about the place.[9]

When it came to refugees, novelists felt free to be more unpleasant, perhaps because they felt less constrained by surrogate-mother obligations. Nevertheless, impatience with the intruder had to be tempered by compassion for the sufferer – ' "poor little beast, but really she is a trial" ' (Stella Gibbons, *Westwood*, 1946) – and there were benefits. Detective novels exploited refugees as convenient red herrings,[10] and they also featured as rivals in love.[11] More generally, the refugee could also expose the insularity of the British. Many characters who encounter refugees in these wartime novels seem to have had little contact with anyone outside Britain. Even the kindly Letty, the secretary in Noel Streatfeild's *I Ordered a Table for Six* (1942), has reservations about the rich Viennese Gerda. Elsewhere colonels and vicars expose their xenophobia: ' "The vicar doesn't *care* for Russians," said Agnes, speaking as if they were a kind of wartime dish'.[12] Novelists also used refugees more positively, as the exotic 'other' to inject colour and warmth into chilly wartime Britain. The repressed Margaret Steggles in Stella Gibbons's *Westwood* (1946) contrasts with the voluble Zita, who is no beauty but attractive and never without a lover; she has 'a succession of young men with whom she would hold interminable conversations in the Old Vienna Cafe at Lyons Corner House on her afternoons off' (101). Like many female refugees in fact and fiction, Zita is employed in domestic work and adapts herself to her British home.[13] But it was not so much their adaptability as their difference which drew the novelist to the foreigner, as Stella Gibbons was to Zita, Richmal Crompton to the balalaika-playing Mrs Stoneberry in *Mrs Frensham Describes a Circle* (1942), and Helen Ashton to Lisel Hahn in *Tadpole Hall* (1941). Lisel ' "goes about the house all day long in a blue dress covered with little red men and women dancing," ' much to Mrs Drake's disapproval – ' "One can't put up with it indefinitely" ' (55). The refugee who turns the tables on those who would exploit her as a domestic slave by capturing the heart of the head of the household, as Vartouhi Annamatta does in Stella Gibbons's *The Bachelor*, can only be congratulated. Ken Fielding, an amiable 45-year-old solicitor, knows that Vartouhi is a grasping opportunist, but he enjoys her youth and vibrancy; she is a refreshing change from the dullness of his sister-dominated routine.

Male refugees were allotted a different range of parts. They may be wise older figures, perhaps a consequence of Freud's arrival in England in 1938. Troubled characters are counselled by psychiatrists or scientists such as Rudi von Ritterhaus in Phyllis Bottome's *Within the Cup* (1943), the Resident Surgical Officer in Helen Ashton's *Yeoman's Hospital* (1944) or Ludwin in Jane Oliver's *The Hour of the Angel* (1942) and *In No Strange Land* (1944). In literature as in life, problems of acclimatisation are more severe for male refugees. Sylvia Townsend Warner's story 'Emil'[14] is all the sadder for the hopes of the well-meaning people who open their houses. Mrs Hathaway announces the arrival of a young Austrian who has escaped to England after the *Anschluss* in 1938: "It's a boy," she said, and blushed, for it sounded so ridiculous, as though she were announcing a birth.' But however open and welcoming it is, the pleasant village of France Green must feel alien to the exile. On Emil's first evening with the Hathaways conversation flags, 'and it was a relief when he said, "You have a piano. I, too, am fond of music." ' Then Mrs Hathaway thinks: 'Now I shall be caught out . . . They are all so intensely musical, and suppose he asks me to play duets with him?' Her dread of the duet acknowledges the status of the refugee, in the home but not a harmonious part of it. The Munich Crisis offers Emil the identity he needs. He becomes the warrior, digging trenches and air-raid shelters, throwing himself into war work, and 'when it was too dark to dig any longer, he produced a mouth organ and the gang marched home with a swagger'. But Emil's hour as local hero cannot last; the crisis passes and the sense of emptiness returns. The story closes with the moment that Mrs Hathaway has feared: 'he stared at the keyboard. Then he turned and looked at Mrs Hathaway – a look of mournful, scornful, listless understanding. "Couldn't we play a duet?" he said.'

Together evacuees and refugees opened up the home; the departure of the servants for the factories and forces made its running a more visible and pressing matter.[15] Domesticity thus defamiliarised became newly interesting. Lady Winifred Peck's *House-Bound* (1942) assumes that her readers will be fascinated by chapter after chapter in which Rose Fairlaw learns how to cook and clean, starting from almost total ignorance, 'watching out of the corner of her eye to see whether you used hot or cold water for the toilet of potatoes and "veg." and if you did or didn't use soap' (60). The new regime is tyrannical, 'the House itself was the supreme god, to which offerings of soap and Vim, floor polish, and most of all, elbow-grease had to be made every day' (77). Although Peck wants to show that housework can be a blessing (Rose thinks often of the Biblical Martha), she is more concerned to use the house as a metaphor for the closed 'bound' self, which the war opens and airs. When Rose's house is partially destroyed by a bomb, her son asks her: ' "Have you lost a tyrant or a friend?" ' and Rose replies, ' "How can I tell?" ' (221) Rose's life is opened up with new possibilities as her house falls around her. But the novel does not free Rose entirely from her house, rather it ends with the domestic revised to include men as well as women. In this new era Rose learns her domestic science from the New World and a man, in the form of an American major stationed near by.

Her husband, old-school Scottish solicitor, manages an inch of reform, and Rose finally hears with joy that her house can be restored, 'her spirits rising incredibly at the prospect of having a home again after all, and a husband who was amused by and sympathetic with domestic details' (227).

Food, in the words of Ministry of Food campaigns, was a 'Munition of War',[16] and novelists deployed it skilfully. Its role in the open house of war was manifold; sometimes it simply offered pleasure, and sometimes it was part of a moral scheme. The scope for pleasure was obvious. Virginia Woolf was not the only author to 'make up imaginary meals',[17] and Susan Ertz opens *Anger in the Sky* with a flourish she knows will entice her readers in 1943: 'Mrs Peters went to the oven and opened the door. Six great deep-dish plum tarts were baking there, and the lovely odours rushed out.' Changes in diet provided useful plot fodder, and new culinary arrivals could prove deadly. ' "And then, of course, came the extraordinary business of the grated carrot," ' comments Mrs Bradley on the murder weapon in Gladys Mitchell's *When Last I Died* (1941, 55). Aunt Flora has choked to death on this 'heathenish food'. Usually though, the appetite with which characters swallow their boring rations is a mark of how authors and characters have committed themselves to the war effort. Shoals of sardines cross the pages of wartime writing: they punctuate the start and finish of the Davenants' stay *At Mrs Lippincote's* (Elizabeth Taylor, 1945), and bond kindred souls in Daphne du Maurier's play *The Years Between* (1944). Richard and Diana demonstrate their togetherness as they laugh good-humouredly at Nanny's offer of spam for supper, 'but I believe I can find a tin of sardines' – 'For the Lord's sake don't do that' protests Richard.[18]

Not to care too much is the right attitude to adopt towards food. After all, people in Britain are not starving, and overly meticulous ration control is a bad sign. It is butter but it might be guns in the hostile Kelway household in Elizabeth Bowen's *The Heat of the Day*, where

> each one of the family had his or her own ration placed before his or her own plate in a different coloured china shell . . .
>
> 'I would offer you some of my butter,' said Ernestine, 'but that would only make you feel uncomfy.' (111)

Relaxation and openness about food are the wartime order of the day. In Angela Thirkell's eyes, 'it is a sign of the changing times that Mrs Belton, who would certainly never have discussed a host's food before the war, unless asked to do so, expressed loud admiration for the freshness of the Vicarage fish' (*The Headmistress*, 1944, 74). Barbara Pym's characters notice a new frankness:

> Harriet picked up the packet of All-Bran.
> 'For constipation' she read. 'How outspoken we are now!'
> I laughed and told her about Miss Moberley, who had pasted a strip of paper over the indelicate words when she had a young clergyman staying with her.[19]

Openness towards foreign food is also a virtue. Mrs Drake criticises her refugee cook in *Tadpole Hall*: ' "Who wants prunes in the stew and nuts in the pastry? When Lisel first came she was always asking for the most peculiar things, wine and cream and red peppers." ' Colonel Heron protests, ' "I like Frau Hahn's cooking," but nobody paid any attention to him' (54). They should have, for by the end of the book this wartime Jane Eyre has cooked her way into his heart. Restaurants could provide a holiday from the regime of rations, coupons and points. Like good holidays, they brim with erotic potential, and many wartime novels and stories set key scenes in restaurants. But this is escape-eating; the real campaigns are conducted in the home. Newspapers, magazines and the BBC gave helpful recipes which used free ingredients such as rooks and snow, and 'Housewives have learned to cook potatoes in two hundred different ways'.[20] Novels did not offer recipes, but contextualised eating as part of the wartime code of behaviour.

The ritual of dinner winds its way through the second chapter of E.M. Delafield's *Late and Soon* (1943), an account of one of the lowest points in wartime cuisine. General Levallois, his widowed sister Lady Valentine Arbell and her daughter Jessica are atrophying in their large, cold country house. The fringe of the Chinese shawl in which Valentine conscientiously dresses for dinner catches repeatedly in the heavy furniture. Its wearer is chained by her sense of duty to this dying world and dinner exemplifies it all:

> The General put on his glasses and read the little white menu-card in its silver holder, that he always expected to find on the table in front of him in the evenings, and that Valentine always wrote out for him.
> He inspected it without exhilaration, and pushed it away again.
> Ivy came in again, changed the plates, and handed round first a silver entree dish, and then two vegetable dishes.

'Do we *have* to have baked cod every single day?' asked Jessica plaintively.

'It was all I could get.'

Much later on, General Levallois addressed his sister.

'I thought we'd agreed not to have the potatoes boiled every time they appear.'

'I don't suppose Mrs Ditchley has many ideas beyond boiling them. And it's not easy to spare any fat for frying them or doing anything amusing. I'll speak to her tomorrow.'

Valentine made these rejoinders almost as she might have spoken them in her sleep, so familiar were they. She knew that the food was uninteresting, ill-prepared and lacking in variety, and she regretted it mildly, on her brother's account, rather more on Jessica's. (19–20)

Valentine is kind but ineffectual; we know it will be cod and boiled potatoes again tomorrow. The meal takes place in slow motion, its elaborate rituals and service accentuate the dreariness of the food.

When Ivy handed round the dish where sardines lay upon dark and brittle fragments of toast, it was not Jessica but General Levallois who complained.

'I thought we'd just been eating fish, Val?'

'I know we have. Really and truly, Reggie, we've got to take what we can get nowadays.'

'Certainly we have. But I don't think this woman has much idea of what's what. *Surely* she can arrange things so that we don't have two fish courses one on top of the other.'

'She can't, but I suppose I could,' said Valentine. 'I must try and manage better another time.' (21)

The stoicism of the shires in the face of the sardine may be admirable but Valentine is too tolerant. This is the house closed: Valentine is trapped by her sense of good form, her fear of offence and her inertia. The arrival of war opens the doors and she is rescued by a *deus ex militia*, a former sweetheart who is billeted on her by the Army.

Other women can escape from their homes only on a twelve-hour pass. Forced out of her house by a time-bomb, Dionysia Campion has a day of freedom in Townsend Warner's story 'From Above'.[21] Her husband James, 'a man full of plans and foresight', has left two heavy suitcases packed, and Dionysia abandons her house with a sense of betrayal:

> She felt as though she were being eyed by countless misjudged and faithful
> spaniels. *You are leaving us*, blinked chairs and tables and ornaments. *You
> don't love us any more.*

On her way out she takes a memento, a small satin child-bed cushion with
'*Bless the Child and Save the Mother* . . . picked out on it in small pins', a fit
companion for her entry into the world, on at least her temporary release.
Once Dionysia is out of the house and in a taxi,

> suddenly everything became clear to her. She would leave the suitcases at
> James's club, he could meet them there for lunch. As for herself, she would
> take a day off, she would go exploring, she would visit St. Paul's.

Dionysia is a Londoner who has never been to St Paul's, but the cathedral
intimidates her. She prefers the 'cosy and reassuring' telephone booth
where she rings her husband: ' "I don't think I *can* lunch with you, not
while your home is hanging on tenterhooks." ' James snaps at her and a
moment of enlightenment strikes her. Not only bombs come from above
in this story, there is also deliverance:

> What on earth possessed me, she thought, to say *your home*? Isn't it my
> home too? Our bed, our rosewood dining-table, our Adam settee? Deep
> within her, eating away like the chemical of a time-bomb, an invincible
> truthfulness responded and said: No! James's home, James's choice, James's
> taste, James's wife, who was James's home's caretaker.
>
> For it could not be denied. The policeman had come to her like some
> draped angel, calling on her to arise and leave the fleshpots of Egypt. At the
> most, he had promised an absolute departure. At the least he had bestowed
> a whole day during which her responsibilities to 11 Albion Terrace would
> be in abeyance, a whole day in which she would be free to gad whither she
> pleased. How ridiculous of her to think she wanted to see St. Paul's. Of
> course she didn't. That sort of wish was merely a copy-catting of James.
> Her wishes were bounded by the West End and solitude, were quite
> simple, base and ordinary.
>
> What she wished was first to have her hair washed and set, her face
> massaged, her hands manicured. Then she would like a simple, base and
> ordinary lunch, macaroni cheese and lemon pie. Then she would like to go
> to the gramophone shop and try over a lot of records, sitting in a little

cubicle furnished with nothing but an easy chair and an ash-tray. Then she
would like a cup of chocolate and a hot muffin. (174)

Dionysia revels in her day of unalloyed pleasure, but when she returns
home to Albion Terrace in the evening she finds that the time-bomb has
not gone off, and 'the child-bed cushion made its get-away and fell in the
gutter'.

Although day-release is occasionally granted, the Albion Terraces of
England must stand firm as Britannia Domestica, the lodestone and
inspiration for an embattled nation. Hence the need for boundaries: too
much toleration, relaxation and freedom could be dangerous. The home
that was invited to be more open in terms of whom it sheltered (evacuees,
refugees), and what it cooked was nevertheless forbidden to open its
bedroom doors as well. Sex was where tolerance faltered. While there was
more frankness and confidence about sexual matters, and more permissiveness too, there was also a need to establish limits. Sexual openness
could too easily be mistaken for promiscuity, a dangerous risk at a time
when female fidelity was national policy. Men fight and their women
support them: women's sexual loyalty was equated with the sacrifices men
were making at the front, and advocated as a patriotic contribution to the
morale of the nation's forces. The advice which poured from women's
magazines exhorted women to be faithful, or at least to be reticent. But
war is a well-known aphrodisiac: 'it came to be rumoured ... that
everybody in London was in love'.[22] The breeze of independence was
blowing strongly for many young women, who were living away from
home for the first time, with more money and confidence and less super-
vision. Women, according to historians Penny Summerfield and Nicole
Crockett, 'learned a variety of things about their own and other people's
sexuality because of their participation in the war effort',[23] and the fiction
of the time maps a mood of growing frankness together with more
tolerant attitudes. While romantic novelists, in the words of the critic
Rachel Anderson, 'set to work with their pens ... to do their bit for
Britain', and in the process became duller,[24] other writers were less
inhibited and more curious. Work, in particular, gave them access to new
areas of observation. Middle-class women conscripted into factories were
intrigued by what they saw of the sexual behaviour – mainly the
confidence – of working-class women. The sexual narratives provided by
work fascinated writers such as Diana Murray Hill, Inez Holden and
Monica Dickens. Murray Hill recorded at length the behaviour of her

new friends from the factory as they toured the pubs, getting into

> one near shave, when a party of airmen, up to no good, pursued them to a
> local café, which ended in a brawl with chairs and crockery-throwing in the
> café. In this the waitress joined, Lil and her friend escaping through a room
> upstairs.[25]

Susan Ertz's middle-aged woman is also curious as she looks about her in
the restaurant in *Anger in the Sky* (1943), speculating on the sexuality of
the beautiful girl in airforce blue:

> What, Mrs A wondered, were that girl's experiences? How did she deal
> with lads soon to die and eager for love? How would she deal with that
> already enthralled young naval officer with whom she was lunching? How
> little one heard, in this war, of 'morality'. In the last war it had seemed to be
> the chief preoccupation of many elderly folk and many more of the clergy.
> Was it that young people were better equipped, nowadays, to look after
> themselves? (42)

Mrs A and her author seem quite non-judgemental, and we can chart a
rise in admissible sexual activity. Fran, the heroine of Christianna Brand's
Heads You Lose (1941), airily admits that she and James ' "have had an
occasional bodge" ' (166). The attractive Alicia in Stella Gibbons's *The
Bachelor* (1944), 'a brave reserved girl, with no creed and no standards
except the contemporary one of not moaning and being a bore' (304), has
an affair with a married man and enjoys three-day parties (she also works in
a factory). When the decent young hero proposes 'she hesitated for a
moment, then said in a cooler tone: "You don't mind about my not being–?"
He shook his head' (312). Pamela Frankau's lovers on leave in *The Willow
Cabin* (1949) could not be more direct: ' "Lord, how I want to make love."
"Oh, me too, but where?" ' (181). While these novels agree that sexual
activity is allowable, they rarely make it sound pleasurable. Indeed, it
sometimes seems distinctly unerotic: Christianna Brand's 'bodge' has little
to commend it. Novelists were unable to ignore the increase in sexual
activity, and disapproval would have seemed prudish. However, they could
not extol the delights of sexual liberation and gratification with impunity.
Female sexual pleasure is often a contentious issue, and it was particularly
so at this time, when official policy firmly decreed fidelity but people's
attitudes were apparently becoming more lenient. Sex seems to have been
acceptable in fiction as long as it was not too enjoyable.

In keeping with the spirit of the age, permissiveness is advocated in women's novels from about 1943 onwards. Phyllis Bottome presents it as a political obligation in *Within the Cup* (1943). Nineteen-year-old Gillian is in moral anguish because her father and her brother are both having affairs with her best friend, who also happens to be the vicar's wife. Her Austrian psychiatrist adviser suggests tolerance, as Europe falls and nearby Plymouth is bombed. Gillian sees the affairs as ' "a sort of treachery . . . to my mother" ', but Rudi objects: ' "Are you not making altogether too much of this business of love-making?" ' (113) He criticises her moral attitude to sex with the implication that she is taking a fascist line; Rudi straightforwardly equates sexual freedom with political freedom and democracy. E. Arnot Robertson's *The Signpost* (1943) also favours open-mindedness in wartime. Tom Fairburn, a wounded RAF pilot troubled by the destruction he has caused over Germany, retreats to Ireland in the summer of 1940. He meets a Frenchwoman on the boat to Belfast and has a brief affair with her which helps to restore his sense of well-being. The couple camp out in a remote fishing village, where the local priest would like to see them 'stoned out of the place' (107) because they are not married, an attitude the novel condemns as backward and inappropriate. Writers could also be open about lesbianism. Mary Renault's *The Friendly Young Ladies* (1944) settles her lesbian couple into a relaxed riverside community as an antidote to a middle England where sexual repression is the norm for girls like Elsie:

> At seventeen her mind was still like Madame Tussaud's Exhibition, with Love, represented by kings and queens in velvet, on the upper floors, and Sex, like the Chamber of Horrors, tucked away underground. (11)

Leo's houseboat is portrayed as an attractive, bohemian 'Noah's Ark' of creativity and sexual diversity. Although Renault compromises at the novel's close (as she admits in an Afterword written forty years later[26]) in marshalling Leo towards heterosexuality, she does make some good points about Leo's need to tell her own story obliquely (for example, the way she tells Elsie indirectly about Helen, and writes her pastiche Westerns). Renault also conveys Leo's difficulty in speaking about her body: ' "Why didn't you tell him you had an off day, like anyone else would?" ' asks Helen, who is a nurse. ' "Maybe they would, in one of your filthy hospitals." "Oh, nonsense. It isn't 1890" ' (117).

When it came to sexual adventuring, permissiveness could sometimes give way to criticism and distaste. The scope offered by the war for sexual opportunism is clearly understood in Margery Sharp's story 'Night Engagement' (1941),[27] in which the engagement is both military and romantic. Mrs Catchpole pragmatically tours her daughter round the shelters of London under fire in search of the 'nice young fellow' so desired by a 'girl that respects herself'. Methods must move with the times, and Mrs Catchpole is relieved when Doris is buried in a cellar with the suitable Arthur, and 'though maybe he didn't know his fate, I and Doris and his Mum did all right'. Diana Gardner's 'Landgirl' (1940) is another sort of sexual opportunist.[28] Una, an unpleasant college girl, wages petty war on the farmer's wife, 'that bitch' Mrs Farrant – tea spilt on the table-cloth to avenge short sugar rations. As Una admits, 'no one can accuse me of being sweet-tempered'. She succeeds in framing Mr Farrant as an adulterer, and his defeated wife leaves the farm. But Una's triumph is Pyrrhic, and her treatment of the decent Mr Farrant is shabby. Gardner's story was accepted by *Horizon* because it conformed to a stereotype of women-at-war: the image of the landgirl was already imbued with notions of sexual availability, and Gardner adds to this an aggressive 'savvy' which is not as smart as it thinks itself.[29]

Tolerance of sexual freedom reaches its limits in Marghanita Laski's *To Bed with Grand Music* (1946), a daring and clear-headed analysis of wartime sexuality which Laski published under the pseudonym Sarah Russell. The novel satirises the sexual mores of wartime London, as we follow the heroine's career from provincial lady to metropolitan whore. After Graham Robertson's departure overseas his wife Deborah jettisons their two-year-old son upon a caring housekeeper, and heads for London and a 'tart-trap' flat. This is the bed-hopping world of Barbara Skelton's memoirs,[30] a wartime London permanently in a 'state of at least slight intoxication' (54), where charming women and transitory men dine in expensive restaurants and talk wittily through air raids, prepared 'to die in the middle of a carefully prepared epigram' (121). Deborah's cynical line on this fast-living world would be refreshing, were it not for her descent into selfishness and immorality. She sleeps with a succession of men for silk stockings and fur coats – 'Geoffrey was succeeded by Martin and Martin by Nils from the Norwegian Navy' (124). For most of the book the narrator sustains an air of amused tolerance towards her transparent hedonist, whose immorality has been bred in the extraordinary circumstances of the war. But by the end reader-disapproval for Deborah is assured. She decides she does not want her husband back and deliberately delays his return home (a favour granted in return for 'being nice' to a man at the War Office); she seduces one of his trusting friends, and she corrupts an old college acquaintance left miserable after her husband's departure. ' "I know just how you feel," ' says Deborah – as indeed she does, because this is where her story began. She tells her, ' "And what's more I know just what you want, and that's a damn good party" ' (158). The two women walk back to Deborah's flat in the last scene of the book, and Laski leaves the reader with an indictment of wartime sexual permissiveness. A corrupter of innocence, a hypocrite who pretends she is part of the war effort to retain her child-minder, Deborah does however possess a degree of self-knowledge which gives the novel a surprising edge: 'There's no going back, Deborah's mind said to her all that night, there's no going back . . . nothing but going forward to gaiety and loss and loss' (150). For all its amused cynicism and understanding of the urgings of the hour, *To Bed with Grand Music* strongly suggests that Deborah Robertson should not have left her home and her son. The message appears to be that some houses have been too open; too much freedom can be destructive. Novels about women who contemplate and reject the idea of having affairs proliferated towards the end of the war: Elizabeth Taylor's *At Mrs Lippincote's*, Betty Miller's *On the Side of the Angels* and Winifred Peck's *There is a Fortress* were all published in 1945.

When women wrote about their wartime experiences, both at the time and subsequently, they seemed to appreciate friendships more than sex, or they claimed to, perhaps as an evasion of the taboo on admitting sexual pleasure. Wartime diaries published more recently are less reticent: ' "What a life," I said, "never knowing if you're going to be bombed or seduced from one moment to the next!" '.[31] During the war many women acknowledged the new importance of female friendship in their lives. June 1940 found Virginia Woolf worried that Elizabeth Bowen had not answered her letter: 'A slaty queasy feeling about E.B. discussed it with L. What a time to quarrel with friends.' Two days later she writes, 'Paris now almost besieged – 20,000 of our men cut off,' and a postcard from Bowen 'warmed & consoled, for if one's friends are to die in the flesh now, what's left?'[32] But however greatly it was treasured, friendship figures surprisingly little in the fiction of the time, and it rarely comes to the forefront. When it does, it assumes the character of something easily recognisable and taken for granted. Townsend Warner's reference to 'one of those wartime friendships, open-hearted and dated as Morning Glories'[33] describes a phenomenon which sounds so common that it needs no elaboration. Later accounts redress the balance.[34] Harriet Pringle, in the *Balkan* and *Levant Trilogies* which Olivia Manning wrote between 1962 and 1980, gains in strength and independence through the friendships she makes throughout the six novels. Women's wartime friendships seem to have been the essential but nearly invisible stuff of life, as they helped to sustain the house opened up so decisively by the war.

4

WORK AND THE RECALCITRANT FACTORY

To most of us the War Effort was a very remote thing, hardly connected with our work at all.

Diana Murray Hill, *Ladies May Now Leave Their Machines*, 1944

Nobody's temper was very good on the bench these days. They were short-handed and in a perpetual rush to get the engines through to schedule.

Monica Dickens, *The Fancy*, 1943

For most women, those 'millions like us', war primarily meant work. This was the biggest single change the war brought to women's lives in Britain. Propaganda promoted the move towards full female employment, and women's writing often registered approval, though not unanimously. This was a moment when women's novels resisted the current of popular feeling. The community might be a positive force in effacing and replacing the divisions of class, but it could also be coercive in the way it controlled women's patterns of work.

Conscription, which legally compelled women to work, was introduced in Britain for the first time in December 1941. The Registration of Women had begun earlier, and it started to expose the contradictory pressures besetting the whole issue of women's work. A radio broadcast in April 1941 by Ralph Assheton, Parliamentary Secretary to the Ministry of Labour, showed the Government's dilemma. On the one hand, 'we cannot allow any healthy young women to remain idle,' but on the other hand, 'we are not going to call up . . . women who are doing essential household work; the home life of this country must go on and many women in this way are enabling others to do important work.'[1] Social historians such as Denise Riley and Penny Summerfield have studied the problems faced by women workers who were compelled to do what the Ministry of Labour agreed in 1942 were two full-time jobs.[2] Work and home were always in potential conflict, and Riley summarises the management's view of women workers as 'an outlandish new workforce with incomprehensible needs'.[3]

The main shift in the representation of women's work during the war was its change of status. Before the war it appeared, intermittently, as a necessity for working-class women, but beckoning middle-class women with possibilities for independence and adventure, an arena for individual choice and self-definition. As work became compulsory its meaning came to lie more clearly outside itself in its value to the nation, an entity which women might not previously have felt they had much stake in. The Government's keenness that women should come willingly to work – 'Mr Bevan's wanting women – in the nicest possible way!'[4] – inspired representations of women's work which emphasised heroism, community and the importance of the jobs being done. These values are particularly visible in those contemporary films which were supported by the Ministry of Information; and radio also harnessed itself to the war effort. Women's novels and stories, less prey to the attentions of propaganda but still mindful of wartime responsibilities, painted a less rosy picture. A comparison between the films and fiction of the period reveals some significant differences. While keeping up with the momentous change in women's lives, fiction had more space to analyse the pressures and contradictions built into women's war work.

Given the hands-on relationship between the Ministry of Information and the film industry, it is not surprising that film carries the most positive representations of women's war work. The MOI Films Division, according to the cultural historian Antonia Lant,

> continued to shape feature filmmaking by vetting all screenplays, rationing film stock and controlling its allocation, facilitating liaisons between the military and the studios (for the making of *The Way Ahead*, *In Which We Serve*, and *The Gentle Sex*, for instance), and calling on filmmakers to follow its opinion that 'film propaganda will be most effective when it is least

recognisable as such'. The official view was that feature films were a more subtle and therefore more powerful device than the documentary for molding British public opinion.[5]

One of the films Lant mentions, *The Gentle Sex*, is about the ATS; it was a popular film and a runner-up for the Best British Film of 1943. Written by a woman and conscious of its task, it stars the idea of the community as its cardinal virtue. Seven young women start out as separate individuals, bidding farewell to parents and husbands on their way to their new lives in the ATS. The training is stressful: shouting, saluting and marching form the women into a uniform squad. Inside this anonymous collective is set the more supportive cohesion of the group the film is following. 'Let's stick together shall we', 'We'll all be doing it together': these are the film's cheering formulae. War as community activity appears in many forms; everywhere in this film are crowds of people all dressed the same. Even leisure activities obey this mandate. The large band of girls who cycle off to play tennis all look the same; the uniformed dancers who pack the floor enjoy dances with some kind of communal element such as the Paul Jones, and sing-songs are a popular pastime. The group of seven women is a microcosm of England as they bond together to fight the war, and even class barriers eventually come down. The frosty upper-class girl has been the unpleasant odd-one-out, but she apologises for her rudeness and Scottish Maggie comments, 'Och, a bunch of women, we're bound to get on each other's nerves sometimes.'

The women's work featured in the film also emphasises community. A fifteen-minute sequence laboriously follows the women as they drive their dull-looking lorries in convoy on a four-hundred-mile trip across England, through day and night, rain and breakdown. The work is resolutely unspectacular: no stunt driving, no exciting precipices, no raids or sabotage. Instead the women drive steadily, often uphill. Their competence and endurance, coping alone in their individual lorries but part of the unglamorous group effort, express the film's idea of female heroism in war. The film also finds room for the more bellicose woman warrior. Although they were not in the front line, the ATS operated anti-aircraft guns, and the film shows the women's guns shooting down a plane. The girl whose RAF fiancé has just been posted as missing weeps, but fluffy little Betty, nicknamed Halfpint and played by Joan Greenwood, grins and waves a clenched fist.

Launder and Gilliat's 1943 film *Millions Like Us* had the more difficult task of persuading women into the factories. Like *The Gentle Sex*, it was made with MOI backing, but even so it could not pretend that women were keen to take their places at the workbench.[6] The heroine Celia, who describes herself as 'ordinary', protests against being pushed into factory work. She prefers to conjure up glamorous fantasies of the women's services, complete with handsome men and attractive uniforms. But Britain needed most of its female workforce in the factories rather than the services, and Celia is converted to factory work and the community spirit. With its recourse to Beethoven's symphonies and shots of purposeful workers, the film unashamedly adopts the heroic tone. Work has meaning: we see the completed plane that Celia and her workmates have made roaring off into battle (a common complaint in factories was that the women had no idea what they were doing and little interest in the war effort).[7] In Celia's factory there seems to be no fatigue or boredom, and as the foreman says, she has the satisfaction of knowing that 'You'll be making something'.

Above all, the community gives meaning and pleasure to life. As in *The Gentle Sex*, the film dwells on people in the mass, whether working or playing. Group dances like the Paul Jones and the Palais Glide are popular, and the premium is on getting on well with everyone, as the genial middle-aged doctor does. The friendly hostel provides a social focus for the factory women, who are spread conscientiously by their creators across the class spectrum. The sophisticated society girl is again the least pleasant, but even she unbends sufficiently to give Celia a set of her pretty underwear for her trousseau. Early in the film Celia is characterised as a home-body, unlike her racy, man-chasing sister who rushes to join up for the 'wrong' reasons. In the course of the film Celia is won over to the virtues of the mass rather than the home, as the community is shown to help the individual: in work which is normalised through friendship and chat, in danger as the group endure the air raid together, and in grief. Through the community-singing at the end, Celia's grief for her dead husband is gently assuaged. The film confirms the worth of work and the importance of numbers, the 'Millions Like You' who are listed in the film's opening credits.

The mood of these films was matched on the radio, as part of the drive for full female involvement in the war effort. In radio talks throughout the war women enthusiastically reported on their strange and wonderful jobs, such as smashing up motor cars, harvesting nettles for drugs and organising baths for troops.[8] These talks by individual women build up an impression of diversity and opportunity, an impression which is confirmed by women's written accounts. Work is the major topic of interest for most women writing about their war experiences, and the publication of so many of these accounts at the time suggests a widespread interest, a desire to document and read about this new phenomenon.[9] The way in which the hardship of women's working lives (those two full-time jobs as the Ministry of Labour admitted) is converted into something to be commemorated with affection points to the meanings with which war work was successfully saturated. In their writing women valued their work not so much for the money they earned, as for more intangible gains and bonds: friendship, community, a sense of worth and a public place in the ranks of the nation.

Although surprisingly little women's fiction centres on war work,[10] there is a definite increase in the work rate. Angela Thirkell provides a useful barometer of shifting middle-class behaviour. In 1939 the amiable Mrs Brandon refers to her flower-arranging as ' "my housekeeping" ' because it is the only work she does. She is well-tended by a large household of servants, and 'would have been hard put to it to find anything useful to do' (*The Brandons*, 19); this is seen as part of her charm. By 1941 and *Cheerfulness Breaks In*, Thirkell's women are all visibly occupied: the young ones with temporary nursing work and the older women with Communal Kitchens, Sewing Parties and Red Cross Evenings, all mildly satirised by Thirkell as 'the Path of Duty'. By 1943 and *Growing Up*, Thirkell feels obliged to account for her heroine's apparent leisure with the explanation that she is recovering after being torpedoed and marooned in an open boat for three days. The following year Thirkell chooses a hard-working and successful teacher for her major protagonist in *The Headmistress* (1944) – though other women in the book may be easier company. Thirkell can glide along this path towards full female employment because some women's work had long been acceptable in fiction, provided it yielded to priorities such as marriage and men's jobs. The war had the effect of revaluing women's work: it is no longer something that a woman does for a taste of adventure or self-fulfilment, or to prove her worth for something else such as marriage.

The new esteem for women's work manifests itself in various ways. Most obviously, work becomes compulsory, even in novels not particularly concerned to be up-to-date. The young women in Patricia Wentworth's 'Miss Silver' detective stories spend their afternoons 'sorting out the most revolting clothes for the bombed'.[11] Romantic fiction finds a new fashion accessory: 'Grace said, "I've taken on ambulance work, in the Chelsea district of course" '.[12] Grace had good reason to be pleased with her efforts. Research by the social historians Jane Waller and Michael Vaughan-Rees shows that fiction in women's wartime magazines kept the high ground for the idle: 'in fifty stories examined, of the sixty-six female characters of working age, some thirty-two were without jobs'.[13] But in novels the non-worker is the anomaly, and avoidance of work is neither possible nor commendable. By 1944 Stella Gibbons can assume that

> the immunity from any form of war work enjoyed by Miss Fielding and Miss Burton will have struck the Gentle Reader. It had not been achieved without a struggle: not a struggle with the local authorities or those hortatory posters which make you feel a social outcast every time you go to the pictures, but a struggle with their own consciences. Miss Burton's struggle was not a hard one; she was soon defiantly taking the line 'Why should I? I'm sixty, and I rolled miles of bandages for four years in the Other War and one war in a lifetime is enough for anyone.' But Miss Fielding's conscience was of quite another calibre; it went deeply into the question: it pointed out that not only must Miss Fielding, if she truly abode by her principles, refuse to join the WVS, she must also refuse to collect her salvage or watch for fires. In short, if Miss Fielding truly abode by her principles, she must try to behave exactly as if there were no war. She had had her worst struggle over the black-out, which, had she followed her principles to the logical limit, should never have darkened her windows at all. (*The Bachelor*, 53)

Luckily Miss Fielding's brother does not share her pacifist views, and buys the black-out material on his way home from work.

The wide range of jobs in women's fiction is further evidence of the growing esteem for women's work. Women nurse and teach, as we might expect; we also find women with jobs their creators seem to have known at first or second hand. The women of wartime fiction work in government offices and Ministries, in military camps, mobile canteens and ATS barracks, in the Wrens and the ATA, in the Land Army and in factories. For the most part, fiction follows non-fiction in its positive representations of work, but we do start to see some significant hesitations, some holding back. Doubts which could not find expression on film or radio surfaced in fiction. In their novels women explored their ambivalence about being part of a war machine and their resistance to being part of a mass.

Traditional women's work benefited from the higher gloss put on female employment. The narrator of Hester Chapman's *Long Division* (1943) establishes and runs a preparatory school; teaching and caring for children prove absorbing and worthwhile. Married to a compulsive adulterer who eventually abandons her (his average proposal rate is one a month), the narrator learns to manage on her own, and sturdily refuses a marriage proposal from a rich and handsome widower because she suspects he will be dull. Nursing is also enhanced by its role in a wartime world, even when it is situated in a provincial English hospital. The action of Helen Ashton's *Yeoman's Hospital* (1944) takes place over twenty-four hours in December 1943, 'in this fifth winter of the war' (7). Although it does not immediately impinge in the shape of air-raid casualties or wounded soldiers, the war makes itself constantly felt: the refugee doctor, the engineer badly burnt at the local airfield, the staff shortages, and above all the pervading sense of general weariness. Nurses are well-represented as an important element of the caring hospital, and part of the novel follows a probationer learning from more experienced nurses. Ashton, who served as a nurse in the First World War and subsequently qualified as a doctor, admires her hospital with its gospel of the job well done. ' "What matters," as the elderly Czech refugee doctor tells his young colleague, (108) "is that you should do good work" ' (222). The news he listens to on the radio is apt:

> There was nothing very special in the bulletin that night. It was just slow slogging fighting everywhere; too much snow in the Apennines and not enough of it on the Russian front, another night-raid on the German factories, a new harbour bombed in the South Seas, an encounter with E-boats in the Channel, two more U-boats sunk in the Bay of Biscay and a convoy brought safely to port. The uphill road to victory seemed a little less steep than it had been; that was all. (222–223)

This is Ashton's bulletin to her hard-working readers in the England of 1944: an uphill road, but if we work together we will get there.

Of course, nursing could and did get much closer to the Front than Ashton's provincial hospital. Rosamond Oppersdorff's 1942 story 'I Was Too Ignorant'[14] is a running, or rather a halting, commentary by a woman with no nursing training who volunteers to work in an under-staffed French military hospital during the fall of France. Oppersdorff rapidly progresses from the outsider who 'had always kept away from blood or anything to do with sickness' to an efficient nurse in sole charge of three wards, relied on by doctors 'to keep cool and clear'. She shows us the intimate face and body of war: mutilated, dirty and matted with blood. Against the refrain of the naive 'I was too ignorant', 'I was foolish enough to think', Oppersdorff sets the pared-down prose of a preoccupied nurse speaking as she works:

> Charts and temperatures come first, of course. I had done these with Nanotte, but never alone. Then, the washing, which alone is also a job. And all the time, through everything, a traffic of stretchers going to and coming from the dressing-room, all in prescribed order.

Seeing the war in such painful close-up, Oppersdorff cannot allow herself too much feeling: 'Pity is the one thing which one cannot offer.' In these conditions work becomes both compulsion and therapy:

> Thank God for work. I go back to G5 after supper, and in the morning rise earlier, hardly able to wait, for I am only happy when I am there.

Mary Renault returned to full-time hospital nursing during the war, 'seeing again terribly ill and dying and bereaved people, and this time, as well, young men suddenly disabled for months or years, often for life, facing their future without complaint'. She postponed writing about what she witnessed until later, 'when the dust had settled'.[15] *The Charioteer* (1953) handles a series of difficult themes with great honesty: the unglamorous aspects of nursing in a hastily improvised hospital of cement floors and filthy lavatories, the pains and disabilities of war wounds, and the thorny issues of conscientious objection and homosexuality. The book's approach to nursing is direct – ' "Odell, have you used the bottle yet?" ' is almost the first nursing voice we hear (44). Renault uses her nursing knowledge to record the progress of a treatment and the aspects of a wound: 'the upper half of the scar had been re-opened; it was thick, purplish, deeply indented, and smelt of pus' (43). She appreciates the ways of the wounded, as 'no one discussed what he had really felt; they took it out on other things. They were an extremely touchy society, but most of them were aware of it' (36–37). But for most of the book Renault forsakes her nurse's-eye view for that of a patient. Laurie Odell is a young soldier, wounded at Dunkirk, who has to come to terms with his lameness and his homosexuality. Through his sensitive, sympathetic eyes we see the other inmates of the hospital. Nurses rarely feature, though Odell has occasional insights:

> As [Nurse Adrian] stood looking down at him in kind anxiety, suddenly he

saw what his own trouble had hidden before, that she was dog-tired and harried to death. Strands of her fair hair were slipping down damply under her cap; her face was shiny like a schoolgirl's after hockey; the inside of her hand was soggy and rough, she must have been scrubbing somewhere out of sight. She had the air of giving up appearances and expecting nothing. He remembered that both the maids and the nurses had always seemed to have a full-time job, and there were no maids today. (50)

Using Odell's vantage-point, Renault observes how badly treated the nurses are, and how the war has caused the over-promotion of women like the matron, 'homesick for her little country nursing home, the gracious cosy chats with private patients . . . She was wretched, but her career was booming' (67). The person who nurses best in this novel is the author, as she turns her trained eye on Odell to note his reaction when he first realises that he will be permanently lame:

he slipped down in bed with the caution of a criminal, lest the counterpane should be disturbed and some nurse come to straighten it. Luckily this fear was a kind of distraction; soon he was able to blot his eyes on the sheet and come to the surface again. (47)

In her treatment of Odell's knee Renault ensures that for the reader, as for the patient, the pain never goes away. While Odell does his best to deflect attention – avoiding give-away low chairs and turning the conversation round – Renault is constantly reminding us of the injury the sufferer can never forget.

Novels about the women's services were entering new terrain, and their responses were mixed. Land Army authors were the most enthusiastic, perhaps because the land and all things pastoral lent themselves more readily to eulogy than factories and barracks. Frances Turk's *Five Grey Geese* (1944) are 'fen flowers' who learn to conquer 'this hard, virile existence' (18), and earn the right to look forward with confidence: ' "Amazons, Barrie! Feminine warriors, teaching the men! We have triumphed. The road is open. The old world is finished" ' (185). Other service novels were less sure about their attitudes to women's work. Margaret Morrison and Pamela Tulk-Hart's *Paid to be Safe* (1948) follows the women of the Air Transport Auxiliary, where the glamour of flying is undeniable. But, as the book's epigraph quotes from the ATA *Pilot's Reminder Book*, 'Remember, you are paid to be safe, not brave.' Safety can be rather a dull virtue, and the women's lives turn out to be an odd blend of strenuous activity, flying jargon, bridge hands and romance.

Edith Pargeter makes a more determined effort to examine the contradictory pressures of service life in *She Goes To War* (1942). Recruited as a
teleprinter operator to the Wrens, Catherine Saxon initially falls in love
with the whole package of job, life and ethos. She even loves her
teleprinter, 'such intriguing things . . . rather like cross-grained pets, of
which all the same, one gets inordinately fond' (28, 74). But by the end of
1941, after eleven months in the Wrens, the heavy bombing of the
Plymouth blitz and personal bereavement, Catherine is tired and openly
critical of the conduct of the war. She does, though, continue to value her
war work, even 'crowing a little' about the small part she played in sinking
the *Bismarck* (209). The ATS women in Pamela Frankau's *The Willow
Cabin* (1949) also assume they are engaged in something worthwhile.
When Caroline Seward is asked, ' "What made you come into this
racket?" ' she replies, ' "It seemed to me a satisfactory and obvious way of
fighting a war" ' (167), and Frankau seems to agree with her. Although
Caroline Seward's work is tedious, dominated by routine and prickling
with strings of initials, its worth is never in doubt. Frankau asks her
readers to admire her ATS women for 'the careless devotion to the job
that made them swear at it and do it well' (228). Nevertheless, the
community spirit which is so socially cohesive in the films of the period
looks less attractive on the page. Caroline Seward's company is stationed
fittingly in a former girls' school where all is 'drab and brown' and a
school atmosphere prevails. It is a world of pointless point-scoring:

> Lockwood said, 'Seward, *what* have you got on?'
>
> 'These, ma'am? Trousers. Battle-dress trousers.'
>
> 'With your shirt and collar and tie?'
>
> 'That is correct, ma'am, yes.'
>
> Lockwood fluttered her eyelashes and said, 'I don't think I understand.'
>
> 'It's quite simple, really,' said Caroline, 'a pair of trousers. Not compli-
> cated.'
>
> 'Did you attend the rehearsal dressed like that?'
>
> 'No, I didn't get on a tram and ride into Newington like this, either.'
>
> 'You mean that you have just put them on?'
>
> 'By God–' said Caroline, 'you're on the right track. I put them on when
> I went into my bedroom.'
>
> 'Oh, I see . . . But Seward, I don't think you should.'
>
> Caroline put down the tooth-glass on the floor. 'If you're serious,' she
> said, 'I think I may be rude, and that would be a pity. Are you suggesting

that I'm not entitled to walk along the landing dressed like this?'

'It's not a question of being entitled. It is a question of the example. One of the orderlies might see you and think that she could wear them.'

'Wear my trousers? Like hell she could.'

Hadow began to scream like a horse in pain. Lockwood said, 'You're impossible. But I must ask you not to wear them again.'

Caroline said, 'And I must ask you, ma'am, to remember that we're at war, not at Roedean'. (171–172)

Life in groups often shows its unattractive side in women's fiction. Sylvia Townsend Warner's 'Poor Mary' has been promoted to sergeant in the ATS, but bears the scars of institutional life in the mass.[16] She returns on leave to her husband, a conscientious objector working on the land, and when he defends his pigs – ' "They're clean animals, really. It's just that they are over-crowded, and dirty feeders," ' – she comments, ' "Sounds like the ATS" '. War has disturbed gender relations in this story, and given Mary not the baby that might have contented her but a starch-bloated body and an empty future:

'Fat! My healthy army fat! When I come out of the army, Nicholas, I shall come out healthy, hideous, middle-aged and without an interest in life. And there will be hordes and hordes of me, all in the same boat. Gosh, what a crew!'

Marjorie Wilenski's band of all-female translators in the Ministry of Foreign Intelligence (*Table Two*, 1942)[17] get on very badly together. Class is an overt barrier to harmony and the women bicker interminably. We can begin to identify a theme in women's war fiction: the working community that does not gell. The pleasure in collective work which films portray is not shared by the novels. As they were less implicated in propaganda, novels could afford to distrust the push towards the mass entailed in the People's War. Large groups of people acting in unison may, after all, be associated with fascism.

It was above all the factory which resisted the call to community in women's novels. Although women who toured the factories could describe them enthusiastically for MOI purposes, and women who wrote critical articles about women's factory work in the press could nevertheless turn their minds to problem-solving,[18] fiction told a different story. Three middle-class women who went to work in the war factories came out with novels which stagger under the strain. To these women the factories offered nothing but sweat, fatigue and poor pay; and this is the point at which fiction diverges most markedly from the representations of women's work on film and radio. Their factories resemble not the model of *Millions Like Us*, but the factory which Celia Fremlin documented for Mass-Observation in 1943, where she found a remarkable 'lack of corporate feeling' among factory women. Fremlin observed,

> the small amount of notice the girls take of each other, outside their immediate circle of friends. Though there are less than one hundred there, it is possible to ask a girl who has been there two years the name of another, who has also been there two years, and she will not know ... Singing at work never spreads all through the room, but remains confined to the corner where it started.[19]

Novelists of factory life were influenced by Mass-Observation techniques and documentary styles from the 1930s; these combined with a duty to realism to push them towards hybrid forms in order to express their experiences. Their work is a mixture of fiction and reportage, its prose spiky and alienated and its structure unharmonious. Inez Holden, who worked in aircraft and Royal Ordnance factories, had a down-beat style well-suited to her environment. Her story may be called 'Fellow Travellers in Factory',[20] but her factory breeds thoughts of war rather than fellowship:

> In the Great War there were, perhaps, soldiers who came to think that the battle might well be between everyone at the front against everyone at home. To-day I thought there should also be a sort of war between everyone who stayed at home and worked against everyone who got away into safe or sunny areas. Besides this, there was a second small guerrilla warfare to be waged against the bourgeois pink political talkers who fight armchair class-battles with left wings folded so securely over upholstered plush elbow rests.

Holden's two factory novels, *Night Shift* (1941) and *There's No Story There* (1944) get progressively bleaker. *Night Shift* manages to follow a series of characters and their stories; there is life outside the factory, and a first-person narrator who listens to her fellow-workers, and is amused and moved by them. But by 1944, and *There's No Story There*, the first person has been effaced, there is no life outside factory or hostel, and life inside them is a disjointed series of casualties and disappointments. Characters either talk non-stop like the schizophrenic Ysabette, or not at all, like Julian who has been wounded in battle. Unidentified women fight each other and a nameless woman dies in an industrial accident, but Holden refuses to develop any plots or relationships. 'In the fifth year of the war' (119) tiredness and factory rhythms crush the narrative impetus. A character explains that the factory is incapable of generating a story, because there is no knowable community in this 'jagged and uneven' life: 'one can't know it all. How can one? – with thirty thousand workers' (186). Holden's factory cannot make a story, and it cannot make sociology either. The character who attempts a Mass-Observation study of it loses his notebook in the snow. Through a collage of disjointed incidents and impressions Holden conveys her experience of factory life: snow imprisons the workers in the factory, and a disabled man limps on to the stage to sing two verses of 'You Can't Change It' (146).

Diana Murray Hill's factory novel, *Ladies May Now Leave Their Machines* (1944), resembles Holden's writing in its hybrid of document and fiction. Murray Hill makes sporadic attempts at facetiousness but her humour falls flat. What the factory calls for is the straightforward report from the new recruit:

> First impressions of Shop B were devastating.
>
> It was all bathed in a hideous yellow gloom. This, as we afterwards found, is due to special vapour lighting. But the effect on the unsuspecting who walk into it for the first time is that they are walking straight into a tomb . . .
>
> This merciless yellow glare is one of the things that was more associated with work in that factory than anything else. Each day, returning, the shock of the dead yellow haze with the stale smell of oil and machinery, struck you again and brought you down to flat level, as a reminder that up till now you might have been a free agent with a certain amount of vitality, but now there you were, back to the same old grind, and everything dead level just as usual. You occasionally got used to it, from force of habit, but when you went out into the open air you soon found what you were missing. (18–19)

The book follows the downhill trajectory of Murray Hill's failure at the work-bench, 'and though I was still trying, I seemed to get worse and worse . . . Lack of stamina, I think, was the real answer, as well as lack of interest' (85, 99). She itemises her accounts to prove that she was earning 'barely . . . enough to eat' (110), and the realistic details of factory work and life give the lie to her assumed cheerfulness. Personal relationships should provide relief, but the women quarrel among themselves, boyfriends are killed or try to take advantage, and the management cancels the Christmas entertainment. Altogether this is a melancholy book, and it closes on an unusually low note. The three women we have been following all leave the factory and go their separate ways, weary, ill and depressed. 'Release from the machines' is the most that can be hoped for, and there is no interest in what lies ahead. This book depicts the factory as the intractable presence, resistant to humour, glamour or higher meaning.

Monica Dickens's *The Fancy* was published in 1943, the year of *Millions Like Us*: the film and the novel contrast strikingly. Dickens draws on her first-hand experience of work in an aircraft factory, but adopts a male viewpoint for most of the novel. Although we see the women at the factory bench through the eyes of their chargehand Edward, there is enough from their own viewpoint to counter Edward's romanticised notions of 'his girls' (280). Edward's sentiment acts as a brake on ours, so that we see the women as well-observed individuals who eat jam fritters, chip their nail varnish and have no idea what they are working on. For them, work is a bore, and community spirit is roundly despised. A union meeting provides an occasion for comedy rather than concerted action: Dickens mocks the pompous procedure, and presents the reasonable request for nursery facilities as comically hopeless. Madeleine yearns nostalgically for the last war:

> It had all been so different in the Ordnance Factory. Was it only because she was younger that the work had seemed easier and she had loved every day of it and had such fun? Nowadays, everything was so much more complicated and scientific, with people trying to teach you to read micrometers, and even the girls seemed to be different from what she and her contemporaries had been. They had never had these off-days and moods and complicated temperaments that had to be humoured. They had grumbled of course, but only in fun. They had been such a jolly lot. She remembered how they used to sing choruses while they worked.
>
> She had suggested this one day and the girls had looked at her blankly.
>
> 'Sing what?' Dinah had asked, breaking off the snatch of crooning that had reminded Madeleine of the old days in the cheerful Filling Shop.
>
> 'Well, you know – choruses, dear. We always used to in the last war, and a fine row we made too. The foreman used to come and tell us to be quiet, he couldn't hear the machines. But we didn't take much notice, I'm afraid.

We were regular terrors for mischief.'

But girls these days were funny. If one did start to sing, as like as not another would start a different song in another key. The rage was all for being different. They even chopped and gathered and pleated their grey overalls to make them look unalike. At the Ordnance Factory, she remembered how proud they had been of looking like an army in their brown overalls and scarves . . .

'Did you see that piece in the paper,' she said chattily to the bench at large, 'about the Granny who works in a factory up North? Worker of the Week, she was. She made a record, turned out more screws on her machine than anyone ever had before. It said how she got a medal and the Queen stopped and spoke to her when she was going round the factory.'

'Fat lot of good that did her,' said Freda.

'I bet she was on piece work,' said Dinah.

'You girls always scoff at everything so,' said Madeleine, 'I know you don't mean it, but–'

'That's to disguise the fullness of our hearts,' said Paddy. (73–74)

These women working long hours together never weld into a group. They live at home rather than in the hostel favoured by *Millions Like Us*, and shy away from collective activity. When Paddy leaves she 'slipped away after lunch' to avoid any celebrations, and when the group does bestir itself its manifestations can be vulgar. The day before Kitty's wedding her workmates hang up a naked doll and a placard inscribed 'All right tomorrow night' (108). Friendship does not flourish easily, and timid Wendy finds no warmth at her work-bench: 'She had nobody to talk to at her end except Ivy, who despised her, and Sheila, who was always shouting up at Dinah at the other end' (134).

Although none of the women enjoys this kind of work or life, and Dickens's attitude seems to be: how could they? there are some beneficial by-products. Comfortably middle-class Sheila is helped out of an unpleasant blackmail situation by bohemian Dinah, a woman she would never have met but for the factory. Sheila begins to emerge from her self-centred cocoon; ' "You've grown up at last," ' comments Dinah; ' "My God, it was about time" ' (276). The factory also gives Wendy temporary respite from her mad tyrannical father, but for none of these women does Dickens offer work as anything particularly positive; it is more the obligatory burden.

In refusing to idealise work or to play the community tune, Dickens bolsters her individual women against collapse into anonymous collectivity. Novels have traditionally expressed their meanings through the individual character, exploring his or her unique qualities and angles of vision; it is fitting that the novelist should put the individual before the group. In refusing to be either the factory's homogenised army of workers or Edward's little rabbits (he is a rabbit fancier and names his rabbits after the women on his bench), Dickens's women strike a modest blow for the individual against the war machine of 1943. They also make a useful contribution to women's war-language. They, and the workers in Holden and Murray Hill's factories, come closest to speaking for some of the two million women in war factories,[21] whose recorded responses from the period are hard to find. In what we do have, we can gauge the pressure of the times. Factory work was dirty, hard and unpleasant, and women left it if they could. When they write it up in their day-to-day diaries their response is unambiguous: it is 'suffocating', 'I loathe and hate it'.[22] But as soon as they step back to survey their experience, it is immediately moulded by the discourse of worth. The joint diary kept by two middle-aged, middle-class women during the three years they worked in war factories reveals the dynamics of this process. For Kathleen Church-Bliss and Elsie Whiteman the deadly tenor of factory life is inescapable: 'another long boring day', 'This is a week of awful days', 'an interminable day', 'we are still very depressed – and often cannot face writing anything in the Diary', 'Factory life is very irksome to us'.[23] Church-Bliss and Whiteman disliked the noise, dirt and time-wasting, and being 'treated as part of the machine' (May 1942); they also record apathy and absenteeism among the conscripts. But these two women had chosen this work for themselves (after watching a fascinating demonstration), and as soon as they stand back after five months to summarise their experiences, drudgery is transformed by meaning into value:

> We are quite convinced that in spite of the dirt, the long tiring hours, the deafening noise and the annoyance of working for rather inhuman employers and the general austerity of our life, we are much happier . . . We are doing what the Government has asked women to do. (1 November 1942)

The diary itself assisted the transformation. Writing it was 'our first duty on returning from the eleven-hour day at the factory', and friends and family who read it 'were enthralled with the saga' (May 1942). Industrial grind converts into narrative pleasure. The rhetoric of work and patriotism operates to gild the tedium, and the diarists entitled their five-volume typescript 'We Had To Laugh'. Paradoxically, it was fiction – the disjointedness of Holden, the trajectory of failure in Murray Hill and the unsocial behaviour of Dickens's women – which could stick most closely to what the day-to-day diary entries reveal. The novels of women's war work show a surprising resistance to the war machine, and a reluctance to comply unquestioningly with the demands of war. This question of complicity was more complicated for those women who worked in surveillance, as we shall see in the next chapter.

5

SURVEILLANCE, ALLEGIANCE, COMPLICITY

Yes, it's funny about the war – the way everybody's on one side or the other.

Elizabeth Bowen, *The Heat of the Day*, 1949

A country at war is a country under surveillance by both friend and foe. During the Second World War many women, including some distinguished novelists, were involved in open and secret intelligence work.[1] If intelligence work suggests power – the one who watches is generally supposed to have power over the one watched – it also entails acquiescence, an agreement to underwrite the male machinery and values of war. Spying has always offered rich pickings to the novelist, with its stories of surveillance and allegiance, complicity and guilt, divided loyalties and double lives. These plots and preoccupations come together in Elizabeth Bowen's *The Heat of the Day*, one of the greatest novels of the war.

Women worked in intelligence at the highest levels: the Director of Home Intelligence at the Ministry of Information was the extremely able Mary Adams. Her brief was 'to provide an assessment of home morale' in the interests of effective propaganda.[2] Convinced that secrecy would be injurious, Adams openly deployed a huge range of informants and an impressive network of 'voluntary spies' – the phrase is Jane Austen's but the organisation was Mary Adams's. Other more or less open surveillance included the monitoring of foreign radio broadcasts at Evesham where, as in Adams's operations, many women were involved. Women excelled at this monitoring of open sources for useful information: fascinating work according to Olive Renier, which demanded careful 'reading between the lines of ordinary passages'. To savour the oddity of this displaced ordinariness Renier used

> on night shift, to reverse the process, listening at 4 a.m. or so to the BBC's Front Line Family Broadcast to Latin America, and wonder what on earth the South Americans made of it all.[3]

Women were employed in much larger numbers in Postal Censorship, a highly visible form of surveillance, with letters to and from abroad opened and stuck down ostentatiously with 'Opened by Censor' labels. Animosity in the wartime press against censorship was deflected from the fact that it was done (it would be unpatriotic to value personal privacy above national security) on to the way it was done. The issue became one of class antagonism and female censors were targeted. A reporter claimed to 'have just discovered the biggest nest of society women pin-money workers established since the war' at Censorship Headquarters in Liverpool; 'Lovelies give up Bridge to be £5-a-week Censors' claimed another newspaper article in 1939.[4] In a way the whole nation was enrolled in a form of surveillance, as suspicion was urged on the population at large. Duff Cooper's invitation to 'Join the Ranks of the Silent Column' insisted, 'We must make up our minds not to believe anything that we are told on mere hearsay'.[5] In conjunction with this suspicion of others should go the awareness of being watched: 'nothing', according to Duff Cooper, 'that is printed or said escapes the eyes and the ears of the enemy. They are listening to us now'. 'Intense vigilance' – the words come from Churchill's 'Finest Hour' speech of 1940[6] – is the stamp of war on each individual. 'Careless Talk Costs Lives', and fear of a fifth column (the frightening notion of an unrecognisable enemy within), heightened after the fall of France in 1940.

Surveillance of a more covert nature was a wartime priority, and many service-women monitored the coded enemy messages transmitted over the air-waves (arduous and usually thankless work). Women's reputed expertise at code-breaking dates back to classical times: according to Herodotus the Amazons could understand the language of men but not vice versa,[7] and many women were recruited to Bletchley Park, where enemy codes were deciphered.[8] Christine Brooke-Rose worked there throughout the war from the age of eighteen, evaluating and prioritising German messages. In her own view, this early trade in codes and forbidden knowledge created her as a novelist;[9] and Bletchley habits permeate her first novel, *The Languages of Love* (1957). The characters are medievalists and philologists who speak many languages and are often incomprehensible to each other. Translating is a constant activity, and when it stops a character worries: 'She suddenly felt isolated, an untranslatable meaning hiding behind a label' (187). Love, as the title suggests, has many languages to be deciphered, practised and learnt. Brooke-Rose has also acknowledged Bletchley's influence in its methodology of reading the war from the enemy point of view: this is akin to what the novelist does, 'learning to imagine the other'. The possession of illicit knowledge 'tinged with absolute secrecy and pleasurable guilt'[10] brings complicity. This realisation surfaces obliquely, fascinatingly, in women's literature of war and surveillance.

Although well-represented in both open and covert surveillance, women involved in such work could not turn it into fiction. Time and the Official Secrets Act forbade. But novelists could feel the codes in the air. Stevie Smith's *The Holiday* (1949), which was written during the war, opens:

> I was working over some figures with Tiny at the Ministry; it was a figure code. Tiny sighed and hummed under his breath.
>
> Oh, Tiny, don't hum.

Smith thus economically establishes three wartime work motifs: the Ministry, the code with its secretive connotations, and the irritation. The claustrophobic atmosphere of places like Bletchley intrigued Elizabeth Bowen, who described a place like it in her 1944 story 'Green Holly'. This story also uses its opening to strike a characteristic note: 'Mr Rankstock entered the room with a dragging tread: nobody looked up or took any notice'.[11] He and a few others are cooped up in a large house, engaged in secret work and considered to be dead for the duration. These hidden watchers have ceased to exist, 'dropped out of human memory', become ghosts; watching can be an all-consuming occupation.

Spy novels were understandably popular during the war, but although women were engaged in undercover activities – for which they subsequently won great fame[12] – when women wrote secret agent novels they usually chose male protagonists. Marthe McKenna had personal experience of spying for the British Secret Service in the First World War, but her bestselling novels exploited cliché rather than reality, a world of gentlemen spies, monocles and 'faultless-fitting morning clothes'. *The*

Spy in Khaki (1941) bristles with agents and double agents – 'Then the truth dawned on Clive. "Arty" O'Brien was an American Intelligence Operator!' (205) – but does have some sound advice for its wartime readers about the need to learn spy's ways: '*Take nothing for granted. Take nothing at its face value. Watch like a cat and stow everything away in memory's locker*' (20). The detective story is considered to have gone into a decline for the duration,[13] although the genre was still alive and reviewed in batches by the *Times Literary Supplement* each week; but in 1941 Agatha Christie herself abandoned her customary murder formula for a spy novel. Her successful *N or M?* differs from most of her other novels in being firmly anchored to a particular time, the spring of 1940. England is in peril, invasion is anticipated and the familiar seaside resort becomes a vulnerable and dangerous place. The spacious country house of the 1930s murder story transmutes into the guest-house of wartime life, filled with bored and fretful people. One of them (but which?) is a fifth columnist; this enemy within is the real menace to England. Tuppence Beresford regrets that ' "the person I like best here is a German!" ' (80) and her superior muses on the enemy:

'We respect our adversaries and they respect us. You usually like your opposite number, you know, even when you're doing your best to down him. (42)

Christie seems to have had fifth-column stories from France in mind when her sleuths uncover an extensive list of great and good Englishmen,

'pledged to assist an invasion of this country. Amongst them were two Chief Constables, an Air Vice-Marshal, two Generals, the Head of an Armaments Works, a Cabinet Minister, many Police Superintendents, Commanders of Local Volunteer Defence Organisations, and various military and naval lesser fry, as well as members of our own Intelligence Force.'
Tommy and Tuppence stared.
'*Incredible!* ' said the former.
Grant shook his head.
'You do not know the force of the German propaganda.' (186)

Articulating the fears of the early years of the war, Christie makes one of her traitors an archetypal upstanding English boy 'with an agreeable but slightly embarrassed smile' (149). Two years later Helen MacInnes's

Assignment in Brittany (1943) complicates the enemy-within story by having her English agent impersonate a French fifth-columnist – a further twist to the double-life theme which runs through secret-agent literature.

During the war the young Barbara Pym tried her hand at a spy novel. 'So Very Secret'[14] is a short masterpiece, crossing comedy of manners with thriller, playing them across each other to show how much there is in common between the spy novel and domestic fiction. That great tradition of women's fiction, the heroine with the buried life, is on familiar ground in the spy's world of double lives, disguise, surveillance and divided loyalties. Pym's heroine opens her novel by telling us she is what she looks:

> I caught sight of myself in the mirror and thought that anyone meeting me for the first time would know me immediately for what I am – Cassandra Swan – a country woman in early middle age, daughter of the former vicar and still living on alone in the family home, quite comfortably off and reasonably happy. (273)

As the vicar's daughter she had been 'one of the most important women in the parish'; now she must settle for less, and even the war disappoints. 'The war had really made very little difference to my life. Our village was so dull that even our evacuees left us' (274). Cassandra's friend Harriet arrives for a visit; her surname is Jekyll, she works in the Foreign Office, and her job is 'so secret that I sometimes wondered if she herself knew exactly what it was all about' (274). The idea of doubleness which is suggested by Harriet's surname resonates characteristically. The sensational duality of Jekyll and Hyde is shadowed by a further, less obvious double, the figure of the Edwardian garden designer Gertrude Jekyll, like Harriet stout and capable.

On the first afternoon of her visit Harriet sets off for the hairdresser – ' "I'm going to risk everything and have a perm!" ' (277). Cassandra lends her Saroyan's *Daring Young Man on a Flying Trapeze*, an apt title for Cassandra herself, about to launch on her daring adventure. Harriet never returns from her perm, leaving behind a few clues and papers which Cassandra guesses are in Russian. She hides them behind a photograph of Bishop Moberley: the exciting, dangerous but unreadable language appropriately concealed by the 'thin sheep-faced' figure of authority. In this story the exterior surfaces of the ordinary conceal much: the innocuous Oxford Sunday tea-party is hosted by enemy agents who drug and search Cassandra. Distington, her home village, recedes into the distance, and her loyalty to that domestic 'quite comfortably off and reasonably happy' life is tested as a world of adventure beckons enticingly.

Under surveillance Cassandra resorts to disguise, the survival kit of spies and repressed Victorian heroines alike. But whereas the beautiful Violette Szabo had to make herself less conspicuous,[15] Cassandra does the opposite and comes out into the light, for characteristically down-to-earth reasons:

> It is not easy to disguise yourself in wartime. I couldn't buy any new clothes because I didn't have my clothing coupons on me. But, I decided, I could go to a hairdresser and smarten myself up a bit. I could have my face made up and varnish on my nails and I could buy a new hat without coupons. (291)

As a disguise this fails and she is recognised instantly. Its more exhilarating consequences are for her inner life:

> It is a very odd feeling to be in disguise – you feel inwardly the same, but the consciousness that you look different makes you feel that you cannot still be yourself. (292)

The 'odd feeling' rejuvenates her. ' "Fancy all this happening to *you*!" ' comments the young undergraduate who should really be the hero of the spy novel, and who offers to take over the surveillance from her (294). In a typical shift of perspective Cassandra's ordinary life looms up; her commitment to it is unquestioning, if a little regretful:

> We walked down into the quadrangle planted with beetroot. I felt rather flat and disappointed now that my adventure seemed to be at an end. But it would be nice to be home again. Tomorrow was Tuesday and I would be at the canteen in the morning and after tea there was bandaging practice at the First Aid Post. (295)

Pym's patterns of characterisation reinforce the mapping together of the twin worlds of exotic espionage and domestic ordinariness. The village dressmaker Miss Gatty, who always adds 'two inches to the hips . . . regardless of the client's measurements' (208) has a sinister double in Miss Nussbaum, enemy agent and murderous dressmaker from Maida

Vale. When confronted by the corpse of Miss Nussbaum's business partner, Cassandra briefly panics – 'It all seemed so difficult and not the kind of thing my upbringing had equipped me to deal with' (298) – but the efficiency with which she has handled the ruffled Miss Gatty (upstaged in the canteen by Miss Nussbaum) shows that her 'upbringing' will stand her in very good stead. One of Pym's Excellent Women, Cassandra is able to cope with most situations. In another pairing, the undergraduate Hugh reminds Cassandra of Adrian, her university flame of thirty years ago. Adrian himself appears for a moment as Sir Adrian when Cassandra blunders into his house. Now a charming, weary politician, he does not recognise Cassandra but deals with her politely:

> One more smile and he was gone. I stared after him. Was this the man whose memory I had cherished for so long? This blank, wooden personality with only a certain facile charm, which could be switched on and off as required? (301)

Thus Cassandra escapes from the spell of long unrequited love which has mildly blighted her life. She has won a second wind as the heroine of the domestic novel temporarily let loose on to the invigorating terrain of the spy novel. Her two lives and the relationship between them are neatly figured in the new hiding place she finds for the Russian papers: she sticks them between the middle pages of her ration book. Dangerous evidence is locked incriminatingly inside the drab camouflage of wartime life.

Cassandra is pursued in her attempts to deliver the Russian papers, and the disguise motif returns when Hugh decides she must borrow his aunt's Red Cross uniform. Domestic fiction lends the spy novel one more theme, the supportive community of women:

> I nearly laughed at my good fortune. My Red Cross uniform would excite comparatively little comment here. I came upon an open door and looked into a room full of women, several of whom were in uniforms exactly like mine. I hurried in as unobtrusively as I could and joined them. (309)

Cassandra is rescued from her pursuer by Nurse Dallow – ' "I never did trust men with beards!" ' (311). She gives Cassandra supper and confirms her temporary double life:

> 'You're in the Secret Service then?'
> 'Not really,' I replied, rather taken with this description of myself.

'I am doing that sort of work at present, I suppose, but usually I just live at home in the village – quite near Oxford – and do ARP and canteen work.'

Sister Dallow seemed to feel that this made me practically one of the family and said, 'Now we must help you to get those papers to Sir Gervase.' (312)

Forbidding Cassandra to go alone, Nurse Dallow furnishes the novel's final double. ' "I know," she exclaimed, "the tandem!" ' (312), thereby transforming the spy novel's device of the double – which usually suggests duplicity and opposition – into a supportive and pleasantly comic double act: 'We must have looked a peculiar sight, the two of us in nurses' uniform pedalling along on a tandem' (312). The spy story concludes triumphantly, and Cassandra heads back to stolid honourable Distington, the domestic circle to which she and her author ultimately commit themselves. Throughout her story Pym has diligently registered the material surfaces of prosaic wartime life in order to identify its distinctive qualities. Sometimes it is literally the materials which occupy Pym's attention: the marocain dress Cassandra suddenly feels is wrong when the more worldly Harriet arrives, the blue ripple cloth dressing-gown worn by Lucy Dallow during an air raid, the pillows at the First Aid Post 'in rather dirty white jaconet covers' (319). All this is the stuff of wartime life, its texture minutely recorded in a comedy of materials as well as manners.

From comedy of manners to tragedy of circumstance: Elizabeth Bowen's *The Heat of the Day* (1949) is both a spy novel and a meditation on the issue of allegiance. One leads to the other. A spy must be suspicious, may have to be disloyal, may choose to betray, may be torn between divided loyalties. Sixty pages into the book Stella Rodney faces a crisis. She stands before her son, holding in her hand what may be evidence incriminating her lover as a spy. Bowen's description of the moment binds suspicion intimately with guilt and betrayal:

This was dynamite, between her fingers and thumbs. That she was terrified of the paper – she wondered, could Roderick see that, too? This secretively-folded, grey-blue half-sheet became the corpus of suspicion – guilt, hers, baseness, hers. What did she feel to be possible? – and, how could she? (63)

This 'corpus of suspicion' is the corpus of the novel: suspicion as the wartime *modus vivendi* with its corollary of betrayal, spying on the beloved. The times are all, and Bowen chooses to complicate this moment of crisis for Stella by having Roderick present, a reminder of Stella's 'division' between her 'two loves', her lover and her son. Divided loyalties are a major preoccupation of this novel, with the problem of allegiance given a personal relevance by Bowen's particular case, the Irishwoman in England.

The Heat of the Day is primarily a spy novel. Forty-year-old sophisticated Stella Rodney is approached by Harrison, who claims to know that Stella's lover Robert Kelway is leaking War Office secrets to the enemy. He hints, ' "If you and I could arrange things, things might be arranged" ' (34), or as Stella puts it, ' "I'm to form a disagreeable association in order that a man be left free to go on selling his country" ' (36). Stella disbelieves, procrastinates, watches and is in turn watched.[16] She visits Robert's family home with him and then travels to Ireland to sort out business at Mount Morris, the Big House which her son Roderick has recently inherited. On her return Stella confronts Robert with Harrison's accusation. Robert denies it, and that same evening proposes marriage. At her next meeting with Harrison, Stella takes up his offer, only to be rejected. Robert acknowledges the truth of Harrison's claim, and after a night spent at Stella's flat he leaves by the roof – leaping or falling to his death – an appropriately opaque death in a story full of opacity and difficulty.

In this spy novel, looking and surveillance are, as we might expect, constant activities. The opening shot which Harold Pinter invents for his screenplay emphasises this aspect: a man (we see the back of his head and his hands) sifts through photographs of Robert and Stella.[17] Looking can be relatively harmless – Robert's nephew and niece demand that he 'look at' them as they do their exercises on the lawn (122). But in this same scene Robert reveals his dislike of looking people straight in the eye and of being looked at in return. This is why he likes Stella's ' "mothy way of blinking and laziness about keeping your eyelids open" ' (119). The act of looking becomes openly menacing with Harrison's promise to ' "look in again" ' on Stella (143). Looking is often fraught and complicated. At Holme Dene, Robert's family home, Stella 'seemed to be looking at everything down a darkening telescope'. Indirect looking can be helpful: she 'brought the scene back again into focus by staring at window-reflections in the glaze of the teapot' (114). Trying to look straight may entail looking crookedly, and perhaps behaving crookedly too. After all, what is the nature of Stella's looking at Holme Dene: has she come to spy, as Harrison later assumes, and she does not deny? Our first glimpse of Stella is revealing. She stands at the window of her flat 'playing with the blind-cord' (22), an augury of the dilemmas ahead. How much should Stella see, how much should she be blind to, and what is the price of seeing? As Stella waits for Harrison she coils the cord round her finger in a prophetic noose. She also looks at the street through the loop of the blind-cord; elsewhere the book contains a multitude of mirrors, glass, reflections of reflections, angled vision. In her final scene with Robert, for example, Stella 'glanced first at the window, then at the window's reflection in the mirror' (274).

The connection between looking and power lies at the heart of the spy novel, and impinges itself forcibly on Stella on her return from Holme Dene. She suspects that her flat is being watched:

> *Her* part – listening for the listener, watching for the watcher – must be the keeping on walking on, as though imperviously: the actual nerved-up briskness of her step, the tingle up from her heels as they struck the pavement, brought back what seemed to be common sense. But, her very decision that there could not be anyone synchronised with the evidence that there was – a match struck, sheltered, then thrown away. This – for how could it not be a watcher's object to stay obliterated up to the last moment? – was bravado, gratuitous. This was a sheer advertisement of impunity; this could not but be Harrison – for who else, by his prodigality with matches, in these days when there were to all intents and purposes none, gave such ostentatious proof of 'inside' power? (127–128)

Not just the watching, but how to read the watching, even in the striking of a match: the attention of character and reader alike is strained intently. Harrison's looking is felt to be malign; people in this book can look too much. So constant is the level of watching that it extends to sounds: the bells ringing for victory in the North Africa campaign 'were a spectacle to be watched passing' (291). Looking and light function negatively – 'exposed' is a word favoured by Bowen to describe characters who are being watched, vulnerable to the gaze of another. The idea of light usually generates positive associations, but in this war and in this novel to be in the light is to be in danger. Safety is in black-out, and the most innocent domestic acts are infected by enforced behaviour with light: 'It was a time of opening street doors conspiratorially: light must not escape on to steps' (46). Climactic scenes (between Stella and Robert, Stella and Harrison) are enacted in excessive 'blinding' sunlight or in the shadowless glare of electric light which mimes the searching brilliance of flash photography or interrogation. No wonder Stella 'put up a hand between a lamp and her eyes' (130).

Spies are of course watchers by profession, but in the war the whole population was roused to vigilance, and *The Heat of the Day* installs suspicion as a wartime condition. Connie is the suspicious reader, the one not to be fooled by the myth and propaganda of the People's War.[18] She and Louie discuss a newspaper photograph of a landgirl, which Connie confidently dismantles to the 'real' picture behind the picture: ' "Oh, *her* – formerly mannequin, that was the point of her. It's not what you do that gets you into a picture, if you notice, it's what you did formerly" ' (154). A certain level of suspicion is endemic, a symptom of the times which bear so heavily on the book. Stella's work professionalises her own vigilance:

> She was now ... employed, in an organization better called Y.X.D., in secret, exacting, not unimportant work, to which the European position since 1940 gave ever-increasing point. The habit of guardedness was growing on her, as on many other people, reinforcing what was in her an existing bent: she never had asked much, from dislike of being in turn asked. (26)

Then Bowen introduces a characteristic pause: 'Or, could that have been circumstance? – for by temperament she was communicative and fluctuating.' The more ingrained habits of suspicion and surveillance emanate from Holme Dene, Intelligence HQ, where all arrivals and departures are strictly monitored. From her armchair Robert's monster mother 'commanded all three windows, also the leaded squints in the inglenook' (108). This house is where the 'rot' started, in Harrison's words (131), the rot of Robert's treason. Spying, the most intense mode of looking, is a treacherous activity. To look can be to betray.

Reading can be as difficult as looking. The first scene deliberately wrong-foots us, by opening with a setting and a light which are strange and dislocating. The angles and values of the evening light are distorted, 'low' and 'theatrical', the darkness paradoxically 'glass-clear' (7). This first scene, an encounter between Harrison and Louie, gets nowhere, which is not what we expect from the opening of a novel. Louie does not reappear until nearly halfway through the book, and we are left dangling, watching out for the next instalment in order to make sense of this one. The first chapter sends us further off balance by introducing Louie at some length, so that we expect to follow her. Instead we move to Stella's flat, where Harrison is about to arrive. He is the spy, the watcher, but the first scene in the park sets him at a strange angle by turning him into the one being watched: 'She [Louie] had given him, the watcher, the enormity of the sense of having been watched' (14). Bowen's awkward sentence structure (its most obvious device is the unusually placed adverb or phrase) suits her subject-matter perfectly. Reading becomes an awkward and difficult activity, and the reader is kept where Bowen wants her, on her toes.

The Heat of the Day has been acclaimed as the one of the best novels of wartime London. Bowen was clearly affected powerfully by the blitz,[19] although she sets her novel for the most part in 1942 – the 'lightless middle of the tunnel' – when dreary slog has superseded the aphrodisiac exhilaration of the blitz. Bowen appreciated the jolt which war gave her: 'I would not have missed being in London throughout the war for anything: it was the most interesting period of my life'.[20] Bowen's roots were in the upper-class Irish Protestant Ascendancy, and she moved between London, Oxford and Bowen's Court, a large house she had inherited in Ireland in 1930. During the war she lived in London and worked as an ARP warden. She may not have been exactly one of millions like us, but she was at least part of some communal enterprise and pleased to think 'At any rate I am taking part in this, I may be doing some good'.[21] On reflection in 1945, Bowen noted that in the war her customary 'feeling of slight differentiation was suspended: I felt one with, and just like, everyone else'.[22] She warmed to the 'village commune' nature of blitz life, where 'we all have new friends: our neighbours'.[23] This suggests that Bowen's encounter with the People's War was pleasurable. Perhaps it informed her choice of subplot for *The Heat of the Day*, the creation of Louie and Connie, women of London and each a recognisable type. Louie is the slack, inarticulate unfaithful service wife, Connie the sharp mouthy cockney who shares Bowen's ARP warden job. According to her biographer, Bowen's 'identification with England in crisis was complete'.[24] This identification was forged particularly closely in the blitz and was part of the meaning of that intense experience for her.

But it is also at this time that we find Bowen proclaiming her Irishness. She told an interviewer in Dublin: 'I regard myself as an Irish novelist,' and unsurprisingly described her 'strong feeling of nationality' as a 'highly disturbing emotion'.[25] This was in 1942; between 1939 and 1941 she was writing a lengthy history of the Big House she had inherited, *Bowen's Court* (1942). Bowen began writing the book in July 1939 when the war was clearly imminent: to write such a book at such a time was a statement of allegiance to Ireland, a testament of loyalty. The house ('merely a great stone box' according to Virginia Woolf who stayed there in 1934,[26]) represented a vision of the civilised life to Bowen, and became a solace in wartime: 'I suppose that everyone, fighting or just enduring, now carries one private image – one peaceful scene in his heart. Mine is Bowen's Court' (*Bowen's Court*, 339). In the book's 1941 Afterword she describes how 'Several times a year I cross the sea to Bowen's Court, to go on with the life that waits there' (333). What she fails to mention here is that her trips to Ireland had an additional, undercover purpose. Stella's secret work corresponds to one of Bowen's wartime guises: not only an ARP warden, she was also a spy.

Between 1940 and 1942 Bowen visited Ireland and submitted confidential reports to London on Irish attitudes to the war. She had dealings with the Ministry of Information, the Dominions Office and the War Office. She was paid about £100 a year for what she called her Activities;[27] but although she was paid by the British she seems to have seen herself as an apologist for Ireland. In 1940 and 1941 she defended Ireland's neutrality in her reports and journalism, arguing that it should be seen as a positive stance.[28] By 1942, according to the Irish historian R.F. Foster, she was more impatient: 'After two years' war experience in London, Irish neutrality seemed less defensible. She thought there was a sense of "moral deterioration" since 1940'.[29] By this time many Anglo-Irish resented Irish neutrality and were, like Bowen, deeply committed to the British war effort. 'Sunday Afternoon', a short story which Bowen wrote in 1941, concisely dramatises the status of the Anglo-Irishman enjoying a respite from the London blitz:

> 'But you'll go back, of course?'
> 'To London? Yes – this is only my holiday. Anyhow, one cannot stay long away.'
> Immediately he had spoken Henry realized how subtly this offended his old friends. Their position was, he saw, more difficult than his own, and he could not have said a more cruel thing. (*Collected Stories*, 618)

Bowen, like Henry, 'cannot stay long away' from London; nevertheless she went to considerable lengths to get to Bowen's Court 'several times a year', lengths which included spying on Ireland. In doing so she was choosing to inhabit more than one country, to take more than one side in the war: a deliberate case of willed conflict.[30]

' "Whatever you are these days, you are rather more so," ' observes a character in one of Bowen's wartime stories.[31] In 1948, the year Bowen was finishing *The Heat of the Day*, she remarked that 'conflict in the self' was 'essential' for the novelist.[32] It is the intensity of Bowen's competing wartime allegiances which fuels *The Heat of the Day*. In the novel she refers to this moment as, for both Stella and the century, the 'testing extremities of their noonday' (134). The title itself reminds us of the force of sunlight – to be out in the heat of the day is not a pleasant place to be. But this is where Bowen chose to put herself during the war, exacerbating that 'conflict in the self' in order to generate a novel about the tragedy of split allegiances. In the book she shows just how rapidly such conflicts can kill. The owner of the Big House, elderly Cousin Francis, is an honourable member of the Protestant Ascendancy. He comes to England,

> to offer that country his services in the war – his own country's abstention had been a severe blow, but he had never sat down under a blow yet. (69–70)

Cousin Francis has been in England for only a day when he is struck down by a fatal heart attack.

Like many other novelists, Bowen was fascinated by espionage. Through her information-gathering work she, like Stella Rodney, 'lived at the edge of a clique of war, knowing who should know what' (174). She also moved in upper-class intellectual circles frequented by Burgess and Maclean and touched by the 'climate of treason'.[33] The worlds of spy and novelist have much in common, and Bowen was attracted to Graham Greene's view that a novelist must be disloyal, a sort of fifth columnist, free from conventional allegiances.[34] But however attracted she was by this idea, Bowen was also affected by a radical unease with the whole business. To spy on is to betray: this premise controls *The Heat of the Day*. Bowen's anxiety about her own spying activities permeates some of the different ways in which spying and surveillance feature in the novel. Some level of suspicion is, as we have seen, necessary – Connie is right to look behind the image of the landgirl in her newspaper. Some watching can be kindly: 'Louie lived on at Chilcombe Street under the surveillance of Connie' (310). Excessive suspicion can present itself almost comically: ' "Milk all right?" . . . "Why?" she said. "Did you put anything in it?" ' (135). But the accusation which Stella goes on to level at Harrison could not be more serious: ' "You succeed in making a spy of me" ' (138). No wonder he winces; the rot has entered her soul. Once she has been warned, Stella can never not be suspicious. The 'guilt' and the 'baseness', as Stella realised in that early crisis with the 'secretly-folded' paper, are 'hers'. Her own brand of scarlet letter appears in her hair:

> Nature had kindly given her one white dash, lock or wing in otherwise tawny hair; and that white wing, springing back from her forehead, looked in the desired sense artificial – other women asked her where she had had it done; she had become accustomed to being glanced at. (25)

Being looked at begins here for Stella with innocent surveillance, natural and artificial confused in an ambiguous sign. Is Stella's white streak a yellow streak, a white lie, or a white feather? Bowen ends her introduction of Stella by handing over to the reader in a telling invitation to complicity: 'Generous and spirited to a fault, not unfeeling, she was not wholly admirable; but who is?' (26).

Complicity lies at the heart of Stella's story. She had – perhaps like Bowen – enjoyed the blitz too much, thrived too vigorously in the 'intimate and loose little society of the garrison', which acts as the breeding ground of her affair with Robert. Angus Calder draws the appropriate moral:

> The price which Stella pays for her excitement under bombardment is the ultimate realisation, in the glum middle of the war, that Robert has made her part of a double life.[35]

Complicity also lies at the heart of Bowen's war. For her too the blitz was a seductive experience, with its compound of danger, communality and sex. She enjoyed the new contacts she made as an ARP worker, she liked being out under fire. In February 1941 she met Charles Ritchie and a close relationship developed between them during the following months, a love affair born out of bombed London, 'a landscape of love', as Ritchie called it.[36] The impact of the blitz on the country as a whole – not so much physically as psychologically – should not be underestimated. Even pacifists were not immune to its unexpected visceral attractions. Deep in the Wiltshire countryside the pacifist Frances Partridge recorded her reactions to the unavoidable diet of bomb stories:

> What surprised me most was to detect in myself a curious feeling of regret at missing some tremendous experience that thousands of people are having.[37]

Vera Brittain's sense of excitement communicated itself across the Atlantic to her daughter who had been evacuated to America. She read her mother's account of London under fire, *England's Hour*, and wrote back: 'you seem to be rather in the midst of things . . . I think it was *lovely*. I wish I was there in some of the experiences you were in.'[38] Elizabeth Bowen, with that eye which Charles Ritchie thought missed nothing,[39] would not have missed the implications of her own involvement in the worlds of violence and betrayal.

To read Bowen's spy story from Stella's point of view is only half the story. The roads of betrayal lead to the spy-traitor Robert Kelway, described by Bowen as 'the touchstone of the book',[40] and for many readers its weakest point. The *Times Literary Supplement* reviewer was perplexed by Bowen's muffled treatment of his treason,[41] and Bowen's friend Rosamond Lehmann agreed in wanting Bowen to be more 'explicit'. She added: 'What bothers me a little is that I cannot see why he shouldn't have been a Communist and therefore pro-Russian, pro-Ally, rather than pro-"enemy" '.[42] Kelway's character is partly based on Charles Ritchie, an Anglo-Canadian and a half-outsider like Bowen herself. Ritchie was a career diplomat, and no particular friend of the People's War. He was fond of taking ballerinas to dine at the Ritz and dreaded a socialist future, 'the eclipse of style, the disappearance of distinction . . . One's soul shrinks from the austere prospect of cotton stockings'.[43] He admired the poetry of Roy Campbell; 'the one fascist poet in England,' Ritchie called him, 'full of vitality, blazing with heat and fire'.[44] Kelway is partly Ritchie, but he is also partly Bowen herself, an example of that 'transposed autobiography' which she conceded was inevitable in any fiction.[45] He shares, as critics have remarked, some of Bowen's attitudes: her 'disaffectedness' according to Hermione Lee,[46] her attraction to order according to R.F. Foster,[47] as well as her scorn for middle-class values. His limp turns out to be a neat piece of 'transposed autobiography' when Bowen likens it to a stammer (90), her own affliction.

Kelway doubles both Ritchie and Bowen in a novel which teems with doubles. Names repeat themselves like Louie Lewis and Roderick Rodney. Roderick's name also echoes Robert's – does the corn on his foot suggest that he might come to double the limping Robert? Harrison is a double in himself, he is that device beloved of spy fiction, the double agent. Stella calls him ' "a counter-spy" ', a ' "spy twice over" ' (39). His doubleness is economically inscribed in his gaze:

> one of his eyes either was or behaved as being just perceptibly higher than the other. This lag or inequality in his vision gave her the feeling of being looked at twice – being viewed then checked over again in the same moment. (12)

The doubling of Robert Kelway's first name with Harrison's, so characteristic of the book's looking-glass ways,[48] has often been noticed by
readers; and Harrison's revelation that his first name is Robert is the note
on which Pinter ends his screenplay. But Robert is also Bowen's own
buried name, as she explained in *Seven Winters, Memories of a Dublin
Childhood*: 'My grandfather had been Robert, my father Henry – there was
no doubt which name was waiting for me' (8). Enquiries for ' "Any news
of Robert?" ' greeted friends and family as Elizabeth's pregnant mother
awaited her arrival. Bowen published this memoir in 1943; by 1944 she
had written the first five chapters of *The Heat of the Day* with its traitor
Robert. But if he shares her name, he does not share her house; instead his
family inhabit the impostor's version. Holme Dene is a bogus Big House,
not permanent and rooted like Bowen's Court but always up for sale, its
interiors as movable as 'touring scenery' (121).[49] *Bowen's Court*, written
like *Seven Winters* in the early years of the war, affirms Bowen's loyalty to
the 'authority of its long tradition', the vital 'attachment of people to
places' (334, 337). However, Bowen was an only child and without a child
of her own, and found herself in the position she gives Stella Rodney: a
member of the landed gentry at the end of the line, standing in history as
'A handsome derelict gateway' (115). If Elizabeth had been Robert, a
man, she might have been able to carry on that 'long tradition' more
successfully. As it was, financial constraints forced her to sell Bowen's
Court in 1960.

In the doubled use of her buried name for Kelway and Harrison,
Bowen expresses her disquiet about her stake in Ireland, about her
dealings between England and Ireland.[50] She and Charles Ritchie used to
tell each other that guilt was a middle-class complaint,[51] so perhaps spying
on a beloved (in Bowen's case a country rather than a person) did not
cause her the guilt felt by Stella. But in her novel she unequivocally
dramatises her conviction that all relationships are contaminated by war.
Stella's tragedy is that the war invades private lives, including and
especially, affairs of the heart. Into her city comes the whole of Europe:
'She began to feel it was not the country but occupied Europe that was
occupying London – suspicious listening, surreptitious movement, and
leaden hearts' (126). And into her personal life sweeps the invasion of war;
as the *Times Literary Supplement* review noted, 'Miss Bowen interprets war
through love'.[52] There can be no private life safe from the world outside.
' "What country have you and I outside this room?" ' Robert asks Stella,
trying to belittle his treachery to his country by substituting his fidelity to
her (267). But the war's invasion is complete:

To her, tonight, 'outside' meant the harmless world; the mischief was in her own and in other rooms. The grind and scream of battles, mechanised advances excoriating flesh and country, tearing through nerves and tearing up trees, were indoor-plotted; this was a war of dry cerebration inside windowless walls. No act was not part of some calculation; spontaneity was in tatters; from the point of view of nothing more than the heart any action was enemy action now . . . (142)

It is the suspicion of Robert's genuineness as a lover rather than as a patriot which undermines Stella and prompts her long, concealed 'watch of Robert's doors and windows' (172). The one remark of Harrison's 'to get her under the skin' is his suggestion that someone – Robert – might be ' "able to act in love" ' (38). The tragedy is that personal relationships cannot be immune, as Bowen observes in a brilliant image of sociability and intimacy invaded: 'But they were not alone, nor had they been from the start, from the start of love. Their time sat in the third place at their table' (194).

War initiates, infects and compromises love, so much so that the language of love and the language of surveillance are, finally, indistinguishable. When Robert proposes he says, ' "I cannot bear you out of my sight" ' – who is speaking here, the lover or the spy? Those with the clearest vision suffer most. Cousin Nettie, the one who sees most clearly in the book, 'an often-rebuked clairvoyante' (207), is half-mad; she has to sit with her back to the window. Stella's curse is to suffer from seeing too much, her eyes 'exposed for ever to what they saw, subjected to whatever chose to be seen' (294): an appropriate curse in a spy novel.

Looking back at her Bletchley Park work, Christine Brooke-Rose acknowledged her sense of 'having been complicitous in war, in male history', adding, 'Like most women'.[53] Like Bowen too, the awareness of complicity runs through *The Heat of the Day*. The book's obsession with fraught and problematic ways of looking can be read as the author's anxiety that she may have done harm by her particular kind of wartime watching. Robert Kelway, Robert Harrison, Robert Bowen: the choice of name is a secret self-conviction of treason. It is fitting that Bowen found what Glendinning called her 'personal celebration' of the end of the war in the spectacle of searchlights playing exuberantly over London:[54] an image of surveillance and light finally and beautifully set free.

6

WOMEN TO BLAME?
ADVERSE IMAGES OF
WOMEN IN WAR

I'm on about a dozen committees.
Richmal Crompton, *Mrs Frensham Describes a Circle*, 1942

The experiences of the blitz bred positive images of women and motherhood: figures of fortitude nurtured England and held the nation together.[1] With the progress of the war women attained a higher profile on the home front but a lower esteem on the page. Nurturing came to look more like bossiness, the good breast turned into the bad, the capable into the culpable. War, as the editors of a recent collection of essays on war and gender remind us,

> must be understood as a *gendering* activity, one that ritually marks the gender of all members of a society, whether or not they are combatants.[2]

In Britain gender roles were shifting with the patterns of demography. Men were obliged to leave their homes and jobs, and women had to take their places. The American critic Susan Gubar has characterised Second World War writing as a 'blitz on women'; her accounts of the hostility towards women in men's writing draw largely on American evidence.[3] If we focus on this side of the Atlantic in order to consider images of women generated by men and women novelists during the war, we also find that all is not well between the sexes. Men writers first.

Evelyn Waugh's *Put Out More Flags* (1942) opens as war breaks out and 'three rich women thought first and mainly of Basil Seal. They were his sister, his mother and his mistress' (9). They all contemplate his death with some enthusiasm: 'Death for Basil, that Angela might live again . . . Rupert Brooke, Old Bill, the Unknown Soldier – thus three fond women saw him' (29). But Basil is a survivor and more than a match for Waugh's mock harpies. Henry Green's *Caught* (1943) takes a less light-hearted view of the gender war in wartime, and here the hostility flows as Gubar suggests, from men to women. Richard Roe despises Hilly, a driver at his Fire Station, for sleeping with him: 'He was irritated, mainly because she had gone to bed with him. He found it made her of no account' (130). So much for women's sexual generosity – in Roe's bitter version women feed off erotic opportunity,

> hungrily seeking another man, oh they were sorry for men and they pitied themselves, for yet another man with whom they could spend last hours, to whom they could murmur darling, darling, darling it will be you always. (63)

Green suggests another motive for Roe's animosity in his resentment of women's involvement in the war. When Hilly says ' "I don't believe there is anyone who hasn't enjoyed the change" ' (101), she confirms Roe's opinion that women are enjoying this war too much: not just the sex, the freedom too. But Roe, who 'had no inkling of the insecurity the war would put him in' (32), needs someone to confide in. A widower, he turns to his sister-in-law to tell her at great length about the terrible air raid he has worked through. She listens, trying to understand, but when she offers a comment he snaps. ' "God damn you," he shouted, releasing everything, "you get on my bloody nerves, all you bloody women with all your talk" ' (196). But the talk has all been his, his outburst fuelled by resentment at needing a woman to listen to him.

The three Second World War novels in Anthony Powell's *Dance to the Music of Time* sequence use women more unambiguously to stand in for the enemy.[4] The Germans never appear but the 'embattled' Audrey Maclintick does:

> small, wiry, aggressive, she looked as ready as ever for a row, her bright black eyes and unsmiling countenance confronting a world from which perpetual hostility was not merely potential, but presumptive. Attack, she made clear, would be met by counter-attack.[5]

Pamela Flitton is even worse, she 'gave the impression of being thoroughly vicious, using the word not so much in the moral sense, but as one might speak of a horse – more specifically, a mare'.[6] The narrator observes the 'unvarying technique of silence, followed by violence, with which she persecuted her lovers' (79); and Pamela declares herself quite openly as the enemy, donning a tin helmet in a 'conscious gesture of hostility' (137). Richard Baxter's *Guilty Women* (1941 and into its fifth edition by 1943) explicitly holds the women of Britain and continental Europe responsible for the war, either because they are Nazi sympathisers or because they supported appeasement. Some of the hostility – Baxter's is an extreme brand – which crawls under the skin of men's wartime writing can be traced to a sense of injustice: men have to fight and women don't, women are usurping men's places at home and work. The segregation of British literary life cannot have eased the strain; Naomi Mitchison noticed ' "anti-women pressure" . . . in literary circles during the war'.[7] The literary world, with its pub-based culture, had little room for women, and it rarely published their writings in the anthologies and magazines which flourished at the time.[8]

Adverse – and adversarial – imagery of women made its way into women's fiction, as women brought the blame back home. But it is important to see the negative in the context of the positive; they are the two sides of the same coin of female wartime competence. During the war there was, unsurprisingly, much discussion about heroism. The historian C.V. Wedgwood acknowledged the danger that 'the adulation of individuals should lead to the heresy of the "Fuhrer-prinzip" ', but she nevertheless regretted the contemporary 'flight from the heroic'.[9] She and others wanted visible icons of heroism, and found role models in their patriotic past. Elizabeth was the name on everyone's lips. 'I said I hoped and thought that we were once again becoming "Elizabethan" ', wrote Freya Stark in 1944.[10] *The Golden Age of Queen Elizabeth* was the title of a play by Clemence Dane in 1941, and in the same year Edith Sitwell was 'reading up for an enormous book I am going to do about Elizabeth'.[11] Everyone was eager to pay homage to the war heroines of the moment, women such as Mary Cornish and Victoria Drummond.[12] For more everyday use writers unearthed models of quiet heroism: in 1943 Vita Sackville-West lauded Saint Thérèse of Lisieux for her 'practical Christianity', her message of the 'Little Way',

> the heroism of . . . little things . . . not to do extraordinary things, but to do ordinary things extraordinarily well . . . by-passing the main road of the heroic.[13]

Women were to win the war through the virtues of constancy and per-severance: these are the province of the middle-aged, a rapidly expanding constituency in the fiction of the time.

By no means a uniform population, though some of them did wear uniform, the middle-aged fictional women of the war span a wide range, from Stella Rodney in Elizabeth Bowen's *The Heat of the Day*, to Valentine Levallois in E.M. Delafield's *Late and Soon* and Sybil Jardine in Rosamond Lehmann's *The Ballad and the Source*. Sometimes their heroism sparkles eccentrically; the aristocratic Mrs Ellsworth in Susan Ertz's *Anger in the Sky* explains her war work in a few dramatic words, ' "I'm living on capital" ' (178). Her guest is duly impressed, and no harm done, Mrs Ellsworth's cook can still produce a good dinner in the middle of an air raid. The sacrifices made by Miss Nimble in Richmal Crompton's *Mrs Frensham Describes a Circle* (1942) for War Weapons Week hurt more:

> Her small peaked face wore a hungry look, and she found herself dreaming constantly of juicy steaks and roast chickens, though she had seldom indulged in such fare even in peace-time. (175–176)

In this newly visible world of middle-aged heroism romantic love does not necessarily conquer all. Helen Temple in Vita Sackville-West's *Grand Canyon* (1942) prefers ' "the quiet thing; only friend-ship, companionship" ' (194). The quiet versions of virtues such as loyalty and courage are exemplified by middle-aged women like Selina Tippett in Bryher's *Beowulf* (1956). Selina tells her partner in the Warming Pan tea-shop that they have a duty to maintain morale during air raids:

> 'The staff copies us unconsciously, and in that way we are influencing not just Ruby, Timothy, and the customers but perhaps hundreds of people.' For if clients came in to lunch and went off cheerfully afterwards, they, in turn, would affect their relatives and their maids. It was inspiring, really, especially on such a cold, dreary morning, to think how much one solitary woman could do in defence of her native land. (22–23)

Selina, Bryher implies, may be a little absurd, but her worth is sterling.

The middle-aged woman as housekeeper, running the house in the absence of its male head, figures frequently in women's writing, but not without ambivalence. Margery Allingham sets her housekeeper Dorothy

Holding in a long perspective in her historical saga, *Dance of the Years* (1943):

> She was one of those women who remain unaltered by any change in the social life of the century. In Saxon hall, Caroline still-room, or the manager's room in the latest block of service flats, wherever or whenever a large household has to be fed, cleaned, bedded and controlled, one of the Dorothy Holdings of the world has bustled there, secret, single-minded, and quite extraordinarily powerful.
>
> In the end, whatever the theories of civilized living, the answer lies in them. Fly to the secret parts of the earth and they are there, looking out casually and with preoccupied eyes from the doorways of the largest huts; come back to the newest communal feeding centre and they are there again, selfless, untiring, thinking of something else. They are the ultimate bosses. (12)

The animosity is unmistakable, Allingham's tribute to female efficiency bristles with distaste. The clue to it lies in the words about the 'large household' which 'has to be fed, cleaned, bedded and controlled'. This large household was the unmanned England of 1943, as Allingham was well aware: two years earlier she had written a book about the effect of war on rural areas. In *The Oaken Heart* (1941) she painted a positive picture of England muddling through with quiet co-operation. By 1943 she has her reservations (which she hides under the *Dance of the Years'* cloak of historical fiction) about women who seek to control the nation from within. Allingham was not alone in her ambivalence towards these 'quite extraordinarily powerful' figures: the fiction of the period is studded with unsympathetic and domineering women. Sometimes she makes a brief comic appearance, like Catherine's mother, busy with her revolver practice in Edith Pargeter's *She Goes to War* (1942). Sometimes she causes disasters through over-management: Jean Ross's *Aunt Ailsa* (1944) is not an evil woman, but her interference fails to bear good fruit. G.B. Stern's *The Young Matriarch* (1942) overflows with combative women and the Rakonitz family is perpetually ' "swarming with Matriarchs" ' (455).

In wartime the state assumes greater powers, altering the living and working patterns of its citizens in the interests of survival and victory. The anomalous role of women in the state of Britain at war is best exemplified by the Women's Voluntary Service, both in its work and in the way it was perceived. Founded by Lady Reading in 1938, the WVS grew rapidly to over a million members by 1941. Starting with evacuation, it came to take responsibility for a huge range of social services and civil defence work. It and other voluntary agencies with predominantly female memberships provided essential services and functions. Such agencies were, in effect, the local and visible enforcers of the huge powers which the Government took in order to run wartime Britain, to such an extent that Lady Reading described the WVS as the 'hyphen between officialdom and ordinary human beings'.[14] In their implementation of the workings of the state these women offered a convenient target; women who organise are often resented. Elizabeth Bowen, looking back in 1969, remembered the enmity between the ARP wardens (she was one) and 'the indomitable WVS . . . we could not abide the sight of them – why, I wonder?'[15] There is an interesting precedent for the powerful but resented woman in wartime fiction: Bellona, the Roman goddess of war, who is described variously as the companion, sister or wife of Mars. She prepares his chariot when he goes to war and encourages warlike sentiments in those about to fight. Her temple was regarded as a symbolic representation of the enemy's territory – a declaration of war would be made by launching a spear over a pillar at the entrance to her temple. Thus, the figure of Bellona has a double meaning: she helps a nation to conduct a war, but she also represents the enemy, that which must be fought. Through her image we may appreciate some of the ambivalence surrounding the middle-aged woman whose powers are now being revealed or unleashed in wartime.

Bossy women charge up and down the margins of wartime novels, billeting, rationing, exhorting, roaring for Ovaltine. ' "Look at me" ' barks Mrs Tylney in Richmal Crompton's *Mrs Frensham Describes a Circle*:

'I run my house, I'm on about a dozen committees and I pull my weight on each – pull *more* than my weight, I might say.' She finished off a ball, tossed it into a basket, flung another roll of wool over the chair-back and had the next ball well under way in a few deft lightning movements. 'I put in regular hours at the Central Hall canteen, I'm organising a Bring and Buy for the WVS and a Bridge Drive for the Red Cross, and I run a weekly War Working Party in the Church Rooms here as well as helping at the Community Feeding Centre. I think I can honestly say that every minute of every day is full and I never leave any piece of work that could be done today till tomorrow. I'm always telling the girls how much happier they'd be if they did the same.'

'I wonder if they would,' murmured Mrs Frensham. (142–143)

Mrs Drake in Helen Ashton's *Tadpole Hall* (1941) bustles about in her Red Cross uniform quarrelling with everyone and making a nuisance of herself as a billeting officer. 'But at least the work got done and the children were well looked after' (168); Ashton and others might mock but they acknowledged that useful jobs were being done. Their bossy women would usually, though not always, be good-natured, harassed and occasionally comic. They were easy targets for the grateful wartime novelist and could be patronised by writer and reader alike. Patronising mockery turns to hostility in representations of the bad mother. Although kindly mothers live on (in the blitz as we have seen, and in novels such as Elizabeth Taylor's *At Mrs Lippincote's* and Betty Miller's *On the Side of the Angels*), they are outnumbered by a host of unkindly ones. Sometimes the bad mother is merely neglectful. Mummie in Noel Streatfeild's *Saplings* (1945) goes downhill after the death of her husband, and becomes an alcoholic with a weakness for American soldiers. Sometimes the mother verges on the monstrous. Ivy Compton Burnett's *Parents and Children* (1941) does not mention the war, but features a blandly manipulative mother. The extent of Eleanor's manoeuvrings remains hidden: father, children and author gallantly collude to shield her from the reader's suspicions. But guilty she is, and this will be a verdict often passed upon the mother by the wartime woman novelist. She is a guilty figure and sometimes a monstrous one.[16] Her crime is not always specified, and even when it is it appears insufficient for the animosity it has aroused. What then is the mother's crime?

If women ran the world there would be no more war: this age-old platitude gains some credence during the Second World War. It would appear that mothers have failed if their sons are killing each other. Katherine Thomas begins her well-informed analysis of *Women in Nazi Germany* (1943) by quoting Charles Kingsley:

> Nations are gathered out of nurseries, and they who hold the leading strings of children may even exercise a greater power than those who hold the reins of Government. (7)

Her first chapter, 'Playing with Soldiers . . .' describes the militarisation of maternity in Germany which is summed up for her in the epitaph: ' "Sleep well! Your children are already playing soldiers." Such is the proudly published epitaph, so sadly typical in feeling, on a German father killed on the Russian Front last year' (9). Thomas records the devastating effects of poverty and Nazi ideology on German women:

Women in Nazi Germany have to live in a man's world, in a world built and governed by the dictatorship of men, where women have duties only and no rights. The moral standards of many of those women have been turned upside down and their general outlook has been narrowed pitifully. They are kept deliberately in a state of permanent fear and insecurity whose peak has not yet been attained. (99)

German women are the victims of Nazism and the world is the loser; according to Thomas, militarism is a fatal consequence of the oppression of women. But this analysis does not fit the allied case and the allied mother. Not over-ruled, but colluding and over-ruling, the women of Britain conform strikingly to the shape of the militaristic Bellona, ambivalent figure and symbolic enemy. Mother imagery entered the war in poor shape: Paul Fussell describes the battery of negative images in First World War literature – 'exposures of maternal self-righteousness, callousness, and egotism' – from which 'the mother cult never recovered'.[17] The prominence of the dutiful mother in German propaganda was another mark against her.[18] War inculcates adversarial patterns of thought, constructing enemies against whom to unite and fight. Mothers are, to rewrite a famous title of the time, not the last but the first enemy, the first no-sayer to the child.[19] The mother must be fought and she will be conquered – such a battle would seem to be sanctioned by all.

The most famous fictional mother of the war, Mrs Miniver, certainly had her enemies. Rosamond Lehmann loathed her eternal rightness (a perennially irritating quality in mothers), and the 'way she has of masking her colossal self-satisfaction with tender self-depreciation'. Lehmann apologised for the vitriol in her review of *Mrs Miniver*,[20] but by the end of 1939 Mrs Miniver's own creator was silencing her for ever, bidding her farewell with a stab in the back. Jan Struther won a prize in a *New Statesman* competition for a parody of Mrs Miniver: 'I felt pretty sure that I could write a far crueller satire on "Mrs Miniver" than could any of my detractors.'[21] Struther left for America, where Mrs Miniver was transformed on screen into America's plucky version of British motherhood at war. Back home British writers were devising maternal horrors such as Rosamond Lehmann's Ma Daintrey:

Ma Daintrey was immense, a monolith. When she sat she went down backwards all of a piece and there she stayed, semi-reversed, gasping, stuck, until she was pulled up again. Barely confined by taut black satin, her stomach protruded with monstrous abruptness, as if worn superimposed, a fertility symbol, to mark the pregnancies which had been her life's achievement. Her person expressed with overpowering force every kind of physical process. Even her voice, gassy, ruminative, replete, seemed a kind of alimentary canal and everything she said regurgitated. I remember when she spoke to us, or of us to our parents, how she seemed to swallow us down into her womanly amplitudes. She was prodigal of that kind of clucking indulgent pity whereby all mankind is castrated, the dignity of the intellect made naught, and humanity in general diminished to its swaddling-bands – the toy, pet, cross of suffering Woman.[22]

Physically unpleasant and unpleasantly physical, the cannibalistic Ma Daintrey dies; other mothers must be fled or fought. Mothers, mothers-in-law and step-mothers, the stock ogres of fairy-tale and comic postcard, stand in for Hitler, the evil to be mocked and scourged. The mother will be easier to conquer and can offer a consoling prophecy of his downfall, a proleptic revenge.

Maternal monstrosity can take diverse forms. Ma Daintrey is a swallower, while the mother in Elizabeth Myers's *A Well Full of Leaves* (1943) attacks with more force:

> She was at her best when she was toppling the entire scene. All her dislike of us and the world in general was extended into whatever she was doing. Under her hands soap suds were angry, clothes sneered, steam menaced, crockery raved.
>
> She was small and energetic. She did everything as though she were being scorched into the act. It was terrible if she did anything for you – buttoned your dress at the back where you could not reach, or if you were ill and she had to wash you or comb your hair. She came at you, and she did things to you, like an executioner, not like a mild good-natured mother such as, in the nature of things, children are led to expect. Not one of us ever had a tender word from her . . .
>
> She was managing and catastrophic and glum. As far as her treatment of my brother Steve went, there ought to have been some outside interference. His limbs were often impatterned with brilliant bruises from her physical cruelty. The other bruises done to his mind in her most ill-natured and rapacious hours were not seen until they had become the *actions* of his later life. (38)

Myers's unnamed mother is cruel and sadistic; in her need to control she takes her children out of school and pushes them into the fire. A would-be giantess, she regards herself as a 'power rather than a person' (91). Sometimes the mother aligns more directly with the national enemy. Kate O'Brien's *The Last of Summer* (1943) is set in Eire at the end of August and beginning of September 1939. The novel's young lovers are divided partly by the international situation (Angèle wants to return home to France at this moment of crisis), but more viciously by Tom's delightful mother Hannah. A force of aggression and division, she plays a subtle game to keep her son. Hannah's campaign is precisely placed in time, and marks the opening skirmish in Hitler's war, the prelude to the battles ahead. ' "You win," ' says Angèle to Hannah at the end of the book and the beginning of the war.[23] The wicked surrogate mother also flourishes in wartime Jerusalem, in Olivia Manning's *School for Love* (1951). Miss Bohun overcharges, starves and neglects the young, recently orphaned Felix. She tells him, ' "I'm a sort of relative . . . and I want to do what I can for you. It's my duty, anyway" ' (15). Felix wants to love Miss Bohun despite her 'almost monstrous' behaviour – she reminds him of a praying mantis (266); but she repels the love he needs to give and take, and he lavishes it instead on the 'sad little cat, as lost as himself' (16). On behalf of the innocent Felix the reader develops a lively dislike for Miss Bohun – for her meanness, hypocrisy, unkindness and officiousness. But by 1951, when Manning published this novel, the fear of women's power which lurks in representations of the monster mother has receded, and old Mr Jewel preaches a gospel of tolerance: ' "We're all human, it's not for us to be too hard on one another" ' (192).

Sibyl Jardine, who dominates Rosamond Lehmann's *The Ballad and the Source* (1944), is one of the most monstrous mothers to come out of the war (though she is not of it, her story has an Edwardian setting); her charm and beauty serve only to heighten her power. The grand tale of Sibyl's malevolent maternity unfolds in a series of reminiscences told to the young Rebecca Landon. The novel has the properties of sensation fiction, but its preoccupations are those of 1944: bad mothering and the fatal seductions of charisma. When she eloped Sibyl Jardine abandoned her baby daughter Ianthe; the damage done to the child and Sibyl's attempts to regain her provide the basis for the rest of the story. Ianthe grows up to run away, in her turn abandoning her three children, Malcolm, Maisie and Cherry. These three are the contemporaries of Rebecca and her sister Jess, who are invited to play with Mrs Jardine's grandchildren and, in Rebecca's case, to listen to the stories. In the last part of the novel we hear of Ianthe's reappearance as a violent madwoman. She destroys a sculpture of her mother which she mistakes for the real figure of her mother. This is a story of the damage done to children by mothers who abandon them – a pertinent story for 1944, with its context of families split by evacuation and war work.[24] The book closes on a more hopeful note than we might have expected: the extent of the potential damage is contained. Ianthe's daughter Maisie manages to protect both her mother and her grandmother; and Rebecca remains uncorrupted by the terrible Sibyl.

Sibyl's version of her life blurs the enormity of her crimes, and the reader must work to establish the truth of what she has been up to. After deserting her baby, Sibyl tries to regain her in a conspiracy against the child's father which involves the child, Rebecca's grandmother, and her maid Tilly. When Sibyl's plan fails, she seeks revenge by publishing a novel which maligns Rebecca's grandmother; she attempts to seduce the grandmother's son (Rebecca's father), and she accuses her ex-husband of incest. In her only meeting with Ianthe, who is now seventeen, Sibyl behaves appallingly. ' "A boy now," ' she reflects, ' "would have seen me as beautiful and been glad . . . I would have won a smile from him" ' (132). Ianthe refuses to succumb to her charm, and Sibyl departs with a last insult to her daughter, ' "I am bored!" ' (134). So much for the mother desperate to regain her child. The next passage between mother and daughter is even worse, but fortunately Sibyl's young listener is unable to understand it. Sibyl colludes with one of her ex-lovers to debauch her daughter in the name of sophisticated education. She tells Rebecca:

'Women need men, you know. They cannot live without them. But are they taught their most important lesson – *how* to live with a man? what to go for, what to avoid? How to please, how to keep their men? Oh dear me, no! I was determined that *my* daughter, at least, should not be flung into marriage ignorant, unprepared.'

'Oh, you wanted him to marry her!' I said enthusiastically, light dawning at last.

'No, I did not,' she said shortly. (141)

The disastrous interlude ends with a mentally ill Ianthe giving birth to an illegitimate stillborn child. At this point Sibyl decides to reject her daughter and direct her urge to dominate elsewhere. Her second husband Harry (reduced by the time we see him to mute alcoholism) and Ianthe's children are her chosen prey. Even the besotted Rebecca notices that Sibyl is 'powerful and cruel' to Maisie, a child whose mother has run away and whose father is dying. Compulsively manipulative, Sibyl intrigues with her grandchildren's guardians, just as she had with her daughter's, and involves their simple Auntie Mack in troubling deceptions. Nor is Rebecca's mother immune to her wiles, invited to tea and consultation about the grandchildren:

> It was the spell of the spell-binder, no more, no less. My mother was prudent and incorruptible, but she too was drawn, irresistibly drawn, to look upon, to listen to Mrs Jardine again. (180)

Triumph comes at last. Sibyl gains possession of her grandchildren, but by the end of the book two of them are dead and she must find fresh subjects to conquer. She selects the young governess Tanya and the sculptor Gil, who manage to escape her orbit by marrying each other.

The events are sensational (Lehmann has gone for gothic), but much of the meaning is in the manner of the telling. The novel dramatises and offers a commentary on the power of story-telling.[25] A series of mother figures narrate the 'ballad' of Sibyl's highly coloured life: the 'spell-binding' Sibyl herself; Tilly, the ancient cockney who was maid to Rebecca's grandmother, and Auntie Mack, the prosaic Scotswoman who helps bring up Sibyl's grandchildren. These characters, in combination with other mothers, and the nature of the child-listener, establish the meaning of Sibyl's autobiography. Lehmann opens her novel with a contrast between two mothers, as Rebecca's mother reads Sibyl Jardine's invitation to Rebecca and Jess. Throughout, Rebecca's mother acts as a counterweight to Sibyl Jardine; and here we read the letter through her eyes as well as those of her ten-year-old daughter who is so easily swayed by language. Mrs Landon reads:

> 'We are getting too old to wander all our days, and Harry's torn roots in England and his childhood home have ached more and more with the passage of the years . . .'
> 'Is that what she says?' I asked. Immediately, I felt attracted towards a lady who expressed herself with such picturesqueness. 'She means he was homesick,' said my mother. (5)

Mrs Landon's eyebrow-raising as she reads Mrs Jardine's description of her daughters as 'little Primaveras', as well as Jess's ' "What on earth does she mean?" ' (6) balance Rebecca's eagerness to fall in with Sibylline ways:

> I personally felt an extreme willingness to lend myself to the inter-
> pretation. My form appeared to me in an indistinct, but pleasing
> diaphanous light, moving over the green hillside, spiritually and gracefully
> gathering blossoms. (6)

Throughout the novel Sibyl Jardine's extravagant version of the act which needs justification – the mother's abandonment of a child – is accompanied by the voices and versions of those other mother figures: the 'temperate' Mrs Landon (208); the sentimental, gullible Auntie Mack, and Tilly, who gives the story a music-hall flavour. Tilly's histrionics are hugely enjoyable for both teller and listener: ' "There was the letter propped up on the mantel – scented and sealed. 'E opens it. *Gone*, 'e reads. *Gone with the one I love*" ' (66). Tilly gets 'irretrievably carried away' (72), and acts out the characters in Sibyl's elopement to turn it into rich melodrama, full of tragedy-queens and curses:

> ' "Be it soon, be it late, I-anth will come back to me. I will have her love.
> And she will HATE her father." And with that she sweeps out like a queen,
> and the front door slams be'ind her.' (80)

Tilly rejects the connections that Rebecca wants to make between the characters in her story and the people now living next door; her story is exactly that, a story, performance sealed off from reality. Rebecca is the perfect listener, but she is only a child and cannot grasp the implications of the mother's desertion of her baby. The little girl is more interested in the fate of Sibyl's pet – 'Though tempted, I refrained from asking "Did she take the monkey?" ' (67) – and takes Sibyl's side against the husband who refuses to send her baby to her:

> 'What a *beastly* man! How could he? She was hers just as much as his.
> Wasn't she?'
> 'Hers that she'd deserted,' said Tilly, with venom.
> 'Yes, but she never *meant* to. She *told* Grandma she was coming for her.'
> (75)

How can the secure child, who does not spend a night away from home without her parents until she is fourteen (314), understand the nature of desertion? Tilly puts the relevant question:

> 'What would you say if your mother was to run off and leave the lot of
> you one fine night? Would you say she was considerin' you and your
> welfare when she done it?'
> Between violent and conflicting emotions: on the one hand to assert:
> 'Yes, I would,' on the other ferociously to repudiate so infamous, so
> unimaginable a supposition, I felt about to burst. (75)

By setting Tilly's version next to the impression Mrs Jardine has already
made upon her, Rebecca starts to grasp the principle which guides
Lehmann's construction of Sibyl Jardine:

> Two irreconcilable sets of facts confronted me. Miss Sibyl was an
> authoress; she had written something horrid and unkind about Grandma.
> Yet, turn the wheel, and she was Mrs Jardine, who loved Grandma so much
> that her voice altered when she spoke of her; who loved me for being her
> grandchild. I could only suppose that grown-ups were like that. (92)

Tilly is an entertainer; 'a consumate actress and mimic', she sings and
dances for the children, 'holding her skirts with quirked fingers' (14), and
entrancing them with tales in her 'magnetic room' (57). Hers is a
beneficial charisma, performance clearly marked as performance. Sibyl
Jardine's, on the other hand, is harmful. As befits her name, Sibyl is a
spell-binder,[26] and *The Ballad and the Source* meditates on the evils of
charisma. 'Charisma', according to the *Oxford English Dictionary*, was a
word gaining in currency in the 1930s and 1940s, particularly in writings
about the authority which Hitler wielded over his audience. 'The power
to bewitch', 'magnetism': the language that the historian Alan Bullock
uses to describe Hitler's dark ascendancy,[27] is also applied to Sibyl Jardine
(44, 53). It may seem excessive to compare a beautiful and charming
elderly lady with an embodiment of evil, but Hitler was never far from
people's minds in 1944, and the issue of power over others is apposite to
real and fictional dictators. Sibyl is no stranger to battle, whether open or
covert. She establishes bridgeheads, engages in frontal combat, and plans
strategies (43, 98, 100); she also plots and counterplots, stalks and
ambushes (100, 230). For both Hitler and Sibyl Jardine speech is the key.
According to Alan Bullock, 'Speech was the essential medium of [Hitler's]
power, not only over his audiences but over his own temperament' (372),
and both dictator and grandmother stand accused of self-delusion.[28] The

force of Sibyl's charisma is such that most of the characters in the novel – and many readers – succumb to it and withhold judgement. The reader must learn to question the heroic perspectives in which Sibyl positions herself, and to remember that she has her less thrilling aspects, as a tedious grandmother – ' "My dentist appears to be the only man in this country with any grasp of bridge work" ' (100) – and an elderly woman boasting of her once glorious complexion and rich voice (120, 133). While we can enjoy and appreciate Sibyl's charisma, we must recognise it for what it is. In this, we are assisted by the unwitting Rebecca.

The first time Rebecca and Jess go to tea with Mrs Jardine neatly illustrates the methods of both Sibyl and Rebecca, orator and audience.

> Mrs Jardine turned to the window, so that only her bleached stone profile was visible to us, and as if declaring herself, alone, before the judgement of the world, said:
>
> 'I have never been a person to be frightened. Physically, I am exceptionally brave. I may say that I have never known danger. Each time I have thought "How interesting! A first class experience. Not to be missed on any account." As for those ignoble anxieties which rule the lives of most human beings – they have never touched me. The world is full of unhappy men and women who feared the opinion of others too much to do what they wanted to do. Consequently they have remained sterile, unfulfilled. Now myself – once I was convinced of what was right for *me*, that was enough! I might suffer, but *nobody* could damage or destroy me.'
>
> I could have listened all day to Mrs Jardine, for the sheer fascination of her style. She enunciated with extraordinary clarity and precision, giving each syllable its due, and controlling a rich range of modulations and inflexions. I wondered at first if she could be reciting from Shakespeare or someone. Then I thought: She's boasting: why? I had heard declarations somewhat similar in the nursery or the 'hall' after a reprimand from authority. (23)

That second response – 'She's boasting' – saves Rebecca. Only a child, she falls under Sibyl's spell, but she is always alert to the methods of the spell-binder and to the effects which can be achieved by performance. And she cannot deny the cruelties she perceives in her behaviour. Rebecca, and the nature of her reception of Sibyl's grand 'ballad' of love and loss, are essential to the meaning of Lehmann's novel. If we take our lead from Rebecca at the tea-table ('She's boasting'), we start to get the measure of Sibyl as a performer. Rebecca does this carefully:

I stole a glance at her. Her nostrils were dilated, her expression dramatic but composed. Her words came so smoothly, with such precision of timing, it was impossible not to feel that she was presenting a part she had rehearsed a hundred times. I experienced a curious moment of disabused vision, and thought I saw myself not as uniquely privileged, selected after a lifetime to receive her secrets, but as one of a long shadowy series of confidential audiences, all gazing, listening, as spellbound, as gratified as I. (110)

Rebecca's well-mothered innocence saves her. She has no idea that Sibyl is referring to sexual debauchery or to incest – ' "Did he have her to sleep with him, then?" I asked, astonished at such intensity of fatherly concern' (125). Her healthy appetite sees her through, as she gobbles down story and tea together. 'She fell silent, breathing deeply. Totally adrift in the storm, I continued to eat scones' (141). The extravagances of Sibyl's oratory (' "*The drop of anguish* – it burns me now" ') fall harmlessly on Rebecca's head: 'Floundering in all this, I began to feel, as I ate my way on through scones and into sponge cake, how unequal I was' (148). As Sibyl's rhetoric reaches a climax – ' "The sin, the bliss, the expiation ... Oh, ecstasy and terror" ' – Rebecca 'had planned to finish up with shortbread biscuits, and began now to complete my design' (154).

To see Sibyl as a tragic figure is to accept her on her own terms, terms which Lehmann has heavily qualified by adding the audience of the adoring but uncomprehending and steadily munching little girl. Not for nothing is Rebecca a debunker with problems imagining God, unable 'to rid myself of an early identification of Him with the Toby jug on the schoolroom mantelpiece', and Sibyl rightly doubts Rebecca's chances of ' "ever becoming one of the faithful" ' (118). Some of Sibyl's best effects are spoiled by the child's reaction. For example, her speech about fertility and the life force – ' "The source, Rebecca! The fount of life – the source, the quick spring that rises in illimitable depths of darkness" ' – must be read through the child's understandable mistake: ' "The source?" I said, puzzled about the spelling' (101). Lehmann makes it difficult to take Mrs Jardine as seriously as she would wish, though we can, with Rebecca, enjoy the luxury of being 'borne along' in the 'elemental welling-up and flow' (101). However, if we ask ourselves why Mrs Jardine talks so freely to a ten-year-old of adult matters, her fondness for 'boasting' to little girls starts to appear rather more sinister. Gil later observes to Rebecca, ' "You must have been an interesting experiment for her" ' (241), implying that Sibyl confided in Rebecca not purely out of affection for the granddaughter of her old friend, as Rebecca supposes. Battles emerge out of battles: Sibyl is perhaps avenging herself on the old friend who had refused to help her years ago. Even Rebecca feels 'a little uncomfortable' and insists to Gil, ' "You do see, don't you, how good she is for children?" ' (241). Mrs Jardine's bravura performances for Rebecca come to an end about halfway through the novel. Thereafter she recedes, and the reader recovers a necessary distance from the charismatic Sibyl which provides a space for reassessment. But she is not dead, and certainly not forgotten (she is discussed in her absence), and the book ends with Rebecca's threatening dream of her: 'I looked in terror over my shoulder, and saw under the dark trees a figure folded in a blue cape, faceless, motionless, watching me' (318).

Mrs Jardine was not the only Sibyl of the war. In 1937 Tchelitchew painted a portrait of Edith Sitwell known as 'The Sibyl', and Sitwell cultivated this image of herself during the war.[29] Her poetry dwells on the figure of the female sufferer poet:

> I, an old woman whose heart is like the Sun
> That has seen too much, looked on too many sorrows . . .[30]

Historical fiction looked back to George Sand as a 'sibyl casting her magic spells and secretive enchantments' over the coughing Chopin in Doris Leslie's *Polonaise* (1943, 150). Jane Oliver's *The Hour of the Angel* (1942) and Margaret Lane's *Where Helen Lies* (1944) both feature over-protective mothers called Sibyl – David Levy's *Maternal Overprotection* helpfully labelled the syndrome in 1943. Lehmann's own lack of immunity to her Sibyl's spells is suggested by Mrs Jardine's return thirty years later in *A Sea-Grape Tree* (1976). Characters who meet Sibyl Jardine at the end of her life describe 'Something about her larger than life size, a touch of the *monstre sacré* – of for instance Sara Bernhardt' (57). She appears from beyond the grave in a dream to the adult Rebecca, who can finally lay her threat to rest by speaking her epitaph: ' "*You are wicked, Mrs Jardine, wicked!*" ' (87).

7

LETTERS

Letters are *everything* these days.
Nancy Buchanan, Letter, 1943

At the heart of women's wartime writing lies an invisible hoard: the millions of letters from this last golden age of letter writing. Because these letters are not fiction they do not, strictly speaking, belong in this study; but putting them beside the novels of the time reveals some surprising shared ground. Letter writers turn out to have much in common with novelists, and this chapter will look at letters both real and fictional.

For friends and family split up by evacuation, war work and military service, letters were often the only possible form of communication. Leave was difficult to co-ordinate and long-distance telephone calls were expensive, with the Post Office reminding its customers that 'Social chatter over the telephone networks may hold up vitally important war talks'.[1] The Phono-Bug, a close relative of the Squander-Bug, was devised to curb telephone abuse. The command, *'Don't telegraph – write!'* was posted up on hoardings after the Central Telegraph Office was bombed in the London blitz.[2] More letters were probably written, posted, lost and received during the war than at any time before or since.[3] They were particularly valued for their beneficial effect on troop morale: 'fresh and frequent news from home was necessary for the soldier's comfort', according to the generals at the front.[4] For troops stationed overseas new technology invented the airgraph, an early version of the fax. The Queen sent the first one in August 1941, 'on behalf,' she wrote, 'of all the women at home'.[5]

It is difficult to overestimate the importance of letters in wartime. The critic Janet Gurkin Altman describes the letter's function 'as a connector between two distant points, as a bridge between sender and receiver'; she observes that 'the epistolary author can choose to emphasise either the distance or the bridge'.[6] Women writing letters in wartime almost invariably emphasised the bridge. Through their letters they could meet a variety of needs, both personal and social. The pen-friend custom testifies to the letter's patriotic work for the war effort. Margaret Harries, a landgirl billeted in a Welsh hostel, had 'pen pals all over the Globe. I was corresponding to the Falklands, North and South Africa'.[7] She and others were encouraged to start correspondences with men they had never met, to cheer, comfort and provide a sense of the home and homeland – those things men were told they were fighting for. Letters could also further courtships,[8] and give couples room to explore their feelings at greater length than might be possible face-to-face. Pamela Moore discussed her 'ideas of sex' with her fiancé, and welcomed the opportunity to 'go over everything to do with this great phase of life' on paper: 'My darling what a success our union should be!'[9] The uses of letter writing as therapy were also clearly understood. Joan Kirby, a nineteen-year-old Wren, wrote to her parents after her brother was killed in 1943:

> Don't for goodness sake either of you, think that you have to write me cheery letters even if you're feeling about as low as a well, because although I like to think of you all being as bright as you can . . . I know just how you're feeling about everything . . . your letters won't upset me if they're written when you're depressed. The more you let it out of your system the better you are for it.[10]

Women in segregated internment camps had to circumvent obstructions of all sorts to send letters to their husbands. Vimmy Grist, held in Changi internment camp from 1942 to 1945, cut up and reordered the script from an old manual on letter writing when she ran out of paper and ink. 'This', she inserted in her own writing, 'will be a case of reading between the lines' – literally as she used and angled the copybook words she inherited to transform a lesson on handwriting into a get-well message for her sick husband.[11]

Succour, courtship, therapy: wartime letters filled many functions. But many women must have shared the mixed feelings expressed by Diana Hopkinson whose husband was stationed abroad. By 1943 she writes, 'we had now each passed our hundredth letter, but sometimes I wanted to throw away my pen.' She wrote to him:

> I hate it as the symbol of the inadequacy of our communication compared to what our life in each other's presence might be. Then it seems a miserable crutch for an unhappy cripple. At other times I cling to it – the one thing that can forge a visible link, almost a messenger itself – a life belt. You know only too well the awful weariness that comes over one from writing – its one dimensional dissatisfaction.[12]

Diana Hopkinson's ambivalence recognises both the bridge and the distance of letters. In a 1942 letter she recalls a 'horrible walk' as a simile for her separation from her husband, leading by analogy to the longed-for conclusion. Simultaneously, the extended description of the walk is the 'walk' of the letter 'running on', 'our only bridge' as Hopkinson calls it:

> At least it is one year of absence over. We shall never have the pain of that absence to live again. Put it away – have done with it. We have to travel on into the almost incredible second year of separation. It is like going for a horrible walk one never wanted to start on and having to go on walking further than one meant to . . . Do you remember that walk up through the rain to St. Gervais to the chalet? I thought it was never going to end, even with you dragging me up half the way. But it did end in wine and a hot supper and a fire to dry ourselves by and that soft sink-in bed, and each other's arms to rest in. And so my letters run on, our only bridge.[13]

For some writers the gulf of separation was insurmountable and letters served only to remind of what was lost. 'Children turn into letters' was the sad phrase coined by parents who had sent their children out of danger, often never to be seen again.[14] Letters which arrived after the writer's death were also hard to bear:

> It was only two months since [her brother's] death, somewhere in the North Atlantic, and his last letters were still coming in, as if washed up by the tides.[15]

For letters to do their work as bridges, their writers needed the skills and techniques of the novelist. Inventing and telling stories, creating character and dialogue, establishing an individual voice: these are the stock-in-trade of novelist and letter writer alike. Fictions of contact and spontaneity, women's wartime letters are masterpieces of simulated conversation. Women seem to have grasped this aspect of letter writing more readily than men. Jock Lewes apologised for writing 'at length' to Mirren Barford but explained to her, 'I am one of the few remaining people who like letter writing and practise it, however ineptly, as an art.'[16] Later he recognised the disadvantages in his approach compared to hers:

> God, what a pompous fool I am! You implore me to relax and here I am aping the stilted language of centuries ago . . . You have never lost your ability to put yourself on paper. (202)

Putting 'yourself on paper', 'I just ramble on as if I am talking to you':[17] women evidently understood and capitalised on what their letters could do. For some women, the conversation was even more of a fiction. Mrs Anckorn's son Fergus was missing for over a year before news arrived that he was captive in a Japanese POW camp. For eighteen months Mrs Anckorn sent her weekly letters off into the void, sustaining a one-way conversation, a monologue pretending to be a dialogue. Occasionally her flow falters: 'Words are such silly things, aren't they, to give any idea of one's thoughts', but she follows her misgivings with more positive sentiments: 'everyone seems to think you'll land on your feet somehow.'[18]

Mrs Anckorn's letters belong to a huge and now largely vanished genre, mothers' letters.[19] As with the mother in the blitz, the mother with the letter is a figure of consolation and support, an embattled and protective Britannia armed with pen in place of trident. Although sons and daughters may not have preserved letters from their mothers, they relied on them nevertheless. Many young adults away from home for the first time felt disoriented and in need of support. Joan Kirby wrote from her training ship: 'Jan gets about five letters a day!! You've absolutely no idea what letters mean here. To see everyone rush for them at "stand easy" would make you gape!! So write often.'[20] Stephanie Batstone, also a Wren, told her mother that she was 'dying for letters'.[21] Jenny Nicholson was in the WAAFs, where, she said, 'We would queue eagerly for hours for the slenderest chance of a postcard from the outside word.' Nicholson stipulated what her mother should write: 'The best letters were long homely ones telling us every microscopic bit of local gossip.'[22] And mothers were willing to construct their letters to meet these demands.

Their long-distance mothering role was to bring not just a person to the one away but a place – home – with its concomitant sense of security and identity for the reader. While the child reads the letter he or she feels at home. The longer the letter the better, simply because it makes the sensation of feeling at home last longer.

In their letters mothers reproduced the kind of dailiness we find in women's fiction. The creation of the everyday, the 'study of provincial life', to borrow *Middlemarch*'s subtitle, is a project which the letter-writing mother shares with the writer of domestic fiction. Those who were absent wished to read about their own version of Jane Austen's three or four families in a country village. Letter-writing manuals such as Charles Warrell's ninepenny booklet, 'I'll Teach You Better Letter-Writing. Give Life To Your Letters – The Warrell Way', encouraged women letter writers to keep their readers 'in the home circle' through the accumulation of domestic detail. What might seem to be unimportant kitchen trivia is thus transformed into realism with a moral rationale. Seasoned writers numbered their letters to enable the reader to follow the order of composition. The letter is to be read not as an isolated expression, it derives its meaning from its place and part in the sequence, and the reader must go down the right narrative path. Mothers' letters produce lives for those away from home, they are a continuous documentation of their real selves, as it were, still existing elsewhere. Letters are the vehicles which bring what is missing to those away from home. In the midst of destruction and institutional anonymity they build home, individuality and affection, replenishing the self sapped by war. Hours of labour were devoted to this work of letter writing, as we can appreciate from some of the surviving collections. Mothers were the marathon writers, corresponding at length and over time. Theirs was the long-haul approach, sustaining the family by remote control, often acting as family correspondent, passing on letters and news, weaving members of the family back into the texture of their domestic and affective lives. Mothers such as Nancy Buchanan and Nella Last wrote at great length, 'four pads going on at once,' wrote Nella Last in her Mass-Observation diary, 'always writing, always trying to interest or amuse my boys.'[23] These lengthy annals can be seen as the people's novels of the war: optimistic, long-running hope operas.

The mother with a young child whose father was absent had pressing reasons to develop the novelist's art of character-creation. In her letters she needed to re-create the child for the father – a child who had no existence for its father other than in words. The busy mother became skilled at what Samuel Richardson called 'writing to the moment', describing what was going on in front of her as she wrote. The nursery bulletin usually shared at the end of the day – the minutiae of a child eating cherries or teasing a cat or banging out the V for Victory rhythm on its high chair – had to be recorded for the absent father. It was only by reading these letters that a soldier or sailor could temporarily feel himself to be a father. After a year's absence David Hopkinson wrote to his wife about their baby son:

> You write of Thomas with the full power to make him come alive for me. I suppose he is your creation like a novelist's favourite character whom he is always talking about. For you Tommy is a creation both in the word and the flesh. For me the flesh has become the word, and not the word the flesh.[24]

For Hopkinson and other absent fathers the child was only a child of words. 'Hugo makes no sense some days,' complained Hugh Williams, separated from his young son and referring to him as if he were a difficult text.[25]

If mothers were the domestic realists of the war, they also had to practise the novelist's arts of editing and selecting. Letters might offer space for creativity and enable the writing self to gain in confidence, but they had to be carefully angled and controlled with the reader in mind. Mothers could not forget for long the function of their letters as surrogate maternal comfort. Jenny Nicholson's mother wrote letters 'with lots of kisses at the end in different-coloured chalk', and thus earned Nicholson's tart comment: 'Mother forgets we are full grown' (56). But perhaps Mrs Nicholson knew well what might comfort and amuse her daughter, who kept up her demands for more letters, which she always expected to be cheerful. These letters were not the place for maternal introspection; suppression and reticence govern what can be said. The spontaneity is a fiction; self-censorship is imperative.[26] Grief is a potentially dangerous emotion in wartime, inviting unpatriotic thoughts. Nancy Buchanan wrote to her son Peter about his brother who had been killed in North Africa: 'It hurts dreadfully. Still as you say, war is bloody – and the only thing to do is to get on with the job.'[27] Advice to letter writers in women's magazines agreed in dissuading all their readers, whether mothers, wives or daughters, from openness and self-expression in their letters. Daphne du Maurier prescribed strict self-censorship:

> Whatever she does, and must feel in her heart, of strain and anxiety, no sign of it should appear in any of her letters . . . There must be no weakness in

these letters of ours, no poor and pitiful hinting at despair. We must be strong, and confident, and full of faith.[28]

In the interests of morale, women were asked to invent pious and noble fictions of themselves on paper, and reticence became a patriotic duty. Advice columnists insisted that 'a husband should not be told of his wife's infidelity while serving abroad'. Wives who wanted to 'confess all' were branded as 'fifth columnists': 'Don't they know what they're doing to the morale of their men?'[29]

So powerful was the genre of the letter in wartime – authenticated by the individual voice of the writer, validated by its guarantee of intimacy and confidentiality – that its influence extended to other media. Films and radio programmes were constructed as letters. A 1941 Ministry of Information film, designed to show American audiences everyday life in Britain, took the form of 'A Letter from Home' from an English mother (Celia Johnson) to her children who had been evacuated to America. Vera Lynn's radio programme, 'Sincerely Yours', was listed in the *Radio Times*: 'To the men of the Forces: a letter in words and music from Vera Lynn.'[30] Books and magazine articles also pretended to be letters. In 1938 Virginia Woolf couched her polemical essay *Three Guineas* in the form of a reply to a correspondent's question: 'How in your opinion are we to prevent war?'[31] Woolf chose the letter as the 'warm' genre of the woman writer, with her strong individual presence, 'the face on the other side of the page', reaching out to forge a close relationship with the reader (41). In subsequent years women's open and published letters plied across the Atlantic on behalf of the war effort. Women's letters from England were published in America in book form: in 1942 Diana Forbes Robertson and Roger W. Strauss Jr edited *War Letters from Britain*, Amy Strachey sent *These Two Strange Years, Letters from England 1939–1941* and in 1941 Jan Struther published *Women of Britain, Letters from England*. She claimed that the letters were written by a cross-section of British women, but they all bear a striking resemblance to Struther's famous fictional creation, Mrs Miniver. This is the war magnificent, and, as one of them boasts, 'It doesn't frighten me an atom!' (45). Struther constructs her women to speak for the nation, with the impression of privacy vouching for their authenticity and sincerity.

The open letter was, by contrast, consciously designed for publication, and it flourished in America as a public ambassador of the People's War. Mollie Panter-Downes's 'Letter from London', which began on

September 3, 1939, appeared regularly in *The New Yorker* throughout the war. The opening paragraph of the first letter sets the tone:

> For a week, everybody in London had been saying every day that if there wasn't a war tomorrow there wouldn't be a war. Yesterday, people were saying that if there wasn't a war today it would be a bloody shame. Now that there is a war, the English, slow to start, have already in spirit started and are comfortably two laps ahead of the official war machine, which had to await the drop of somebody's handkerchief. In the general opinion, Hitler has got it coming to him.[32]

Here Panter-Downes grounds her letters as the voice of England. Phrases such as 'everybody in London had been saying', 'people were saying', 'the English', and 'in the general opinion' assert the mood of England as solid, singular, united. The message to American readers is that here is a nation undivided, except for the 'official war machine', an old-fashioned vehicle which is already lagging behind in some unspecified sporting event.

Women's wartime letters, both public and private, invent and offer the benefits of communication. But in women's fiction novels letters tell a different story. They resonate with trouble and danger, secrets and sorrow. It is as if the strain of supporting the war in their letters – and converting them in the process into contrived fictions of well-being – emerges in the openly fictional letters of the time. *She Goes to War*, Edith Pargeter's epistolary novel of 1942, is an exposition of letter writing itself as a politicising process. Catherine Saxon joins the Wrens, and the novel charts her shift of mood in the sombre year of 1940–1941, as she becomes radicalised through war work and letter writing. After a brief courtship, Catherine's fiancé Tom is posted to Greece, the doomed campaign. The letters he sends from there are given authority by the manner of their composition and delivery. He writes two versions, and sends 'the kinds of letters one can't send through His Majesty's mails at this time' via an American newspaper man (170). Pargeter shows war invading Tom's letters with a startling immediacy:

> Even between the sentences of this letter, Catherine, I have killed one man. A searchlight held and blinded him as he fell, and I shot him dead in his harness, with a tommy gun in his hand. And then came back to you, and can you find the blot he made between us? (294)

Tom dies safeguarding the retreat from Crete, a campaign he recognises and criticises as botched. Catherine is a more surprising critic, as she writes herself to the left. This is the work of the war for her:

> Did there have to be a war to make us stand up and open our eyes and see how we're being cheated? Could only this unbelievable disaster make socialists out of people like me? (241)

Catherine was a journalist before the war, and she determines to return to her profession afterwards to assist the progress of the class war. The private middle-class letter writer enlists herself as the public writer for the new democracy: 'I shall never be silent, and I shall never turn back. They called me to war. Well, let them be satisfied. I am at war' (313).

When it comes to men as letter writers, Edith Pargeter's articulate soldier is the exception. Most of the warriors in women's novels have epistolary shortcomings. The RAF hero in Jane Oliver's *The Hour of the Angel* (1942) turns to his car for inspiration much as his predecessor Hotspur had turned to his horse:

> He headed the page meticulously with the number of his squadron and the full postal address of the Station. Then he typed the date in Roman figures. Then he sat and stared at it for some time. Finally he typed on.
>
> 'MY DEAR, – There isn't any news. I got back in good time after a cissie trip. Made it in one hour twenty dead. Car isn't running too well, though. Must have her de-coked. Spent the evening with the boys at the local. Young John's getting married. Nobody seems to take a high view of the idea. Can't say I do myself.
>
> See you soon, I hope. Take care of yourself.
>
> Love,
>
> Robert' (41)

Robert subsequently marries Moira but his letters do not improve, giving his author scope for some timely advice about the necessary asymmetricality of male/female correspondence. Moira's sister explains that Robert's half page,

> 'written when he's dead tired or sick with worry about his job or on his way to the pub to forget it means the very same thing as your half dozen pages when you've got all the time in the world to write them.' (102)

Moira acquiesces – ' "Yes. I ought to have seen that" ' – and joins the mass of women letter writers who expect little in return.

Letters in women's novels can signify disaster. Moira is sent the worst letter of all, the priority telegram which is read before it is opened. Letters can also mean trouble. Margaret Lane's *Where Helen Lies* (1944) starts with a time-bomb bundle of love letters between Charles and his mistress Eileen. Charles's wife finds the ten-year-old letters and burns them, but the fire serves only to rekindle Charles's passion for Eileen. For the rest of the novel, and on the verge of war, Charles searches for her, hindered principally by his mother-in-law Sibyl, 'the old serpent' (218). Sibyl is continually associated with letters; we first see her 'sitting idly on the hearthrug and surrounded by scattered letters and writing materials' (93). ' "She never stops," said Isabella, fretfully admiring. "She wrote between thirty and forty letters yesterday. I don't know how she does it" ' (95). Sibyl uses letters as weapons: she prised Eileen away from Charles with one ten years ago. Charles distrusts letters and prefers face-to-face communication. ' "It's got to be faced" ', he says as his marriage ends and the war begins (217).

Stella Gibbons dramatises the malignant power of the letter in *The Rich House* (1941). Mrs Vholes makes corsets for the good ladies of Seagate and she also sends them poison-pen letters. Omitting the sender's name, the anonymous letter is a mutation, and Mrs Vholes's have an extra twist. Poison-pen letters tend to be unpleasant threats or insults; Mrs Vholes's are more sinister:

> The notepaper was pale blue and cheap, the writing was rounded and childish.
>
> 'DEAR MADAM
>
> I have often thought how happy you must be with your dear son and husband, and your beautiful home, I should say a perfect life really wouldn't you. No worries. It isn't many that can say that nowadays. You are a very lucky woman.'
>
> That was all. (57)

Although they are not explicitly connected with the war, Mrs Vholes's letters exploit prevailing vulnerabilities. People who had not experienced suffering would be waiting for it, perhaps feeling guilty for escaping it. Mrs Vholes – Mrs Hitler as her daughter calls her – mines this vein of guilt until she is caught, and Gibbons then gives us the letter beneficial. Mrs Vholes's daughter Reenie is rescued from her mother's clutches by the labels on the tins of food from exotic places. These 'letters' from afar fascinate Reenie; she buys an atlas to find out more, and finally emigrates to New Zealand where she marries a prosperous sheep-farmer.

Harmful letters feature again in Margery Allingham's detective novel *Traitor's Purse* (1941), this time in their millions. These are the baleful letters of bureaucracy, and the master-villain's plan is ingenious:

> The plan by which false inflation was to have been induced overnight in the most civilized island in the world was an exquisitely simple one. Each of the envelopes was of the familiar Government colour and pattern. *On His Majesty's Service* was printed across the front of each in the standard ink and type, as was also the black frank-mark, the familiar crown in the circle. (198)

The 'familiar' brown envelopes (Campion picks up one addressed to Mr P. Carter, Allingham's husband) contain counterfeit banknotes and a printed slip:

> The Ministry of Labour, Whitehall, London, S.W. SRG.20539.
>
> Dear Sir/Madam,
>
> The enclosed sum of £7.0s.0d. has been awarded to you on the War Bonus Claims Committee's recommendation.
>
> This money is paid to you under the arrears of remuneration for Persons of Incomes Below Tax Level Board (0.in.C.AQ430028), as has been announced in the public press and elsewhere.
>
> *Note.* You will help your country if you do not hoard this money but translate it into goods immediately.
>
> R.W. Smith,
>
> Compt.

Allingham's official letter gives the clichéd mad-dictator plot a nasty kick. By 1941 many such envelopes containing incomprehensible instructions would have been delivered throughout the country, as the Government assumed more and more wartime powers. 'To what unlawful end?' is the question which adds a frisson to Allingham's novel. Luckily Albert Campion comes to the rescue and the 'brown snow' of envelopes is safely contained.

The harm that letters can do overshadows Elizabeth Taylor's first novel, *At Mrs Lippincote's* (1945). Near the end of the book Julia Davenant tears up a large pile of letters (204). With good reason: this is a novel about the inadvisability of reading letters, in which letters bring much grief and little

satisfaction. The discretion and reticence drilled into letter readers and
writers by wartime advice columnists make sense to Taylor. In her novel,
letters signify deception and failed communication. Julia leads an unsettled
life as an officer's wife; her husband Roddy is unfaithful throughout the
book to her knowledge but not to ours. On the second page, as they unpack
in their new lodgings (Roddy's commanding officer has told him to send for
his wife in a bid to mend the marriage), Julia rummages in Roddy's coat
pockets for a handkerchief. Right at the end of the book we learn that on
that occasion she found a letter but did not read it, ' "Not any of your
letters" ' (214). Julia has not read the letters in the interest of saving their
marriage, ' "And if I didn't read it because I didn't care," she thought, "I am
absolutely done for" ' (214).

Julia is a non-reader of letters, but not because she is incurious; far
from it. She spends the first afternoon in the new lodgings investigating,

> with calm unscrupulousness, Mrs Lippincote's bureau. Roddy, who had
> been carefully brought up and would not have done this for the world, very
> sincerely protested, and Eleanor [Roddy's cousin] who had intended to
> look at the photographs but probably not the letters, as soon as she was
> alone, protested too. Neither of them would glance at the treasures Julia
> kept discovering. Oliver [Julia and Roddy's son] was lying on a shelf in the
> conservatory reading.
>
> 'Oh, not the letters!' cried Roddy.
>
> 'Cards first,' said Julia, who descended one by one the shelving levels
> towards absolute (she hoped) intimacy. (21)

Julia delights in calibrating the social strata in the wedding photograph –
' "I suppose she must have married beneath her" ', then it is tea-time and
' "letters another time" ' (22). This is to be another set of letters which
Julia does not read, even though the perfect opportunity arises when
Roddy and Eleanor are out:

> She had nothing to do. Mrs Lippincote's bureau held no interest for her. It
> would have been sordid to have pried into it when she was alone in the
> house – a strange nicety which Mrs Lippincote herself might not have
> appreciated. (36)

Taylor underlines her theme of not reading letters by reminding us of
their outsides, envelopes. These are often associated with Julia, the
non-reader of letters. Looking in vain for her handkerchief, 'She found,

however, some talcum powder and a packet of envelopes which she needed' (6). The back of an envelope comes in handy to draw diagrams of sexual reproduction for Oliver in a scene of comic miscommunication; when she wants to note an address she asks the Wing Commander for ' "An odd envelope or something" ' (76). The title of the novel itself, *At Mrs Lippincote's*, adopts the form of address written at that time on envelopes when the addressee was staying at someone else's house, a reminder of the unrootedness of many wartime lives.

What letters there are in the book fall lamentably short of true communication.

'My dearest Julia,
    Don't keep supper for me as there is a new intake and I may be late.
    Love, sweetheart.
    RODDY.' (177)

Julia tears this note up; later we realise it is because she has recognised its falseness.[33] The correspondence which dribbles on through the book is a story of inadequacy and insincerity. Eleanor writes to a prisoner-of-war:

'My very dear Reggy,' she wrote, without feeling any surprise whatsoever. She had not known Reggy well nor cared to know him better when he had gone overseas four years before, and had begun to write to him – 'Dear Reggy' – simply because it was in her anyhow to be a prodigious letter writer. Then he was killed and she found that, barring Roddy, he was all she had to offer up for her country, and wept. But after a month or two, he was not killed, but a prisoner-of-war. In her relief, he became 'My dear Reggy'. It was obvious that she was still only a short way up that scale which culminates, one supposes, in 'Darling', 'My Love', 'My Own'.

She wrote her letter, signed it 'Your E', wrote on the envelope that monstrous word *Kriegsgefangenenpost*, and put it proudly on the mantelpiece. (24)

Eleanor makes new friends and the correspondence becomes a chore:

'Dear Reg,' she wrote – it was as well that her fluctuations were a matter of indifference to Reg himself ... Eleanor wrote: 'I hope the cigarettes arrived and that you are well,' – a bleak enough little sentence to chill anyone's heart ... 'I hope this ... I hope that,' Eleanor wrote, with indifference. (128–129)

Then there is the handkerchief letter, the evidence which convicts Roddy of adultery. The Wing Commander gives him back the handkerchief which should have been Eleanor's but was his mistress's:

> He folded the handkerchief again and was about to put it in his pocket when he caught sight of the name 'Muriel Parsons' printed on the hem. (197)

The book opens with the handkerchief/letter evidence in Roddy's coat-pocket (Julia looks for a handkerchief and finds an incriminating letter instead), but unlike Othello Julia refuses to be jealous. It is not *Othello* but another literary text which lies behind *At Mrs Lippincote's*.

Seven-year-old Oliver is the only character to have any success with his letter writing, perhaps because he is honest about its deficiencies. On the last day at Mrs Lippincote's he says goodbye to the one friend he has made:

> Oliver picked two spotted-laurel leaves and with a pin wrote 'Felicity' on one and his own name on the other. 'It's a child's game. Keep it next to your skin and if the writing turns brown it means we always – like one another. It's only silly, because, of course, it always does turn brown.' She took hers and slipped it down the neck of her jersey. Oliver suddenly wanted to throw his away but he was a kind little boy and rather self-consciously opened the front of his shirt and dropped it in. (208)

Later Felicity sobs on her bed, and then takes the leaf from her liberty bodice to find that

> 'Oliver' was engraved on it in brown. Although he had said this invariably happened, she was a little comforted and lay, with the leaf against her cheek, in the peace that follows violent emotion. (209)

The novel begins with arrival and ends a few months later with departure; the transitoriness of wartime life and the knowledge of her husband's infidelity contribute to Julia's unhappiness. But there is more. Mrs Lippincote's house has a tower with a locked attic, and 'it is acknowledged . . . that we none of us speak the truth about the rooms which we keep locked' (16). The locked attic is one of the many references to *Jane Eyre*; Oliver, Julia and the Wing Commander discuss the Brontës more than once. ' "*Jane Eyre* is NOTHING to *Villette*," ' is the Wing Commander's verdict and Julia agrees (49); *Villette* is the message buried in Taylor's novel. Julia cooks her baked apples according to a recipe in *Villette*, and Oliver calls the dressmaker's dummy Madame Heger (Charlotte Brontë's model for the prying Madame Beck). Alone for the evening, Julia sits under a pear-tree 'considering men and their small idiocies' (38). It was under a pear-tree that Lucy Snowe buried her letters of love for Dr John. The secret in Julia's locked room is not only her knowledge of Roddy's betrayal; it is also her grief for her dead daughter. Only once does she mention her, to the Wing Commander:

> 'My daughter's birth was so benign, only tiring in the exhilarating way that it is tiring to climb a hill to see a great stretch of country . . .'
> 'But what happened to the child?'
> 'Oh, the child was dead in no time,' she said in a shocking, light voice.
> (147)

Some doors must be kept locked; lightness and reticence hold the barricade in place.

About the small things of life Julia cheerfully admits to being inquisitive – about the wedding photograph she scans so often, about the Masonic book left behind by Mr Lippincote, about other people's conversations in restaurants. But when it comes to Roddy's affairs she chooses not to find out. Apart from the final scene, her anger is roused only when Roddy accuses her of trying to find out his secrets (83). This she has resolutely refused to do, so that she can maintain at the end ' "Nothing has happened" ' (214). Roddy comments:

> 'You are inquisitive about little things, but about this . . .'
> 'I am a coward,' she agreed. (214)

A coward perhaps, but Julia, who flirts with and rejects the 'Madame Bovary' world of 'secret notes' (72, 204), proves the worth of that discretion urged upon the wartime wife 'for the duration'. In a fitting finale to the book, which is itself a sealed envelope colluding in suppressing Julia's knowledge of Roddy's infidelity until the end, Julia draws the curtains tight shut:

> And with a great rattle and flourish she drew Mrs Lippincote's damask curtains across the window for the last time. (215)

Sadder than unread letters are lost letters, and one of the saddest stories

of the war is Rose Macaulay's 'Miss Anstruther's Letters' (1942).[34] Miss
Anstruther loses her lover's letters in an air raid; Macaulay wrote the story
a year after her own flat had been bombed and its contents destroyed.
Miss Anstruther, whose lover is dead, is a displaced version of Macaulay,
whose own lover was dying. The story is about displacement and loss.
Bombed out on the same night in May 1941 as her creator, Miss
Anstruther rushes back to her flat to save a few random books and objects.
She remembers too late the letters from her lover which are locked in her
desk and stretch back over twenty-two years. Later she scrabbles among
the ruins, but the only fragment she finds dates back twenty-one years
and reads: ' "Leave it at that. I know now that you don't care twopence; if
you did you would" . . .'. Miss Anstruther judges her failure to save the
letters as a second lapse in loving. This is a story of 'instead ofs', the
displacement of one thing by something else of less value or infected by
war. These substitutions punish Miss Anstruther for substituting
something lesser than love twenty-one years ago.

Miss Anstruther herself is a displaced person. When we meet her at the
beginning of the story she is temporarily rehoused in a substitute for her
flat, an 'unhomely' bedsit. Displacements proliferate as she remembers
the air raid: 'high explosives and incendiaries had rained' instead of the
water which 'had run short', and the basement tenant who searches for
her motoring trophies finds only a battered saucepan. In the raid 'the
whole front' of Mortimer House comes 'crashing down', to be replaced
by a 'wall of flame'. The 'green gardens' which Miss Anstruther had
contemplated as she wrote are replaced by 'the pandemonic red garden of
night'; the whole orderly civilisation of 'carpets, beds, curtains, furniture,
pictures and books' are now deformed into inchoate 'drifts of burnt
rubbish'. Through this rubbish Miss Anstruther searches desperately
because, on the night of the raid, she made the terrible substitution of a
few random possessions for her lover's letters.

Letters themselves are already a kind of substitution, a second best,
they stand in for face-to-face communication. Letters have 'stood in' for
Miss Anstruther and her lover for twenty-two years – presumably the
couple wrote when they could not meet. Since her lover's death Miss
Anstruther has been unable to read his letters and 'they had lain there, a
solace waiting for her when she could take it'. They speak of love, in
lyrical phrases that she can remember only disjointedly: 'Light of my
eyes. You are the sun and the moon and the stars to me.' These letters
Miss Anstruther has kept locked in her desk, and her story is the tragedy
of the locked-up. We never know Miss Anstruther's first name and the

formality of the title 'Miss' keeps intimacy at bay. People in the story who talk to her may be friendly but they never get close. They are always thinking of other things. The kind basement tenant is 'thinking about her motoring cups', the warden is 'wondering what had happened in North Ealing, where he lived'. One of the random objects Miss Anstruther salvages from her flat is 'a tiny walnut shell with tiny Mexicans behind glass', she herself is like the walnut shell with its hard carapace and passionate but glassed-in Mexicans. Twenty-one years ago her lover accused her of lack of love. If she had loved him more, the fragment of his letter suggests, she would perhaps have given more, unlocked herself a little.

As Miss Anstruther realises that the letters are burnt, the 'hell' and 'inferno' of the raid become the hell and inferno of loss. The 'disjointed phrases' of love which she remembers mutate horribly into wounding weapons of war: 'As each phrase came back to her, it jabbed at her heart like a twisting bayonet.' The scrap she finds triggers the last and worst displacement of the story. The past, frighteningly self-destructs:

> The words, each time she looked at them, seemed to darken and obliterate a little more of the twenty years that had followed them, the years of the letters and the starred places and all they had had together. You don't care twopence, he seemed to say still; if you had cared twopence, you would have saved my letters, not your wireless and your typewriter and your china cow, least of all those little walnut Mexicans, which you know I never liked. Leave it at that.

Miss Anstruther condemns herself to desolation, a life without a past that she feels she has no right to. After her failure to love,

> She was alone with a past devoured by fire and a charred scrap of paper which said you don't care twopence, and then a blank, a great interruption, an end. She had failed in caring once, twenty years ago, and failed again now, and the twenty years between were a drift of grey ashes that once were fire, and she a drifting ghost too. She had to leave it at that.

8

THE INDIRECT FACE OF WAR

Once in a while something invisible seemed to skim the expanse of water, causing it to wrinkle and contract through all its surface.

Rosamond Lehmann, 'The Red-Haired Miss Daintreys', 1941

War, the unstoppable intruder into the fiction of the time, made its presence felt in indirect as well as direct ways. Genres and subjects which seemed to have nothing to do with war could not help but be affected. This chapter charts some of the disguised faces of war in women's fiction, some of the displacements, and the reasons for them. If the times were inescapable they might also be impossible to transcribe directly; suppression was the order of the day. Moreover, the war itself did not always have a direct presence in Britain. After the intensive blitz of 1940–1941 the war tended, with exceptions of course, to be experienced as something happening elsewhere, an absent presence insidiously affecting the whole of life. The idea of the unseen force which Rosamond Lehmann's young observer sees disturbing the surface of the water in 'The Red-Haired Miss Daintreys' is a suggestive image for the action of war in some of the literature of its time.

The strategies of indirection and camouflage were particularly necessary in order to negotiate emotions which might be a liability to a country at war. The nation had to take lessons in repression: the stiff upper lip, characteristic of the upper-class male warrior, became the uniform of the patriot. Men had the advantage in their ability to exploit the props of nature, and women noted the new popularity of the moustache. ' "Nobody likes it," ' says a young officer in Susan Ertz's *Anger in the Sky* (1943), ' "but it makes me feel different, as if I'd got a new personality. It helps me to impersonate a warrior" ' (58).[1] For women, moustaches were generally not an option, and their emotions tended to be nearer the surface. Wartime fiction carries a small cargo of bereaved mothers who comfort one another – ' "I think it helps to talk," ' says a mourning mother in Winifred Peck's *House-Bound* (1942, 121) – and wives who wait anxiously for news. Monica Dickens's *Mariana* (1940)[2] is a solitary nocturnal vigil. At the beginning of the book Mary hears on the nine o'clock news that her husband's ship has been sunk by an enemy mine. The night passes in suspense and flashback while we wait until morning and the end of the book for the news that Mary's husband is safe. Winifred Peck's Miranda Winter (*There is a Fortress*, 1945) also waits for news, this time of her son's painful recovery from wounds received in France. Peck describes Miranda,

> going through her round of household duties, attending her canteen and first-aid classes, too tired and spent by conflicting emotions, like most other women, to feel anything much at all. (226)

Numbness had its protective uses for the wartime reader too, and unambiguously sad and troubled figures are carefully rationed. Emotional limitation could be an attraction, and C.A. Lejeune accounted for the popularity of the film of *Gone With the Wind* on the grounds of its shallowness:

> A mind that is heavy and disturbed does not want to reach very high or delve very deep. It wants to be carried along, distracted by many and even little things. Great emotion at such a time is painful and dangerous.[3]

Emotion as pain and danger is a text for the times. Pamela Hansford Johnson makes emotion the enemy within in *The Trojan Brothers* (1944), a novel which mentions war explicitly only in its title. The solid, likeable working-class comedian Sid belongs to the Trojan Brothers partnership, a successful music-hall act involving a tin horse. But the real Trojan horse is Sid himself. Inside his dependable exterior lurks a destructive passion which drives him to murder the woman who rejects him. Rosamond Lehmann's story 'The Gipsy's Baby' (1941–1942) is also displaced from the war, and is itself about the processes of displacement and the projection of violent emotion. Set in the comfortable Edwardian child-hood of Rebecca Ellison, the story concerns Chrissie Wyatt, the wild child who comes from down the lane and the bottom of the social pile. Chrissie claims that gypsies have left a dead baby in a gravel pit, but later denies it. This imaginary murdered baby is a terrible proposition, suggestive of the horrors lurking inside the child's mind. Chrissie has already seen cruelty in the social awkwardness of the nursery tea to which she and her brother and sister are invited at the Ellisons. She tells another child: ' "It was horrible, awful in there anyway, a kind of torture chamber: nobody was allowed to talk, *not even to smile* at the tea-table" ' (33). Rebecca herself has felt the social unease forcibly enough, and guilt too, compounded by the fact that the Ellison dog has killed the Wyatt cat. Rebecca also passionately fears the gypsies because she thinks they will steal her. Her emotions find abrupt expression and ejection via the wild Chrissie, a scapegoat to be exiled to a foster-family until she 'mended her ways' (52).

On the whole suppression is assumed to be the inevitable corollary of war, though the costs of sending emotion underground are carefully counted. Mollie Panter-Downes's story, 'Goodbye, My Love' (1941),[4] covers the days in Ruth Vyner's life before and after her husband's departure overseas. Here is emotion impossible, British reserve as both resource and curse, defence and defeat. Ruth hangs up after a stilted telephone conversation with her mother-in-law, and 'suddenly remembered a French governess out of her childhood who used to rage, weeping with anger, "Oh, you British, you British!" ' Adrian's mother treats Ruth and Adrian's farewell visit 'as though this were just an ordinary visit, with nothing particular about it', and Ruth is 'grateful now for the lack of outward emotion which had so often chilled her'. The story starts by situating these British tactics for being at war on a cliff garden 'border facing the sea' – this is a story of ledges, of borders which must not be crossed. On these vertiginous edges of war communication must be kept at a distance. The elderly Major who buttonholes Adrian after church with his prophecy of heavy fighting upsets Ruth, who resorts to the language of an earlier age when she wants to discuss personal matters. She tells Adrian of her desire to bear his child through Shakespeare: ' "You know, the Sonnets and all that– " ' Modern life has no room for the large heroic gestures which war invites – after all Ruth and Adrian may both be killed in the service of their country. But circumstances are unpropitious:

She wasn't going to the station, so they said goodbye in the hall, a tiny cupboard built for a man to hang his hat in, for a woman to read a telephone message in – not for heroic partings.

As with settings, so with words:

> Language was inadequate, after all. One used the same words for a parting which might be for years, which might end in death, as one did for an overnight business trip. She put her arms tightly round him and said,
> 'Goodbye, my love.'
> 'Darling,' he said. 'I can't begin to tell you–'
> 'Don't,' she said. 'Don't.'
> The door shut, and presently Ruth heard the taxi driving away.

The story ends with what is paradoxically its worst moment, reprieve. Just as Ruth is recovering her equanimity, Adrian rings to say that his departure has been postponed for ten days and that he is on his way back. The process of parting will have to be endured again, as it was so many times for families and friends during the war:

> Ruth heard the click as he hung up, and she hung up slowly, too. For a moment she sat quite still. The clock on the table beside her sounded deafening again, beginning to mark off the ten days at the end of which terror was the red light at the end of the tunnel. Then her face became drawn and, putting her hands over it, she burst into tears.

Sometimes the policy of suppression seems to have been so well enforced that there is indeed, in the words of Carola Oman's 1940 title, *Nothing to Report*. Occasionally Oman's agreeable provincial surface is ruffled, and a woman reading a soldier's last message from Dunkirk has 'to stand at the window for a long moment after she had read the letter' (282). And occasionally there is a brief outburst, as in Elizabeth Taylor's story 'A Sad Garden' about a woman giving her niece a swing.[5] Sybil sits in her sad garden, bereft of husband and son, and discounting her own presence so unthinkingly that she tells her sister-in-law ' "There is no one to eat the fruit" '. But Sybil is possessed of 'power ill-concealed', and pushing her niece on her son's old swing turns into an act of frantic violence. The girl's terror intensifies the moment, which is both a thrusting away of grief and a release:

> The child, whiter than ever, was unable to speak, to cry out. She sensed something terribly wrong and yet something which was inevitable and not

surprising. Each time she dropped to earth, a wave of darkness hit her face and then she would fly up again in a wild agony. A strand of hair caught in some twigs and was torn from her head.

Sybil stood squarely on the grass. As the swing came down, she put up her hands and with the tips of her fingers and yet with all her strength, she pushed. She had lost consciousness and control and cried out each time exultingly: 'There you go. There you go' – until all her body was trembling.

The intensity of wartime emotion, together with the idea of war as an absent presence, an unwelcome invasion, colours Elizabeth Bowen's wartime stories of haunting and menace. 'Am I not manifestly a writer for whom places loom large?' asked Bowen,[6] and for her wartime was just such a place: 'I see war (or should I say feel war?) more as a territory than as a page of history'.[7] In 'The Happy Autumn Fields' (1944)[8] the territory is the other country of a Victorian autumn afternoon in County Cork, a moment of piercing sweetness suffused with premonition: 'She apprehended that the seconds were numbered'. The landscape and the hour, which is the moment before a young man declares his love, materialise inexplicably in the mind of a woman lying on an 'uncovered mattress' in her London house during an air raid. Mary is escaping from her shaking house into sleep, and her dream visualises the penultimate moment. We gather that the young man died that very evening and that the girl he would have proposed to – and through whom we experience the moment – never married. But this is not a simple tale of lost happiness. It is more the loss of emotion itself, of intensity, which interests Bowen. Lying in her house as it is battered and bombed, Mary says:

'So much flowed through people; so little flows through us. All we can do is imitate love or sorrow . . . I cannot forget the climate of those hours. Or life at that pitch, eventful – not happy, no, but strung like a harp.'

Bowen wrote this story while bombed out of her own house and her experience of dislocation finds its way into the story. The people from the past are not related to the woman who dreams about them. That Mary should be invaded by someone completely other and unknown relates to Bowen's own wartime experience:

Sometimes I hardly knew where I stopped and everyone else began. The violent destruction of solid things, the explosion of the illusion that prestige, power and permanence attach to bulk and weight, left all of us, equally, heady and disembodied. Walls went down; and we felt, if not knew, each other.[9]

According to Bowen, 'one counteracts fear by fear, stress by stress'.[10] As the walls of Mary's blitzed house go down, Sarah, the girl from the past, invades her in a hallucination which Bowen diagnoses as 'an unconscious, instinctive, saving resort',[11] although not necessarily a comforting one. It is as though Mary's crisis summons Sarah's, the blitz opens a route back to the past terrain of powerfully felt emotion.

Invasion on a wider scale is the subject of 'Mysterious Kor' (1944),[12] which Bowen opens from the moon's-eye view:

> Full moonlight drenched the city and searched it; there was not a niche left to stand in. The effect was remorseless: London looked like the moon's capital – shallow, cratered, extinct . . . The futility of the black-out became laughable: from the sky, presumably, you could see every slate in the roofs, every whited kerb, every contour of the naked winter flowerbeds in the park; and the lake, with its shining twists and tree-darkened islands would be a landmark for miles, yes, miles, overhead.

This is also the bomber's-eye view.[13] Bowen's city is invaded, though not by enemy bombers, 'The Germans no longer came by the full moon'. But 'Something more immaterial seemed to threaten and to be keeping people at home'. Except for Arthur and Pepita, a soldier on leave and his girlfriend, who have nowhere to go. As she walks, Pepita transforms London into mysterious Kor, the ruined moonlit city of Rider Haggard's *She*,[14] her imagination converting sexual frustration into an 'avid dream' of an empty city. Pepita's chaste flatmate Callie is the moon's hand-maiden; her name suggests a reference to Callisto, a favourite female companion of Artemis, the virgin huntress goddess associated with moon and night. After hospitably waiting up for the late-returning couple, Callie retires to bed and puts out the light.

> At once she knew that something was happening – outdoors, in the street, the whole of London, the world. An advance, an extraordinary movement was silently taking place; blue-white beams overflowed from it, silting, dropping round the edges of the muffling black-out curtains.

The moon is a hostile military presence: 'A searchlight, the most powerful of all time, might have been turned full and steady upon her defended window.' If hostile, the moon is also magical, seductive and creative: 'finding flaws in the black-out stuff, it made veins and stars.' 'Gained by this idea of pressure,' Callie slowly opens her curtains to the moon. War and sex coincide in the moon's power, its 'advance' is both martial and sexual. Bowen sustains an ambiguous relationship between moon and earth: 'Something – was it a coin or a ring? – glittered half-way across the chalk-white street'; the coin suggests the price the moon has paid to possess the earth, the ring suggests a betrothal. Callie submits to the moon's attack, and 'Light marched in past her face' to search and transfigure the room. Photographs express the secret thoughts of their sitters, a drab dressing-gown becomes 'silver brocade'; 'And the moon did more: it exonerated and beautified the lateness of the lovers' return'. In a 'rapture', entranced by the idea of the lovers, Callie entertains a 'mysterious expectation', a 'love for love'; she has been seduced by the moon. But by the end of the story the rape of the city by the moon is over:

> Indeed, the moon's power over London and the imagination had now declined. The siege of light had relaxed; the search was over; the street had a look of survival and no more. Whatever had glittered there, coin or ring, was now invisible or had gone. To Callie it seemed likely that there would never be such a moon again; and on the whole she felt this was for the best.

Sex and war again cohere dramatically for another sort of invasion in 'The Demon Lover' (1941),[15] a story of fear and possession in an ordinary London suburb. The story opens calmly enough:

> Towards the end of her day in London Mrs Drover went round to her shut-up house to look for several things she wanted to take away. Some belonged to herself, some to her family, who were by now used to their country life.

Bowen characteristically collocates time and place to great effect: the late August afternoon, the tense stormy weather with 'the next batch of clouds, already piling up ink-dark', and the house with 'some cracks in the structure, left by the last bombing', now empty and unfamiliar, 'a cracked cup from which memory, with its reassuring power, had either evaporated or leaked away'. The crisis, as so often in wartime, is precipitated by a letter. It has been left on the hall table, but the caretaker is away, so how did it get there? Mrs Drover feels watched, 'intruded upon', but 'no human eye watched Mrs Drover's return'. The letter is short:

> Dear Kathleen: you will not have forgotten that today is our anniversary, and the day we said. The years have gone by at once slowly and fast. In view of the fact that nothing has changed, I shall rely upon you to keep your promise. I was sorry to see you leave London, but was satisfied that you would be back in time. You may expect me, therefore, at the hour arranged. Until then . . . K.

As Kathleen Drover searches the bedroom chest for the things she has come for, the memories of twenty-five years ago return:

> The young girl talking to the soldier in the garden had not ever completely seen his face. It was dark; they were saying goodbye under a tree.

But what looks like a familiar sentimental vignette is shot through with coercion. The girl is 'intimidated' by the soldier, his gestures of love hurt her as he presses her hand 'without very much kindness, and painfully, on to one of the breast buttons of his uniform. That cut of the button on the palm of her hand was, principally, what she was to carry away'. His eyes are 'spectral glitters' in the dark; he speaks 'without feeling' to remind her. ' "You know what we said . . . I shall be with you . . . You need do nothing but wait" ', and then 'she was free to run up the silent lawn'. But she is not free from the 'unnatural promise' which she felt 'drive down between her and the rest of all human kind'. Then the nameless, featureless soldier is reported missing, presumed killed, and Kathleen gradually recovers from years of 'complete dislocation from everything' to marry and settle down with her husband and three sons.

Back in the present of 1941 Kathleen rapidly packs and attempts flight in a classic nightmare panic.[16] Her sense of an intruder persists. The draught moving in the airless house 'emanated from the basement: down there a door or window was being opened by someone who chose this moment to leave the house'. Mrs Drover manages to escape, even to find the much wished-for taxi. But how does the driver know which direction to set off in before she has ' "said where" '?

> She leaned forward to scratch at the glass panel that divided the driver's head from her own.
>
> The driver braked to what was almost a stop, turned round and slid the glass panel back: the jolt of this flung Mrs Drover forward till her face was

almost into the glass. Through the aperture driver and passenger, not six inches between them, remained for an eternity eye to eye. Mrs Drover's mouth hung open for some seconds before she could issue her first scream. After that she continued to scream freely and to beat with her gloved hands on the glass all round as the taxi, accelerating without mercy, made off with her into the hinterland of deserted streets.

The title of Bowen's story refers to the ballad in which a man goes back to a woman after 'seven long years and more' to 'seek my former vows/That ye promised me before'. The woman has married another man, but sails away with her former lover in his 'glorious' golden ship, bound for hell.[17] True to his namesake, Bowen's demon lover is implacable and irresistible. Probably from hell, he is certainly from war, cruelly impressing his betrothed with its mark, the uniform button.[18] The 'sinister troth' Kathleen 'plighted' during the First World War is enforced during the Second World War, but another 'troth' lies behind it. The soldier's letter is signed with Kathleen's own initial, and Kathleen seems to be meeting part of herself in her demon lover. When she reads his letter she turns in panic to the mirror and then away, 'turning from her own face as precipitately as she had gone to meet it'. This prefigures the last scene in the taxi, where Kathleen's 'face was almost into the glass'. Not so much a Drover as one of the driven, Kathleen has been possessed by the faceless demon of war. 'He was set on me' is her later summary of their relationship, which involved 'the complete suspension of *her* existence during that August week. I was not myself'. Not myself: in 1916 and now in 1941, this time with three male children, Kathleen Drover has been possessed by the force of war, and she is powerless to resist. As K said in his letter, 'nothing has changed'.

War and the emotions it excites could, then, be sent underground, to emerge in brief violence or strange haunting. War could also insinuate itself into genres which seemed to be offering escape from the troubles of the times. Historical fiction, romances and detective fiction often bore its scars in displaced ways, however much they liked to welcome readers to a war-free zone.[19] In her Foreword to *Findernes' Flowers* (1941), George Preedy (Marjorie Bowen's pseudonym) prescribes 'nostalgia' as an aid to forgetting 'what now all of us want to forget – something of the burden of our own [lives]'. *Findernes' Flowers* is a historical romance about a family which disappears leaving nothing behind of itself, an apposite theme in 'this year 1940, with all of the implications that lie behind that date', as

Preedy's Foreword reminds us. Sometimes it seems as if all roads must lead to war and even a novel starting in Biblical times finishes in the RAF (Jane Oliver's *In No Strange Land*, 1944). Historical novels may head for the escape-hatch, but what is striking about many of them is their fondness for other wars. One war is written about in the guise of another; the writer can say things about her own war that she cannot say directly. Daphne du Maurier's three historical novels, published between 1941 and 1946, show this with particular clarity.[20]

Frenchman's Creek was published in 1941, when the threat of invasion was still strong. It is not surprising that du Maurier should address this theme; what is more remarkable is the excitement with which she flirts with it. The idea of being temporarily invaded offers a welcome diversion to Dona St Columb, an aristocratic mother of two whose body and land are fused in the action of the novel. The threat of invasion comes from the dashing French pirate who enjoys creeping into Cornish harbours by night. ' "Our womenfolk" ', claims Lord Godolphin, ' "sleep in terror of their lives, and not only their lives." "Oh, he is that sort of pirate, then?" murmured Dona' (35). Rape is supposed to accompany the pillage, but it is the English women who ' "won't leave [the French sailors] alone. They creep out of their cottages, and stray upon the hills, if they think *La Mouette* is at anchor near their shores" ' (104). Some English people seem to like being invaded. The Frenchman proceeds to penetrate the houses of the English landed gentry and the creek, given to him in the title of the novel. The creek is Dona's; here he illicitly anchors his beautiful ship and teaches her to fish, to fix his wriggling worm on a hook. He also takes her, dressed as a cabin-boy, on pirating expeditions which Dona discusses with the faithful servant William:

> 'I have a wager with your master that I shall not succumb. Do you think I shall win?'
> 'It depends what your ladyship is alluding to.'
> 'That I shall not succumb to the motion of the ship of course.' (98)

Double meanings saturate the language of this moist book. Romantic scenes take place on or near water: in creeks, inlets, rivers, in the 'narrow twisting channel' and on the open sea. Water was supposed to protect the island of Britain in 1941; here it offers scope for invasion, excitement and gratification. Since the novel's English landed gentry are a bunch of oafs, we can enjoy seeing them worsted by a stylish Frenchman with a wonderful line in maritime cuisine (so tempting in 1941 and duly appreciated by Dona). Hidden in history, du Maurier's heroine flirts with violence, relishing both transgression and aggression: 'Soon there would be danger, and excitement, and the reality perhaps of fighting' (110). Women were not supposed, of course, to carry weapons in the Second World War, and here Dona's transgression is two-fold in imagining fighting her own side, in a one-woman civil war. The image of woman as fifth columnist, the enemy within, flickers briefly. But escape and opposition can be 'only for a night and for a day' (143). Dona has two children and cannot abandon them. The Frenchman is allowed to go unpunished but Dona does kill his wicked double, the seducer Rockingham. Her weapon is a huge family shield, 'some trophy of a dead St Columb' (194). 'Heavy and dusty with age', the weight of landed England finally asserts itself.

Frenchman's Creek was du Maurier's most upbeat wartime historical novel. *Hungry Hill* (1943) is a family saga set between 1820 and 1920, but the solid comforts usually associated with family sagas are withheld. There is too much suffering, too many frustrated hopes. The Brodricks are an Anglo-Irish family with unattractive colonising ways. They exploit the land and its wealth (copper and tin) and put nothing back, forsaking the great house cherished by earlier generations. Nor are the Irish people portrayed sympathetically: they feature intermittently as an ignorant and vindictive peasantry. The novel shows du Maurier mid-war, wanting but failing to find solace in the family of Britain and its literary genre, the extended family saga. The Brodricks share much in common with many Second World War families: in each generation we find a single parent having to raise children on his or her own. The graceful gilt chairs in the drawing-room of the Big House have wobbly legs, which seems to characterise the status of historical romance for du Maurier at this point in the war.

By 1946 du Maurier's historical camouflage is the vehicle for late and post-war weariness, 'a great war-sickness'. *The King's General* is a post-Civil War novel, and du Maurier's sympathies lie with the defeated Royalists. She shows 'the agony of war' and its aftermath in its most negative aspects, from the perspective of the loser: 'Long faces and worsted garments, bad harvests and sinking trade, everywhere men poorer than they were before, and the people miserable' (12). Apart from a small interest in professional soldiering – there are debates about how to run a war[21] – du Maurier emphasises damage and destruction. She still acknowledges the exhilaration of war which had beckoned Dona St Columb in *Frenchman's Creek*, but this now appears as a drug, 'that life of strain and folly, anguish and enchantment' (284). Honor Harris, the narrator-heroine, is an invalid and although the cause was a riding accident it is difficult not to see her as a casualty of the civil war devastating the country. In a characteristic twist du Maurier energises and empowers the invalid. Honor becomes a mobile woman with a difference, propelling herself in what must be one of the earliest wheelchairs in historical fiction. She becomes a camp follower – a 'pursuivant of the drum', she calls herself (223), allowed a more relaxed attitude to extra-marital sex than Dona. But the novel ends in exhaustion and self-destruction; the roll calls of the men who have fallen in battle sound through the book.

Du Maurier was not the only historical novelist to plunder past wars. Clemence Dane's hero-worship of Nelson inspired her 1944 novel *He Brings Great News*, which is set in the Napoleonic wars and highly critical of profiteers and the 'strangely ungrateful . . . light minds' who denigrate war leaders (122).[22] Margery Allingham's *Dance of the Years* (1943) also opens on the Napoleonic Wars and the prospect of imminent invasion. Molly Keane's *Two Days in Aragon* (1941) is set in the Irish Civil Wars of the 1920s and characterises the English as imperilled and not particularly sympathetic colonisers. Elizabeth Myers's *The Basilisk of St James's* was published in January 1945; it expressed the mood of the moment through its 1712 setting, when 'England had been at war with the tyrant Louis XIV for ten years' (Foreword), and the people longed for peace. More famously, Kathleen Winsor's *Forever Amber* (1944)[23] invites its readers into an irresponsible world of post-war excess and pleasure. Its Restoration setting promises, by analogy, licence after austerity. This is a world of wonderfully enjoyable consumption, embodied in its heroine Amber, 'popping a crisp plump shrimp into her mouth' (99), and refusing to behave like the whore she is. Her sexual adventuring provides the plot but the food seems more important. 'Every dinner was a feast' (375); 'There were so many things to eat here in London that she had never had before: elaborate sweets called marchpanes, olives imported from the Continent, Parmesan cheese and Bayonne bacon' (92). In contrast to the home-grown sparse utility fare of the 1940s, here is exotic food richly decorated and layered, often sweet and comforting: 'A French cake, split and covered with melted butter and rose-water, sprinkled with almonds' (100), 'an orange pudding baked in a dish lined with a crisp flakey puff-paste and decorated with candied orange-blossoms' (257). This is a generous novel, stuffed with the ingredients of Restoration London – Plague, Fire, political intrigue, Nell Gwyn and all – and it does not disappoint: 'the meal was everything that Amber had hoped it would be' (256).

Escape from war turns out to be almost impossible, even in historical novels apparently removed from a warlike context. Eiluned Lewis's *The Captain's Wife* (1943) is set in late nineteenth-century rural Wales, but even this tranquil spot is inhabited by recognisable wartime shapes. The book opens with a child waiting for her absent father:

> Papa coming home! She knew she ought to be glad, she ought to be happy, but she couldn't even remember what he looked like, having a confused picture in her mind made up of memory, hearsay and the picture on her mother's dressing table. (11)

Once again a middle-aged woman holds the fort, keeping her family together and anticipating her husband's long overdue telegram. Moreover, the very idea of the impossibility of escape becomes a theme of the time, with the motif of the flawed Eden. The 'Interlude in Arcady' which Chopin shares with George Sand in Doris Leslie's *Polonaise* (1943) should be the perfect retreat: 'Valdemosa! The very name was poetry; their monkish dwelling a haven of peace, crowning the lofty mountain side and girdled by terraces of vine and olive' (166). Leslie soon punctures the dream. Valdemosa in winter is a hell of rain, scorpions, vermin and hunger: 'Life narrowed to a battle for existence' (169). The idyll disappoints; a sick Chopin and a chastened George Sand return to Paris.

The failure of Eden in wartime is also picked up in fiction more directly about the war, as novelists registered their failures to evade or overcome the pressures of the times. Martha Gellhorn's *Liana* (1944) is set on a tiny and beautiful French Caribbean island after the fall of France. This should be a haven from war but characters feel ' "locked in . . . there is no escape" ' (80); ' "it is like prison" ' (9). *Liana* is a sad story of isolation and misunderstanding. Pierre, the French schoolmaster who has tried to escape from the war in Europe, feels cut off and in desperate need for newspapers. Escape is not the way to cope with war, and Pierre is impelled to return to France.[24] Back in England, and on a smaller scale, the 'Wonderful Holidays' of Rosamond Lehmann's late wartime story (1944–1945) are continually endangered. Mrs Ritchie is a romantic; both her 'self-indulgent daydreaming' and her real hard work seek to protect her children and herself in a cocoon of wonderful holidays. But the war persistently intrudes. Bombers and gliders pass overhead, rumours about the second front fill the village, and the eighteen-year-old boy she enjoys dancing with must leave for the Army and the possibility of death. At the end of a long, exhausting day Mrs Ritchie puts the cherry blossom the boy has gallantly given her by her bed:

> Beautiful, beautiful, triumphant consolation. But one branch was withering already; and as she watched, a whole flurry of petals dropped down out of the sheaf and fell on the table. (192)

The pressures and violence of war have often been remarked upon in *Between the Acts*, the novel which Virginia Woolf started at the beginning of April 1938 and finished at the end of November 1940; it was published posthumously in 1941.[25] The novel takes us through the events before, during and after a pageant put on in the grounds of a large house in the summer of 1939. We meet the people who live in Pointz Hall and their visitors; we also meet Miss La Trobe, the author and producer of the pageant. Woolf moves fluidly in and out of these characters, and she also creates a backdrop of unattributed voices, snatches of gossip and comment. We also get the pageant itself: songs, processions, music and three short plays within the play. The tone of much of the book befits the occasion: it is sophisticated and light. On one level this is Angela Thirkell territory and indeed Thirkell's own novel from 1939, *The Brandons*, devotes two chapters to the vicarage fête, scoring it for the same kind of voices which Woolf uses for her disjointed and sometimes comic chorus. But Woolf is working on many levels and she darkens her novel with the shades of war, ' "The doom of sudden death hanging over us" ', as one character puts it (70).

Mitchell Leaska's monumental and painstaking edition of the two Typescripts of 'Pointz Hall' (Woolf's title for *Between the Acts* until February 1941)[26] is an inestimable gift, a window into the mind of the novelist as she works. We can follow Woolf through the years of 1938, 1939 and 1940, and the different stages of her novel. The story is set on a June day in 1939, but much of it was written well before that date. By the end of 1938 Woolf had written 125 pages of the first version (what Leaska calls the Earlier Typescript) of what she estimated would be a 220 page book. There was a Later Typescript before the published version of *Between the Acts*, and within each Typescript some scenes went through several drafts. There are substantial changes between the Earlier and Later Typescripts, many less between the Later Typescript and the published text. *Between the Acts* is then a palimpsest, as of course are many novels, but with the important difference that Leaska's edition allows us to overlay the versions and map the changes. In this way we can read the novel (which examines the processes of history[27]) as itself a witness to the passage of history through its changing states. Comparing the versions is another way of reading the events of the years in which they were written. Leaska finds that the section of the book which gave Woolf most problems was the ending; it went through a number of revisions. The rejected endings all concentrate on the encounter between Giles and Isa, as does the published text, but are more violent. One early version of the last words of the book reads, 'It was their part to tear each other asunder' (*Pointz Hall*, 188), compared with the last words of *Between the Acts*: 'Then the curtain rose. They spoke' (130). In Leaska's view, 'The first ending is in fact so different from that of the published text that everything leading up to it must be read with different emphases and focuses of attention' (*Pointz Hall*, 29). If we take our lead from Leaska's observation and the muting of violence in the final version of the ending, we can see, in many of the revisions Woolf made, a case of emotion muffled and effaced.

In one of her earliest diary entries about her novel Woolf wrote, 'PH is to be a series of contrasts'.[28] These contrasts are much more pronounced in the Earlier Typescript. There is more agony and pain; there is also more faith in the power of art to harmonise. Emotions which are explicit and painful in the Earlier Typescript have disappeared or been altered by the time they reach the final version. Take, for instance, Isa's response to the Elizabethan part of the pageant in the Earlier Typescript: 'She shifted and looked at Rupert Haines. The plot was only there to breed emotion. And there were only three emotions: love; hate; fear' (*Pointz Hall*, 103). When she thinks of adding another emotion it is 'death', then 'sorrow': 'You plaited them like a horse's tail on a fair day: love; hate; fear; sorrow. Four emotions made the ply of man's life' (105). In the Later Typescript, 'She shifted and looked over her right shoulder. The plot was only there to breed emotion. And there were only three; love; hate; anguish' (329). Again Isa adds a fourth, this time 'Peace was the fourth emotion; love, hate, anguish, peace' (330). The final version in *Between the Acts* cuts the numbers: 'There were only two emotions: love; and hate' (56), and again Isa adds one: 'Peace was the third emotion. Love. Hate. Peace' (57). The fear, anguish, death and sorrow of the earlier versions have been dropped. Peace, absent from the first version, now offers a resolution in a simplified dialectical pattern.

In other scenes Woolf makes emotions which are strong or painful in the Earlier Typescript less explicit in the final version. Owen Felkin (who later becomes Cobbet) condemns the behaviour of Mrs Manresa with Giles as 'disgusting' and thinks of 'the automatic action, say of bluebottles on a plum cake' (115). He lingers in the Barn during the interval,

> noting that the human body, perpetually oozing at various orifices, smells; when those bodies are confined in an enclosed space, the smell . . . [*sic*] he raised his head the better to appreciate (if that word is not too strong) the odour that now filled the Barn. (116)

In *Between the Acts* he merely 'saw through her little game' and thinks about watering his plants (67). Cobbet is one of the many characters about whom the Earlier Typescript is more explicit, usually about their suffering. We are told of Giles's 'torture' in trying to communicate with Isa (159), and Isa confesses to William Dodge that she is unhappily married and in love with Rupert Haines (121). Even the briefly glimpsed Mrs Chalmers, going to lay her daily flowers on her husband's grave, is given a history of suffering which disappears from the final version: 'it was well within memory that he had treated her, regularly, every Saturday night to a hiding' (174). Comic pain is also effaced. The evidence of 'our passions' in the story of Roddy bursting into tears 'when the gardener, taking it for pure water, poured weed killer over the plants' (168) is deleted from the final commentary after the pageant. Unpleasantness is also toned down. The 'poison' in Isa's silent comments as she looks at Mrs Manresa's rings, and the explicit mention of Ralph Manresa's name in the reference to ' "liars and cheats" ' at the end of the pageant are two examples of what is removed from the final version. Rupert Haines's character as a philanderer – he has got a girl in the village pregnant and is the father of William Dodge's child (*Pointz Hall*, 193) – is also suppressed.

If the unpleasantnesses are curtailed in the final version, so too are the possibilities and powers of art. The moment in the empty dining room before lunch and the arrival of Mrs Manresa is very brief in *Between the Acts*:

> Empty, empty, empty; silent, silent, silent. The room was a shell, singing of what was before time was; a vase stood in the heart of house, alabaster, smooth, cold, holding the still, distilled essence of emptiness, silence. (24)

More than a page has been cut, in which Woolf poses the question, 'Who noted the silence, the emptiness?' and meditates on the nature and triumphs of the creative imagination:

Certainly it is difficult to find a name for that which is in a room, yet the room is empty; for that which perceives pictures, knife and fork, also men and women; and describes them; and not only perceives but partakes of them, and has access to the mind in its darkness. And further goes from mind to mind and surface to surface, and from body to body creating what is not mind or body, nor surface or depths, but a common element in which the perishable is preserved, and the separate become one. Does it not by this means create immortality? And yet we who named other presences equally impalpable – and called them God, for instance, or again The Holy Ghost – have no name but novelist, or poet, or sculptor, or musician, for this greatest of all preservers and creators. But this spirit, this haunter and joiner, who makes one where there are two, three, six or seven, and preserves what without it would perish, is nameless. (61–62)

This miraculous power of art to 'make one' and harmonise is given to Miss La Trobe and her pageant much more successfully in the Earlier Typescript. Later versions emphasise her sense of failure. In the Earlier Typescript, when Mrs Manresa hums along with 'My home is at Windsor', Miss La Trobe 'sighed with relief. The producer's great terror – that the gap will never be bridged was gone; it had been skimmed at any rate' (96). She can cope with Mrs Swithin's late arrival. In *Between the Acts* there is no clear sense of relief and the lateness is terrible. ' "O," Miss La Trobe growled behind her tree, "the torture of these interruptions!" ' (50). During the first interval in the Earlier Typescript Miss La Trobe rejoices at 'the most splendid sight that human eyes can behold; faces upon which "I, with nothing but sixpenny brooches and dish cloths to help me, imprinted my ideas" ' (108). *Between the Acts* withholds the 'splendid sight' and allows only 'relief from agony' before Miss La Trobe decides, 'She hadn't made them see. It was a failure, another damned failure! As usual. Her vision escaped her' (60).

Why did Woolf make these alterations, abating both the horror and the glory? We know that she had a natural tendency to conceal. In July 1940 she complimented her friend Ethel Smyth on the candour of her autobiography: 'you can confess so openly, what I should have hidden so carefully'.[29] The progressive subduing of the contrasts and muting of the emotions could be seen as Woolf 'hid[ing] so carefully' what surfaced in the first and most outspoken version. She started work on 'Pointz Hall' in the months leading up to Munich, a crisis during which she found herself close to the mainsprings of the action. Kingsley Martin, the editor of the *New Statesman and Nation*, summoned the Woolfs to his office, where, amid much commotion and many phone calls to the BBC, 'we sat and discussed the inevitable end of civilisation'.[30] A few days later the Woolfs visited Vita Sackville-West at Sissinghurst, where they learnt that war had been averted. Harold Nicolson, who was at that time in the Cabinet,

> had just rung up Vita and said she was to show us his diary. This was very interesting. They had all been convinced that war was inevitable. The cabinet had tried to control Chamb – the younger members that is. They were certain he was going to sell us.[31]

Witnessing the actions of press and government in close-up, what were the responses of the Woolfs? That week Virginia wrote to a French correspondent, 'We were so angry here in Sussex, and so afraid and so ashamed.'[32] They knew that war had only been postponed – six months perhaps – and judged it 'peace with dishonour'.[33] And so the strain went on through the early months of 1939.

Woolf's composition of the Earlier Typescript, the first version of 'Pointz Hall', was rapid until the outbreak of war; thereafter her pace slowed.[34] The action of the book is kept pre-war, although only just, in June 1939. This choice of moment means that Woolf cannot refer directly to what was happening during the later months of composition and revision: the blitz and the Battle of Britain. Woolf had first-hand experience of both: her London house was damaged by a bomb, planes flew and fought overhead in Sussex. Woolf's biographer, Hermione Lee, considers the descriptions in Woolf's diary of blitzed London to be 'some of her most powerful writing',[35] but none of this could get directly into *Between the Acts*. What does happen is an over-writing of the work of the months of Munich and early 1939, the time of anger, dishonour and waiting for war. The emotions of these months have been edited, flattened, diluted. *Between the Acts* presents an indirect face to us, in its displacement of its original impulses. It still rumbles with unspoken anger, but Woolf has made its characters nicer. She has also permitted art to do less.

Words themselves, the stuff of plays and books, reveal themselves to be inadequate and wanting.[36] Often blown away on the breeze, muttered, spoken most loudly when silently – 'He said (without words) "I'm damnably unhappy" ' (105) – words finally won't do. ' "We haven't the words – we haven't the words," Mrs Swithin protested. "Behind the eyes; not on the lips; that's all" ' (35). This is a novel of interruptions, gaps, words not spoken, not heard or not owned. In the last months of her life

Woolf was thinking about how the words on the page often point us to what is not there, to what is between the words. A passage in 'Anon', the work she started writing after *Between the Acts*, compares the reader of a book to a spectator at a play. The reader has the advantage of being able to 'read directly what is on the page, or, drawing aside, can read what is not written'.[37] The very title of *Between the Acts* asks us to contemplate not acts themselves but what lies between. Woolf did not fix on this title until the book was finished;[38] until then she referred to it as 'Pointz Hall', emphasising the unifying image of the large country house. By changing her title Woolf radically decentred her book, 'displaced' it, feeling perhaps by 1941 that 'the centre cannot hold'. What lies between acts can be either gaps or bridges. In this book what is 'between' is often felt as empty space: Mrs Manresa felt 'a vast vacancy between her and the singing villagers' (49). Words should be links, go-betweens, but in this book they fail. People do not hear each other, cannot communicate, 'the breeze blew gaps between their words' (84). *Between the Acts* stresses the fragmented, the dispersed. 'Dispersed are we' wails the gramophone over and over again.

Against this fragmentation Woolf sets a desire for unity, ' "What we need is a centre. Something to bring us all together" ' (117). In the Earlier Typescript it is art which can create the 'common element in which the perishable is preserved, and the separate become one' (61). Woolf wrote these words in July 1938. As the months passed it seemed to her that it was not art but war which provided the 'common element'.[39] 'As an English citizen in wartime,' according to Lee, Woolf was 'intensely aware of the dissolving of her private feelings into those of the community . . . Her individual feelings kept being swallowed up in "the communal feeling": "We're in for it" '.[40] But neither war nor art can bring together the scattered and fill the gaps in *Between the Acts*. The Earlier Typescript passage in celebration of the powers of art is deleted, and Miss La Trobe dismisses her pageant as a failure. There is however some measure of unity achieved and it is largely through the agency of women.

In August 1940 Woolf wrote 'Thoughts on Peace in an Air Raid', in which she pursues the case for the gendered nature of war which she had argued in *Three Guineas*. Women 'can fight with the mind' is her rallying call here,[41] and this is what she shows the women of *Between the Acts* doing. Mrs Swithin was 'off, they guessed, on a circular tour of the imagination – one-making. Sheep, cows, grass, trees, ourselves – all are one' (104). Miss La Trobe produces a pageant in which the presiding monarchs are all female: Elizabeth, Anne, Victoria – even Queen Mary gets a mention (64). Miss La Trobe and Mrs Swithin 'belonged to the unifiers' (72), and Woolf insists that the harmony of Miss La Trobe's pageant cannot be achieved through words alone:

Music makes us see the hidden, join the broken. Look and listen. See the flowers, how they ray their redness, whiteness, silverness and blue. And the trees with their many-tongued much syllabling, their green and yellow leaves hustle us and shuffle us, and bid us, like the starlings, and the rooks, come together, crowd together, to chatter and make merry, while the red cow moves forward and the black cow stands still. (73)

What Roger Fry makes us see in Cezanne, according to Woolf in the biography of Fry which she was writing at the same time as 'Pointz Hall', is what she lets Miss La Trobe achieve briefly with her pageant, 'the bringing together from chaos and disorder of the parts that are necessary to the whole'.[42]

As the pageant ends Miss La Trobe hides behind a tree, using it as camouflage in her wish to ' "remain anonymous" ' (115). In similar vein Woolf, increasingly interested in anonymity towards the end of her life,[43] hides her anger and shame about Munich behind the camouflage of her edited and rewritten book. But Miss La Trobe does emerge from hiding and Woolf rewards her: 'Glory possessed her – for one moment'. The moment passed, gloom descends: ' "A failure," she groaned, and stooped to put away the records' (124). And then the miracle happens:

Then suddenly the starlings attacked the tree behind which she had hidden. In one flock they pelted it like so many winged stones. The whole tree hummed with the whizz they made, as if each bird plucked a wire. A whizz, a buzz rose from the bird-buzzing, bird-vibrant, bird-blackened tree. The tree became a rhapsody, a quivering cacophony, a whizz and vibrant rapture, branches, leaves, birds syllabling discordantly life, life, life, without measure, without stop devouring the tree. Then up! Then off! (124)

Miss La Trobe's transfigured tree, radiant, both rhapsody and cacophony and utterly impermanent, stands as an emblem of Woolf's view of her own art.[44] As she finished 'Pointz Hall' she remarked that she had 'enjoyed writing almost every page'.[45] Writing it was a relief from the strain of writing her 'duty' biography of Roger Fry, of waiting for war to come, for bombs to drop. A frisk, a gallop, a pleasure: these are the words she uses in her diary to describe the composition of 'Pointz Hall'. But it was this very context of war which made her increase the threats to civilisation and diminish the powers of art. The ten aeroplanes flying in perfect formation and drowning out the vicar's words in the Earlier Typescript grow to twelve in *Between the Acts*; Miss La Trobe's thirty-five minutes of glory are cut to twenty-five in the final version.

9

WAR WOUNDS

War is never fatal but always lost. Always lost.
Gertrude Stein, *Wars I have Seen*, 1945

Martha Gellhorn's long experience as a war reporter led her to conclude,
'There is a single plot in war; action is based on hunger, homelessness,
fear, pain and death.'[1] This, by and large, was not how the war was
experienced by women in Britain. They lived and wrote in the sub-plots
of war, and their fiction illuminates the effects rather than the acts of war.
In their fiction war figures as something which wounds badly, wounding
those who win as well as those who lose, those who fight as well as those
who do not. This chapter explores the different sorts of damage which
women novelists located in the war, not so much the physical damage as
the less tangible harm done to and by the self in war.

Why people make war, what war does to people, how to think about
the enemy: these preoccupations exercised many women before and
during the war. In 1937 the psychoanalyst Joan Riviere argued that
aggression is an inescapable element of the human psyche: 'we have only
to look at the international situation, or at the behaviour in any nursery to
see that'.[2] Riviere cites the pleasure we take in minor and vicarious acts of
aggression, cutting retorts and the frisson of cruel stories. In her analysis
the enemy offers a convenient group for the 'conduit for aggression and
hate, "just as we provide ourselves with compartments and receptacles in
our houses which can safely receive the offensive or injurious discharges

of our bodies" '.[3] But part of the enemy is within – that very aggression which has to be nurtured in order to combat the enemy. British women novelists also addressed this issue of aggression in the years before the war. They linked it to the rise of fascism in dystopian novels which characterised fascism not as something 'out there', but as already arrived in England. Some of these novels focused on the male dominance integral to fascism, others asked readers to contemplate the Nazi 'in ourselves'.[4]

Storm Jameson's *In the Second Year* (1936) is set in the second year of a fascist state taking 'the first awkward steps towards dictatorship' (88); her England in the near future resembles 1930s Germany. There is economic depression and crass nationalism, fear of communism and much talk of war. The narrator, returning from abroad, struggles to decipher events in a half-understood world of shifting factions, threats and veiled violence. His brother-in-law is the head of the National Volunteers, a man of action prone to drunken pronouncements: ' "England for the English. No more foreigners allowed, except as envious visitors. No French, Boches, Eyetalians, or Scythians. The women shall spin English wool and the men wear it, and they shall eat English mutton and cabbage, and keep early hours" ' (41). Women are the second and suffering sex in this cult of male barbarism, 'a fearful sort of public school' (111). Murray Constantine's *Swastika Night* (1937) addresses gender issues more explicitly, exploring the misogyny inherent in fascism.[5] Her dystopia is set in the 'Holy German Empire in this year of the Lord Hitler 720' (5). This long-established militaristic totalitarian state venerates Hitler as the only Son of God the Thunderer, 'not born of a woman but Exploded' (5), and commemorates him as a magnificent blond giant who never let women into his presence. Hitlerdom celebrates the cult of the 'Holy Mystery of Maleness' (9); women are segregated, shaven and despised, ' "Of course women have no souls" ' (99). Constantine traces this oppression to its source in Christianity's fear of women. In her dystopia the Christians are the most enlightened group, now outcast, but even they treat their women ' "as if they were good and well-loved dogs" ' (185). Hitlerdom is still in place at the end of the book, and women have no voice; but Constantine suggests that their biological revenge might bring this Reich down. Only male children are being born, an ironic sign of sterile male triumphalism. Meanwhile the male population is locked into a perpetual militarism, conditioned only for war and fit for nothing else.

Phyllis Bottome's *The Mortal Storm* (1937) also criticises Nazi anti-women policies, this time as the Nazis rise to power in 1930s Munich.

Bottome's politicised love story was highly successful, the first novel to
appear as a Penguin Special.[6] The young medical student Freya
nonchalantly dismisses Nazism:

> Freya did not care for these new politics very much. She was a good
> German, a fiery Bavarian, and she thought that there might be something
> in Hitler; but Nazis did not seem to have room in their tremendous
> schemes – restoring the German Reich and shaping the world over again –
> for women. (9)

The energetic Freya experiences Nazism as an inexorable force which
manifests itself first in pettiness – ' "We don't much like girls driving on
the road" ' (369) – and then in the thickening atmosphere of oppression.
Freya's two half-brothers join the Nazi party and murder her lover
because he is a Communist. He is also a peasant: the novel opposes a
genuine peasantry against the decadent German upper classes. Freya has
a child by Hans, and the reaction to unmarried motherhood serves here,
as in other wartime novels, as a litmus test of liberalism. With Hans's
family it gives her 'fresh dignity and strength, while down below – in her
own social world – the same fact would make her feel ashamed and
despised' (321). As an unmarried mother and a half-Jewish student barred
from University, as a Communist sympathiser and critic of Nazism, and
as a woman, Freya has no future in Nazi Germany. She leaves her baby
with her lover's family and sets out optimistically for America. ' "What
you object to in women," ' she tells her Nazi half-brother, ' "isn't their
weakness – it's their strength" ' (369). But the hopes of survival invested in
Freya are dimmed by the fate of her wise and generous father, an eminent
Jewish scientist, who is put to death in a concentration camp.

Clemence Dane's *The Arrogant History of White Ben* (1939) examines
the psychology of the mass movement when a fascist dictatorship
establishes itself in Britain under the same preconditions as Jameson's:
economic depression and weak political groupings. White Ben begins his
career as a scarecrow in the garden of a house where the men have been
killed in 'the disastrous war of the nineteen-fifties' (1). Dressed as he is in
the clothes of dead men, Dane's dictator is literally constructed out of the
trappings of male authority. The clothes make the man:

> He had been garmented with religion, diplomacy, the art of war, the art of
> healing; for he wore a priest's vestment, a soldier's gauntlets and civilian
> mackintosh, a gentleman's pleasure hat, a surgeon's coat. (20)

Ben is brought to life by a little girl; in this novel women serve as the sometimes unwitting handmaids of male dictatorship. Dane's heavy colour-scheming – all Ben's followers must wear white, the antithesis of his crow-enemies – is a reminder of the black and brown tides sweeping across Europe in the 1930s. Witch-hunts, house-burning and 'crow-fever' infect the land, and Dane explores how a nation can be sucked into irrationality. It is Ben's eyes which compel. They are made from cinders, and one of his disciples explains: ' "He could stare at you with those chunky eyes till you couldn't stand it, and . . . in a minute or two I was saying to myself: I'll do what you say sir, and like it. Oh yes, he had me eating out of his hand from the first" ' (57). Another character caught in his 'spell' concludes that 'tonight she had known the meaning of glamour' (82). White Ben the scarecrow shares with Hitler the power of charisma.[7]

The little girl who needs White Ben's broomstick for her game of rounders is able to destroy the scarecrow made of clothes singlehandedly. Virginia Woolf's three essays, *Three Guineas* (1938), take the same trope of clothes, but Woolf's clothing is more resistant. Her devastating critique of militarism, nationalism and patriarchy targets not so much the aggression innate within us all (Riviere's idea) as the aggression instilled through education:

> Need we collect more facts from history and biography to prove our statement that all attempt to influence the young against war through the education they receive at the universities must be abandoned? For do they not prove that education, the finest education in the world, does not teach people to hate force, but to use it? (35)

Clothes provide Woolf with the perfect ammunition for her argument, and her campaign starts lightly. Photographs of pompous judges and bishops in procession illustrate her critique of the absurdities of ceremonial male dress in Britain:

> Your clothes . . . make us gape with astonishment. How many, how splendid, how extremely ornate they are – the clothes worn by the educated man in his public capacity! Now you dress in violet; a jewelled crucifix swings on your breast; now your shoulders are covered with lace; now furred with ermine; now slung with many linked chains set with precious stones. Now you wear wigs on your heads; rows of graduated curls descend to your necks. Now your hats are boat-shaped, or cocked; now they mount in cones of black fur; now they are made of brass and scuttle-shaped; now

plumes of red, now of blue hair surmount them. (23)

Having used her characteristic glance 'sidelong from an upper window' (71) to make us laugh at the bedecked men heading Britain's institutions, Woolf waits until the great closing passages of *Three Guineas*. Then she turns her attention to the man in military uniform. 'His hand is upon a sword'; 'his body, which is braced in an unnatural position, is tightly cased in a uniform . . . And behind him lie ruined houses and dead bodies – men, women and children' (162). Woolf argues forcefully that this tyrant is a 'human figure', with whom we as fellow human beings are 'inseparably connected'. Clothes and education are, for Woolf, two straitjackets, both of which are removable. Clothes can be taken off and 'centuries of tradition and education' (123) brought to a halt. Woolf invites women to form an 'Outsiders Society', dedicated to pacifism and the radical redefinition of nationalism. In her famous words, 'As a woman my country is the whole world' (125).

The effects of war upon those engaged in it was an issue which exercised many women during the war. The French philosopher and activist Simone Weil offered a pessimistic analysis of what she called 'force', a concept similar to Riviere's aggression. In an article on Homer's *Iliad* Weil clarified her thinking on the contemporary situation.[8] 'The true hero', she begins, 'the true subject, the centre of the *Iliad* is force'; and its workings are ineluctable. 'In whatever aspect, its effect is the same: it turns a man into a stone.' Weil uses the *Iliad* to illustrate her argument that when might is right there can be no winners, only losers. 'Force is as pitiless to the man who possesses it, or thinks he does, as it is to its victims; the second it crushes, the first it intoxicates.' She quotes from Homer: ' "Ares is just, and kills those who kill" ', and comments that, 'perhaps all men, by the very act of being born are destined to suffer violence'.[9] By 1945 even *Good Housekeeping* magazine had got the message about the negative effects of war on the warrior. The alienated imagery of stone, slavery and imprisonment used by writers such as Weil, Woolf and Gertrude Stein to describe the action of force finds an echo in Louise Morgan's article, 'When They Come Back'. Morgan portrays the soldier about to return home as 'a cog in the machine . . . a mechanised man, trained to do one thing only – kill the enemy'.[10] Although her advice might seem inappropriate – 'regard your husband or son as a boy home from school' – her recognition that trained killers need to be resocialised probably struck a chord with many women in 1945.

In their attempts to understand the mentality of the trained killer two writers took the unusual step of moving their stories inside the enemy. Sylvia Townsend Warner and Monica Stirling wrote stories from the German soldier's perspective, deliberately reversing that process of differentiation which writers from Hegel onwards have seen as crucial in constructions of the enemy.[11] These two writers envisage a seepage between the German soldier and the country he is invading which is fatal to the armoured identity of the killer-soldier. Townsend Warner's 'A Red Carnation' follows private Kurt Winkler on his journey with the German army to Spain.[12] The trope of the clothes making the man takes on a sympathetic reality:

> Kurt Winkler looked at his boots with new appreciation. Such fine boots, good leather, thick soles! ... At first it had hurt his feet, wearing such boots; now he was used to them, could not imagine himself without them.

Kurt veers between his simple 'soldier's duty to fight the Red menace' and his romantic excitement at the thought of Spain: 'Spain! He would see Seville, the orange trees, the bullfights, those girls who made cigarettes. He would walk about holding a red carnation between his teeth.' He has to remind himself sternly that Spain is 'a battlefield merely, a preliminary battlefield'. Meanwhile his friend Heinrich commits suicide rather than go to Spain; those neat ranks of soldiers, 'like a clipped garden', have a history of casualty. The Spain which Kurt eventually discovers in a hot walk round a city confuses him. Garages look like churches and churches look like prisons; where he had hoped for welcome he meets blankness, spitting and hatred. The fatal meaning of his presence in Spain is revealed to him in the last paragraph:

> And I am dying on their behalf, he thought dolefully. Till now it had never occurred to him that in coming to Spain to fight he might also have come to Spain to die. But from then till the hour of his death the conviction never left him.

Gunther Riesel, the German soldier in Monica Stirling's 'Marie Bashkirtseff and the Hitler Youth',[13] is also invaded by that which the Germans seek to invade, in his case the lovely streets of Paris and a 'new, painful curiosity about alien ways'. In his lodgings Riesel finds the three volume *Journal of Marie Bashkirtseff*, and 'with a little sigh like that of a very thirsty person who finds a pleasing drink within reach, turned back to the first page and began to read steadily'. Riesel falls in love with Marie, 'a precocious, violent, absurd, lovable schoolgirl riding in her carriage', with her 'touching egotism' and her passionate outburst against her early death: ' "so many hopes, so many desires and plans . . . all to die at twenty-four on the threshold of everything" '. Riesel, the soldier who must also prepare for early death, starts to fall apart:

> Marie Bashkirtseff's values were ones he had been taught to despise, but because he loved her his power to direct his contempt was slipping from him. And it was here that his training betrayed him. For whereas no one had ever told him of the existence of tolerance, a great many persons whom he respected had told him that when there are two opinions on any one subject one is wrong. Of the possibility of there being more than two opinions no one had spoken to him at all. In consequence the discovery that a Russian artist who died sixty-six years ago had taken a view of life different from that he took himself filled young Riesel with alarm. For it was clear that one of them was wrong, and infatuation drove him to suppose himself this one . . . The trappings of young Riesel's mind were fading as the colours fade from the walls of an Egyptian tomb when it is exposed to the air after being for centuries hermetically sealed.

Riesel tries for a posting at the front, then goes to Marie Bashkirtseff's tomb in Passy and shoots himself.

Townsend Warner and Stirling's impressionable young soldiers are the victims of war and conditioning; and Townsend Warner traces the curse of the fatal training back to childhood in her story 'Apprentice'.[14] The beautiful ten-year-old Lili embodies the perfection of German maidenhood. Her mother is one of the 'establishment' of women which Major von Kraebeck has brought with him to Poland, and Lili is its 'littlest dove'. 'Back in Germany Lili had learned in school how what you fight for and take from others is sweetest of all', and with his box of chocolates the Major teaches her that food is power: 'She sat on his knee and ate them from between his lips'. Lili is an apt apprentice, and is soon torturing the starving Polish children with the food she offers and then snatches away. The story abounds in animal references. Lili likens feeding the children to feeding her dog; the cleaning woman looks round like a cat before running off with some scraps, and the Poles howl with hunger like wolves. Townsend Warner suggests a terrible confusion between animal and human categories in the minds of the invaders.

The wounds which are the most visible in war feature relatively little in women's fiction. Writers are less interested in the getting of the wound, and more preoccupied with its consequences. Monica Dickens's study of the wounded soldier, *The Happy Prisoner* (1946), seeks to turn loss into gain through the contemporary philosophy of 'holy elementalism'. Writers such as Elizabeth Myers and Dorothy Cowlin were investing everyday life with a transcendental intensity, the domestic transfigured;[15] and this philosophy provides the cure for Oliver North. He has been severely wounded at Arnhem, and Dickens shows him feminised and sensitised by invalidism. A man of action, previously impatient of books and 'idle musing', he now spends hours examining the delicate moth which has landed on his Jane Austen novel. He learns to appreciate the invalid's pleasure of watching other people's lives – ' "like having a seat in the stalls of *Private Lives*" ' (162) – and starts to enjoy ordering their emotional lives (his Jane Austen was *Emma*): 'He felt despotic, positively matriarchal. He felt he ought to have a lace cap' (250). This is a temporary but beneficial phase in North's life; we are led to believe that the man of action emerges from the 'cocoon' (39) of invalidism a better person. Josephine Bell turned her soldier's wounds to more dynamic advantage. The eponymous *Martin Croft* (1941) has been wounded in the trenches of the First World War; his injuries at Dunkirk baptise him anew, and restore him to vigour and decisiveness. But some wounds write themselves on the body more indelibly, as Townsend Warner shows in her powerful story 'The Level Crossing' (1943).[16] Alice is dumb and badly disfigured after being injured in a kitchen fire, from which 'the flames seemed to have burned off youth and sex and personality'. One of the young 'family' of soldiers billeted in her uncle's cottage early in the war is attracted to her, because he thinks she can accustom him to his own fate:

> 'When I saw Alice . . . I couldn't bear to look at her. Then I thought: Suppose I do look at her? Maybe I'll get used to it, forgive it. *For that's what will happen to me!* I know it, I've known all along.'

But he changes his mind about marrying Alice and is moved on elsewhere. More soldiers arrive, and Alice 'looked after these as efficiently, as commandingly, as she had looked after those others, and moved among them firmly, and seemingly content'. Alice is to the end an enigmatic figure, a level-crossing over which those on their way to war must travel, a caring mother to the soldiers, but also a figure of silence and mutilation.

The war-wounded take many shapes in women's novels. The victim in

Vera Brittain's *Account Rendered* (1945) is still paying for the legacy of the First World War. Francis Halkin is a sensitive musician who was wounded in the trenches and suffers intermittently from shell-shock. As France falls in 1940 he goes into a trance and kills his wife. This bizarre plot opens the way for Brittain's message:

> This is what happens when a civilised community goes to war, thought Ruth Alleyndene. Every great war renders its account to the society that made it, but those responsible are seldom the ones who pay. It's civilisation itself, not Francis Halkin, that ought to be in the dock. (191)

Richmal Crompton looks back even further in history to take stock of the wounded. *Weatherley Parade* (1944) covers the years from 1902 to 1944, and begins with Arthur Weatherley's home-coming from the Boer War, a war from which he never fully recovers.

The internal wounds of war have no easy remedy. Pity for those victims of war who, though able-bodied may be beyond help, colours stories such as Anna Kavan's 'Face of My People'.[17] Kavan suggests that the wounded of Europe cannot always be understood, they speak a different language from those safe in the big houses of England, one of which, in her story, has been converted into a psychiatric hospital. Kling (his name shortened by brisk British tongues) strives to suppress painful memories of his dead father, and the many thousands whose graves he has been forced to dig. But when treatment brings release, his words are in a language no one can understand. Those at home may suffer from other wounds: anxious and bereaved mothers can also be counted among the casualties of war. The mother in Sylvia Townsend Warner's story 'The Mothers'[18] is an unpleasant and 'superior' village schoolmistress. She protects the swallows nesting in the school porch: 'the swallows' nest became an obsession with Mrs Pitcher. If the birds had been building in her stomach she could not have been more painfully aware of them' (108). Her two sons are serving abroad, and 'In January 1942 the pictures of Singapore had to be removed' (106). Mrs Pitcher's other son is in North Africa,

> And hearing the first squawks of the fledglings she began to sweat and tremble. Still the nest was untouched. She could not make out why. She had not noticed that the children realised – better than she, maybe – how jealously she watched over the nest in the porch, and so found it more convenient to go birds'-nesting along the hedges. (108)

But ultimately Mrs Pitcher can no more protect the birds from the attacks of aggressive boys, than she can protect her sons from the depredations of war:

> 'Any more airgraph letters from your boy in Libya, Mrs Pitcher?'
> 'No.'
> 'Ah, well! Of course he's busy just now, isn't he?' (110)

'War is too hard on women, no one realizes how hard it is on women,' reflects a character in one of Martha Gellhorn's stories.[19] The woman in another Gellhorn story, 'About Shorty', is not so much wounded as blotted out by war.[20] 'I do not remember her name,' begins a war-correspondent's account of her one-time friend, and 'Shorty' comes to represent the many women victims of war. A German on the sidelines of the Civil War in Spain, Shorty is unfaithful to her husband while he is at the front. The male war-correspondents disapprovingly class her as one of the 'whores de combat', but the narrator realises that 'she loved all these passing men and continued to love Otto'. Otto is killed and Shorty disappears, 'crossed off as a war casualty, and forgotten'. She reappears in Paris, remarried and radiant, confident that the baby she is carrying will be a girl. 'Why? Because it must not be killed in a war. I did not argue this. She had forgotten the sexually impartial effectiveness of aerial and artillery bombardment.' This is 1939 and Shorty does not survive the next war. A German anti-fascist with no papers and fearful for the safety of her small child, ' "one day she walked out the front door and disappeared" '. Shorty is one of the many nameless casualties on the edges of the main battlefield and a reproach to the narrator who admits, 'I would like . . . to forget Shorty as I have forgotten her name'.

Many who were not physically hurt or bereaved seem to have felt themselves marked, if not wounded, by the war. In a time of increased vulnerability, identity could be fragile. Elizabeth Bowen explained, 'You used to know what you were like from the things you liked, and chose. Now there was not what you liked, and you did not choose.'[21] Agatha Christie had had the 'idea behind' *Absent in the Spring*, which she published under the name of Mary Westmacott, since 1929, but it was the war which provided the impetus for the story's composition. *Absent in the Spring* (1944) is about vulnerability, and its heroine resembles Christie herself, a comfortably-off, middle-aged, middle-class woman. Joan Scudamore is stranded on her own in the Syrian desert for three days, and without her family and house to organise, she starts to go to pieces. She rereads her past and recognises that she has been cold and cruel. Overcome by panic, she has a temporary breakdown. Christie wrote the book 'in three days flat' at a time when she too was isolated, cut off from husband and family, and facing the war alone. This analysis of the moment when the self begins to crack was, she said, 'the one book that has satisfied me completely'.[22]

Vulnerability also dominates Rosamond Lehmann's story 'A Dream of Winter' (1941).[23] A woman lies in bed feverish and voiceless with influenza; it is 'the middle of the great frost' and she looks out on 'a mineral landscape: iron, ice and stone'. The bee man comes to take the swarm which has been buried for years inside the wall of her country house.

> 'Be a long job this,' called the bee man. 'Looks like they've got down very deep.'
> A sense of terror overcame her, as if some dreaded exploratory physical operation of doubtful issue, and which she would be forced to witness, was about to take place. This growth was deep down in the body of the house. The waves of fever started to beat up again. (103)

The story throbs with fever and fear, the violation to be done to the house is felt upon the body of the woman. When the bee man tells her that there will be very little honey she feels an understandable disappointment: in these times of sugar rationing she had hoped to 'save herself a little longer from having to tell the children: No more sugar' (105). To her the episode becomes a moral fable, fed by feelings of class guilt and maternal inadequacy which are exacerbated by the war:

Her Enemy, so attentive since the outbreak of the war, whispered in her ear:

'Just as I thought. Another sentimental illusion. Schemes to produce food by magic strokes of fortune. Life doesn't arrange stories with happy endings any more, see? *Never again*. This source of energy whose living voice comforted you at dawn, at dusk, saying: We work for you. Our surplus is yours, there for the taking – vanished! You left it to accumulate, thinking: There's time; thinking: when I will. You left it too late. What you took for the hum of growth and plenty is nothing, you see, but the buzz of an outworn machine running down. The workers have eaten up their fruits, there's nothing left for you. It's no use this time, my girl! Supplies are getting scarce for people like you. An end, soon, of getting more than their fair share for dwellers in country houses. Ripe gifts unearned out of traditional walls, no more. All the while your roof was being sealed up patiently, cunningly, with spreading plasters and waxy shrouds.' (106)

This slightly melodramatic self-castigation is accompanied by the down-to-earth chat and business of the bee man and the comings and goings of the woman's children. A little honey is finally salvaged, the woman's temperature starts to come down, and the story ends with the children by the fire in their mother's room. John tries to revive a bird caught by the cat, but it flies straight into the fire.

In a split second she was there, plunged in her hand, out again. Smell of burnt feathers, charred fragments flaking down. It was on the hearth-stone. Everybody stared.

Suddenly it revived, it began to stagger about. The tenacity of life in its minute frame appalled her. Over the carpet it bounced, one wing burnt off, one leg shrivelled up under its breast, no tail; up and down, vigorously, round and about.

'Is it going to be alive?' said Jane.

'Yes,' said John coldly, heavily. 'We can't do anything about it now.' (112)

Lehmann's imagery in 'A Dream of Winter' conveys the meanings and emotions of war indirectly. Betty Miller's *On the Side of the Angels* (1945) confronts more explicitly what the war is doing to those engaged in it. To write such a subtle study of militarism and aggression was a remarkable feat during the war.[24] Miller's interest in the psychology of warfare – where it comes from, what it does to people – follows Riviere's pre-war diagnosis of the innate aggression in the human psyche, 'The Enemy in our Midst', as one of Miller's chapters is called. The title of the novel comes from Disraeli, as does the epigraph, ' "The question is this: Is Man an ape or an angel? I, my lord, am on the side of the angels" '. Miller's project is the exposition of the ape in us all, which must be suppressed for the sake of civilisation. The novel takes place in what Angus Calder calls 'Deep England',[25] an idyllic summer Cotswold scene, but even so not immune from air raids. Set in and around a military hospital, Miller's terrain is a multiple battlefield. The wounds gained in battle, though severe, are the easiest to bear; Miller describes the soldiers who 'exhibited a serenity and high humour to be found only in those who, physically maimed, are yet whole in their own estimation' (81). It is the wounds to the psyche, both individual and collective, which Miller wants to search, as she studies the effects of the war on non-combatant life. Colin Carmichael, the pin-striped 'rising young doctor' from Worthing (104) who is now in the Royal Army Medical Corps, his wife Honor and her schoolteacher sister Claudia live near the hospital where Colin works. Claudia is engaged to Andrew, a lawyer who has been invalided out of the Army with a weak heart. A Commando arrives, is idolised, and later arrested as an impostor. Nothing much happens – a sports day, a dance, two small air raids, some dinners and drinks, nearly an affair, Colin is nearly posted abroad. Nothing much, but the text is a battlefield upon which war rages incessantly.

War conquers all in *On the Side of the Angels*. Everything must be interpreted in its ubiquitous language and grammar. Adversarial attitudes shape the book into a series of triangular power struggles. Colin is pulled between his wife Honor and the despotic Colonel who runs the hospital; he also contends with Herriot, the fake Commando, for the Colonel's favours. Honor is torn between Colin and Claudia who disapprove of each other. Predictably, Claudia fights over Andrew with his mother (138); more pressing is the rivalry between Andrew and Herriot over Claudia, in the triangle which carries the book's argument. Every relationship catches the infection of war: an aunt breaks off 'diplomatic relations' with a nephew (17); an elderly lady runs her house like a 'beleaguered fort' admitting 'only those who knew the passwords' (70), and even the barmaid waits for her customers 'in readiness for the assault' (55). Nature too: the cuckoo sings 'in light-hearted code' (27), and the only safe zone seems to be the world of Honor, the breast-feeding mother. A series of conversations between Claudia and her fiancé Andrew thread their way through the novel, discussing the 'serious moral problem' which Rosamond Lehmann welcomed as a rare treat.[26] ' "In a sense – we're all prisoners of war," ' suggests Claudia. Andrew reverses her idea to form the book's main thesis:

> 'Prisoners of war, you say – but don't forget the Prisoners of Peace – the people who've had to live battened down, all their lives, pretending to conform, pretending to be what they aren't. And that applies to most of us – Hence war, in fact. Call it a general amnesty, if you will–' (69)

Andrew sees war as the inevitable unleashing of suppressed aggression:

> 'It's the force of pent-up human emotion that wrecked Amsterdam, Leningrad, Coventry, Cologne. Why? Because it's compressed, tightly packed down into the shell-case of civilisation. Hence our joy in those

"beautiful bombs". They say it all for us – everything that we've been forbidden to say or think or do . . .' His hand relaxed. 'As a result of our unnatural way of living,' he said, 'civilisation has become so costive that it needs a regular dose of high explosive to achieve a catharsis!' (77)

Miller finds the attractions of war embedded in Western culture, as her references to *Julius Caesar*, Dying Gauls and Trojan horses remind us. War's worship of brute force and violent death has a devoted follower in Colin. Dazzled by the new order, the doctor who should be the preserver of life is glamorised by death, keen to be sent overseas. What dismays him is not death but life after the war, a return to 'the greyness and uneventfulness of every-day life' (127). In her sustained analysis of war as the 'flight from reason' (141) Miller is not afraid to strike to the heart of wartime mythography, the icon of the collective group. In war films, group dances often represent the uplifting community spirit. The Palais Glide at Miller's hospital dance comes out rather differently:

> the individual could sunder neither mind nor body from the mind and body of his neighbour, but must move as he moved, feel as he felt, obedient to the strong impersonal will, the incalculable personality, which now controlled and animated them all. Locked together, moving all in unison, they swung past, men and women alike gazing before them with shining eyes, with fixed tranced smiles. The floor thundered beneath them: a wave of intense physical energy passed out from them. (149)

'War Dance': the punning chapter title traces the primitive in the collective.

Disguise crops up frequently in Miller's study of the lures of war. She uses the word to refer, for example, to the way local girls make themselves up to look like film stars (87), and to Claudia's personality as Miss Abbott the schoolmistress (12). None of these disguises are watertight, discrete from the wearer's self. When the girls smile 'the disguise cracked apart' and the 'homely girl beneath' appears; Claudia herself is sometimes 'in some doubt as to where camouflage ended and the field of her own spontaneous nature began' (12). In wartime many people had to wear uniform (servicemen and women of course, also those with jobs in areas such as transport, catering, welfare), and Honor shares Miller's fascination with disguise as she contemplates her husband's metamorphosis from the rising young doctor of Worthing:

> She looked at him standing there in his khaki tunic, neatly belted and

buttoned. It was as if the anonymity conferred on him by uniform gave him a new sense of freedom and irresponsibility: as if he were masked, and, being masked, privileged, in a sort of carnival spirit, to conduct himself in a manner wholly alien to his normal way of life. The discipline of military life did nothing to correct this: on the contrary: being an imposed discipline, to be accepted whole and without question, it seemed to permit, in compensation, the relaxation of those personal standards, self-imposed and self-maintained, by which up till now as a private citizen he had chosen to live. (104)

Colin has been liberated by the mask of uniform, ' "It's unbelievable" ', says Claudia, ' "the effect war has had on that man" ' (156). The effect that the disguise of war has on others is demonstrated perfectly by Herriot, the fake Commando. The women and boys in the street, and the girls at the dances all read the violence of the Commando flashes on his sleeve with pleasure:

'They can kill a man instantly just by gripping hold of him in a certain way.'
'Or by sticking something sharp into his eardrums–'
'They black their faces, too. I've seen it on the pictures. Cor, fancy meeting one of them in the dark–'
'You're telling me!'
'I don't know what you mean.'
'Of course not.' (147–148)

'Of course' the girls know but cannot openly admit the sexual thrill of violence. This is the attraction for Claudia when she turns from the pale, weak-hearted Andrew to the 'rough soldier' Herriot, creating a fiction out of her own desires, as Andrew remarks later (232). Herriot invites Claudia to acknowledge her own impulses: ' "Isn't it about time you made your own acquaintance, Claudia?" ' (186) Claudia is the 'creature caught in the trap of its own nature' (202), unwilling to give in, but unable to resist. While she recoils from the 'ape' likeness she sees in Herriot (186), she is almost mesmerically attracted to him, torn apart in 'a state of perpetual civil war' (99). On her way to join Herriot in Oxford to embark on their affair, she has a moment of 'self-revelation' which is devastating in the context of its wartime composition (the novel was finished early in 1944):

We are not outraged at the murder of Abel, she thought. On the contrary.

We hate Abel, the guiltless man, the victim: it's Cain we love: Cain, the
killer. And we permit war in order to justify that love in our hearts. (214)

So much for the rhetoric of the just war. According to Miller, we need war
in order to express both our own aggression and our love of it in others. In
her novel she daringly shows 'the very ecstasy of love itself' on the face of
the housemaid Edith as she watches the German pilot's swastika-draped
coffin (161). Andrew's comment that ' "There's a Fifth Columnist inside
every one of us" ' (78) echoes Miller's own 'Notes for an Unwritten
Autobiography', which are subtitled 'Meditations of a Fifth Columnist'.[27]
And Claudia struggles ' "to learn how *not* to be ourselves – to have the
courage, the strength to be something else. Otherwise there never *will* be
any progress" ' (187).

The twist in the unmasking of Herriot is that the would-be
Commando cannot be easily dismissed as someone compensating for an
unsatisfactory life. ' "Commercial traveller, gigolo, swindler," ' guesses
Claudia (233), but the truth is quite the opposite. Herriot's life was as
fulfilled as any ordinary civilised life can be: ' "A married man, the dutiful
husband of a hard-working and capable housewife: the affectionate father
of three boys attending the local Grammar School . . . Town councillor
and part-time ARP official" ' (234). Herriot thus represents what Andrew
identifies as the hidden ' "criminal in all of us . . . the anti-social
impulse" ' (133) which war transforms into virtue. Andrew and Claudia,
the two civilians, must stand apart from the adulation of aggression,
which they resist in the name of progress and civilisation: ' "No way out
for us. Caught in the trap of our own reason. Like a rabbit with its paw in
a gin. On the side of the angels, in fact, with a vengeance" ' (235). They
are a pair of insomniacs; the price of civilisation is eternal vigilance.

There is also Honor. As Nancy Huston reminds us, the rivalry between
mothers and warriors runs deep in our culture, 'the act of giving birth
itself' is 'considered to be profoundly incompatible with the act of dealing
death'.[28] The rhythms of Honor's child-centred house start, punctuate
and end the book, the rhythms of afternoon sleeps, tea-times, bath-times
and especially breast-feeding. Her 'innate distrust of the spoken word'
(163) places her in the realm of Lacan's pre-symbolic order, the space
which exists before the world of the mother is usurped by that of the
father.[29] In a kind of 'understanding that did not reach the level of words'
(201), Honor opposes the inroads of the war on her family:

She looked round for her needle, her wool. Slipping the wooden

mushroom into the heel of a sock, she began to darn; pricking the long
needle in and out: resuming that essential maintenance and repair work,
emotional no less than practical, which derives from the feminine desire to
preserve at all costs the *status quo*. (168)

Preserving the *status quo* is the most, Miller seems to be saying, that
mothers can do. Honor is utterly opposed to Colin's Commanding
Officer, Colonel Mayne, who finds the very hint of breast-feeding
indecent (146), but her two sons will presumably grow up to follow the
way of the father. The book closes with the war brought home to Honor's
house. Claudia picks up one of Peter's lead soldiers:

It had been trodden on. She looked attentively for a moment at the tiny
Guardsman, faceless, shouldering resolutely his damaged rifle. With a
sigh, she set it down on the hall table and went upstairs. (237)

Upstairs is Honor with her baby, 'her blouse was unbuttoned, one breast
hanging disregarded, with its big blown nipple' (238). This is the
powerful yet vulnerable world of maternity (Colin has just rung to signal
his allegiance to his new Commanding Officer), the house of honour to
which Andrew and Claudia finally commit themselves.

The wounds of war long outlive the war, and the literature of these
wounds is still being written. Martha Gellhorn was one of the few women
writers to take the reader to the front, where she herself had been a
war-reporter. She could see how long the shadows cast by this war might
be. *The Wine of Astonishment* (1948) follows a group of American soldiers
fighting their way back and forth across France, Belgium and Germany in
the winter of 1944–1945. The attrition of war bites into every page.
Whether the character is a soldier or a Red Cross worker or a waitress in
a town occupied and reoccupied by opposing armies, the war has gone on
too long. 'He was sick and tired of the whole business. So was everyone
else' (245). War ages and exhausts, 'It tired you, there was no question
about that. And it made you old' (248). Lieutenant Colonel Smithers
looks back a few months to 'when they were young and had roared across
France' (247). War has written itself on to him:

He had grey hair too, alongside his temples and streaking the brown up
from his forehead. This grey hair alarmed him, yet it seemed to belong to
another man. You looked at it and wondered what had happened to the guy

that would give him grey hair at twenty-eight. You weren't ready for grey hair yourself. It was some other fellow, showing these signs of strain and anxiety. (248)

Smithers has escaped physical injury; his driver Jacob Levy has been wounded twice and 'held the sombre conviction that his third wound would be the last' (11). Levy's third wound, though not physical, is indeed the worst: he is destroyed by what he sees at Dachau. 'News from the world of darkness' (277) dominates the closing pages of the book, a detailed and rational documentary of insanity. Levy drives away from Dachau overwhelmed, filled with horror and hatred. Some Germans are standing in the road near the camp, talking and laughing:

> Jacob Levy saw them as he had seen no one in his life before. They strutted there, proud and strong as if they owned the world. Their bodies boasted how fat they were. The grinning pink faces dared him to bother them. They didn't have to move for anyone. They'd gotten away with it. Laughing, he thought, laughing out loud in the street to show me.
>
> The people in the freight cars must have screamed a long time before they died. When the wind was right, the ashes from the chimney must have blown down this way. Not a mile away, not even a mile. They knew, they didn't care, they *laughed*. Hate exploded in his brain. He felt himself sliding, slipping. It was hard to breathe. He held his fist on the horn and pressed his foot until the accelerator touched the floor. At sixty miles an hour, Jacob Levy drove his jeep on to the laughing Germans. (292)

10

OLIVIA MANNING: FRONT LINE OF ONE

'Wherever one is,' she said, 'the only thing certain is that nothing is certain.'

    Olivia Manning, *The Great Fortune*, 1960

This study has restricted itself to novels published before the mid-1950s, but the war has continued to inspire many excellent novels by women. Novels such as Muriel Spark's *The Girls of Slender Means* (1963), Penelope Fitzgerald's *Human Voices* (1980), Jessie Kesson's *Another Time, Another Place* (1983), Penelope Liveley's *Moon Tiger* (1987) and Maureen Duffy's *Change* (1987) bring new perspectives to our understanding of war. There is no room here to consider all these, but a study of women's Second World War fiction would be incomplete without Olivia Manning's two great trilogies, *The Balkan Trilogy* (1960–1965) and *The Levant Trilogy* (1977–1980). In her six-volume epic of a woman in the zones of war, Manning has succeeded in her complex project of getting history into fiction: this is what critics applauded when her Balkan novels were first published in the 1960s.[1] Anthony Burgess's praise of *The Balkan Trilogy* as 'one of the finest records we have of the impact of [the] war on Europe'[2] reminds us of the European dimension in Manning's work, so often – necessarily – missing from British war novels. Alan Munton's recent assessment of the two trilogies as belonging 'to the conventional novel of manners, made significant by the proximity of war'[3] needs to be tempered by the appreciation that Manning's war is very much *in* Europe, and that her cast are characters of history. History is not only in her fiction, it is in her characters; they carry the spirit of the times in them.

In Britain information about what was occurring inside Europe was hard to come by after 1940, and difficult to trust (a frequently cited reason for not believing accounts of Nazi atrocities). Mainland Europe appears in women's fiction during the war as the lost domain. Sometimes it stands as the place of suffering about which it is better not to enquire too closely; sometimes it is the place of present danger or past pleasure (pre-war foreign holidays are nostalgically recalled), and it can offer the gift of imaginative solace. The elderly Laura in Barbara Pym's story 'Goodbye Balkan Capital' (1941)[4] follows at a distance the diplomatic career of the man she danced with years ago at an Oxford Commemoration Ball. Laura endows Crispin's career with all the excitement missing from her own life, imagining in detail the hasty flight from the Balkan capital where she thinks he is posted. To Laura wartime brings air raids, danger domesticised in Pym's closely observed air raid. It also brings Crispin's obituary in *The Times*. He had retired from the Diplomatic Service five years earlier and,

> The remembrance of her wonderful imaginings about his journey made her feel foolish and a little desolate, when all the time he had been perfectly safe in an Oxfordshire village, his life as dull as hers.

But the 'Balkan capital' Laura has invested in Crispin's career survives to yield interest in the years to come:

> Why, she thought, when the siren went that evening, I might get killed by a bomb! And yet that would not be right. It was always Crispin who had had the dramatic adventures, and after all these years Laura did not want it to be any different. In life or in death people are very much what we like to think them. Laura knew that she might search in vain in the Oxfordshire churchyard among the new graves with their sodden wreaths to find Crispin's. But it would be easy in the Balkans, in the dangerous places. There would always be something of him there.

As Laura's Crispin was leaving, Olivia Manning was arriving. In 1939 she married Reggie Smith and went with him to Bucharest where he was employed by the British Council. They left Romania for Greece in 1940 and subsequently fled to Egypt, forced out by German advances. Uncertain and dangerous times, but Manning saw their positive side.

Writing for *Horizon* in 1944, she makes a strong case for the artist abroad.[5] She is defending the European poets in Cairo from the charge made by a critic in England that ' "It is surprising how quickly they have lost touch" '. While the title of Manning's article, 'Poets in Exile', acknowledges exclusion (she particularly regrets missing the London blitz), she is well-placed to diagnose the 'inbreeding' which she sees as a weakness in English war writing. Exile in Egypt has its rewards: the wider perspectives of a different culture and 'the sense of a greater, past civilisation'. The European poets in Cairo have, 'whether willingly or not, ... become cosmopolitan'; and this is the gift which Manning herself brings to the fiction of the Second World War. It may seem unfair to put her trilogies beside the novels being written by women in Britain during the war. They were forcibly cut off from mainland Europe, while Manning was part of the wider picture. She has the advantages of both proximity and hindsight. Her novels deserve our consideration here not just for their own merits which are considerable, but for the light they shed on women's wartime fiction as a whole. Back in England, at a time when men were engaged in battle and the rest of Europe was suffering in unknown ways, it might be difficult or inappropriate for women to admit the exhilaration and excitement of war. Manning's heroine on her front line of one can be read as a concentrated version of what many women went through, confronting danger and turning it into gain and growth.

Manning's experiences in Europe and North Africa took time to assimilate, and she did not start publishing her two trilogies until 1960. Before 1960 she alternated between home and away settings, as she worked towards the meaning of war to be developed at length in her trilogies. The stories and novels which she set in post-war England and Ireland languish in an atmosphere of staleness and stalemate. ' "I was ordered to take a holiday ... no, not really ill. Just a bit shagged. We all are" ' says an Englishwoman on holiday in Ireland just after the war.[6] The title of the story, 'Twilight of the Gods', refers to the disillusion this woman feels on re-encountering a once-attractive artistic friend; post-war life is inimical to glamour. The name of the English seaside setting for Manning's 1953 novel *A Different Face* says it all: Coldmouth is a chilly world of exhaustion, shabbiness and discontent. Europe, by contrast, is the place of adventure and danger. The early story 'A Journey' establishes fear as the medium of the woman's war for Manning, and dramatises a woman's initiation by immersion.[7] Undertaking to report on the Hungarian occupation of Transylvania on behalf of a journalist friend, Mary Martin leaves the safety of Bucharest and her 'kindly, comfortable husband'. The city she visits, Cluj, is a world of 'incipient rioters'; people and furniture are on the move, shops and communications shut down. Mary and the peasant leader she tries to interview speak five languages between them, none of them in common. But Manning wants us to appreciate that the 'star of anxiety' burning in Mary's solar plexus is partly self-inflicted. Cluj may be frightening but it is also exciting. Mary and her English friend Ellie, who is married to a Hungarian, respond to that spirit of adventure which Manning finds exhilarating, the attraction of being ' "out in the wilds" '. Here, and elsewhere, Manning and her heroine find temporary safety on a train. The restaurant-car is the ideal setting for Manning's woman at war. It offers nourishment and immunity, but at the same time it is on the move and impermanent.

Manning's first novel with a war setting, *Artist Among the Missing* (1949), is an interesting false start. Apparently in the belief that war novels should have male protagonists, Manning has moved women to the periphery. But she needs a non-combatant to register her angle of vision on the war in the Middle East, and she chooses Geoffrey Lynd, in peacetime an artist, in war a staff officer barred from active service by ill-health. Although he feels guilty for his absence from the front, it is the men of action who come across badly. They condemn themselves out of their own mouths when Geoffrey overhears

> every word of a story a naval officer from Alexandria was telling with elaborate casualness at the next table: '. . . and we got 'em. A lucky shot. Down they came, one after another, the bloody wops, and floundered about in the sea. They looked pretty scared. They knew they'd asked for it. We put a boat out. They were all alive when we got 'em aboard. As a matter of fact, they were all more or less alive when we threw them back in again.'
>
> The girls yelped delight at this conclusion. One spilt her wine over her dress.
>
> 'Oh dear,' the naval officer pulled out his handkerchief.
>
> 'Mustn't spoil the pretty dress. Mustn't spoil the pretty dress,' he repeated over and over again as he rubbed the girl's satin lap as she lay giggling helplessly. (143)

War presents a succession of intolerable faces throughout the novel, which range from these restaurant erotics to a helpless nihilism. A front-line officer remembers 'coming on a gun emplacement where the whole crew'd been wiped out. One of them had printed on a piece of wood: "In memory of a gallant comrade" but they were all dead. No one knew which chap was which, the state they were in. It made me think – I know one shouldn't think such things – but it made me think: well, what the hell good is it being brave or anything else?' (151)

Manning uses two drunken officers in the last scene of the book to show how the war has become an end in itself for the British Army:

'And when we're finished with these bastards, whose turn next?' 'Anyone you like. Keep the show going. This is the life!' (256)

For most of *Artist Among the Missing*, Geoffrey is stranded in Jerusalem with a group of refugees, trying to get back to his wife and job in Cairo. Beset by the common wartime trinity of boredom, frustration and loneliness, Geoffrey also has to experience the Manning wartime phenomenon of fear, but here Manning overdoes it. Convinced that he has been bitten by a rabid dog, Geoffrey is driven insane by fear, but this is fear without excitement. It does nothing to help accommodate Geoffrey to the war zone, from which he still feels alienated when he recovers. Manning has not yet found the right way into war, and true to its title, *Artist Among the Missing* dismisses art as a casualty of war, not as an aid in its representation.[8]

After *Artist Among the Missing* Manning seems to have recognised that her own experiences in central Europe and the Middle East would generate the kind of war writing she wanted, and that with a female protagonist a new war story could develop. Her two trilogies form a female odyssey. Unlike Ulysses's which takes place after a war has finished, the woman's odyssey is constituted by a series of travels and temporary halts round the edges of war.[9] Harriet Pringle is an explorer in the new terrains of marriage and central Europe, both places of incipient war which share the major feature of uncertainty. After the first political crisis of *The Great Fortune*, Harriet begins the process of adaptation: 'Harriet attempted philosophy: "wherever one is," she said, "the only thing certain is that nothing is certain" ' (82). Her new lives of war and marriage begin on a train in the opening scene of *The Balkan Trilogy*. Harriet has just married Guy Pringle and they are heading for Bucharest, where Guy teaches at the University. 'In the confusion of a

newly created war, the train was stopping every twenty minutes or so'
(9); Guy talks to a refugee from Germany, nodding, 'indicating that all
he heard was exactly what he had expected to hear'. While Guy talks
Harriet is on the look-out for the unexpected and peers out of the train
window; this is the difference between her and Guy. What Harriet sees
is difficult to understand in the twilight:

> Between the girders a couple fumbled and struggled, every now and then
> thrusting a foot or an elbow out into the light that fell from the carriage
> windows. (9)

Fumbling and struggling: love and war can look the same. As the train
jolts towards night and war, Harriet thinks, ' "Anything can happen
now" '. But when she turns to Guy for help in this new territory and asks
for an interpretation of the German refugee's words, 'Guy put his hand
on hers to keep her quiet' – not an auspicious gesture.

Bucharest reveals itself to Harriet as a world of excess. The food on
display in restaurants and markets is piled too high for her eye, as are the
melons in the park.

> A peasant had brought a handcart laden with melons into the town and
> tipped them out at the park gates. He lay among them, sleeping, his arms
> crossed over his eyes. The melons were of all sizes, the smallest no bigger
> than a tennis ball. Harriet said: 'I've never seen so many before.'
>   'That is Rumania [sic],' said Guy. (62)

Harriet is 'repelled by their profusion'; and as melons, so morals.
Bucharest is a world of ease and over-indulgence, decadence among the
aristocracy, hypocrisy and callousness elsewhere. As the war inches nearer
– ' "Where is the war now?" Harriet asked. "As the crow flies, about three
hundred miles away" ' (66) – Manning carefully maps the inroads made
by fascism. She documents incidents such as the Minister of Information's
censorship of journalists' reports of the assassination of the Prime
Minister by the Iron Guard, in order to show how fascism takes hold in a
country. In this climate of 'alert unease' and imminent crisis, Harriet
hopes to establish her marriage and home as solid bulwarks. She envies
the permanence of the solid family life she sees in the wealthy Jewish
Drucker household (124). Her words to Guy when they leave their hotel
for their own flat assert her faith in domesticity: ' "Tonight we are going
to eat at home" ' (125). But Harriet's private world is part of the public

world; this is the first of many homes which she attempts to found and has to abandon.

In Manning's politicised fiction personal behaviour complements and expresses public situations. On one level Prince Yakimov is a comic monster, a charming and ruthless sponge who picks Guy's pockets in order to cram himself with rich food. 'Rich food was an obsessive longing. He needed it as other men need drink, tobacco or drugs' (200). But Manning gives Yakimov's greed another dimension: his desire to 'absorb into his own person the substance of the earth' (44) finds a parallel in Germany's attitude to the rich and fertile land of Romania. Guy's expansive friendliness takes on an air of coercion as Manning describes his reluctance 'to let anyone pass from his sphere of influence' (171). Strategy dictates his welcome of Yakimov as a house-guest: he wants Yakimov to appear in the play he is producing, and needs to keep him under his eye.

It is with Guy's production of *Troilus and Cressida* that Manning establishes the most sustained parallels between the personal lives of her characters and the public events in Europe. The final section of *The Great Fortune*, 'The Fall of Troy', maps the play and Guy's production of it on to the invasion of Europe and the fall of Paris. The episode neatly expresses Manning's European perspective on the British stance. Using the production as a 'bolthole', Guy dominates the British community so that 'They had no time to brood on present anxieties. They lived now to pursue a war of the past' (253). The fall of Europe passes them by while the actors ape masculinity, padding out their tights with cotton-wool and earning the Minister's admiration for ' "the mixed grill put up by the Legation" ' (284). Guy's retreat from political crisis into successful theatricals parallels simultaneous events at Dunkirk, another British defeat which was converted into triumph. Harriet brings the news of Dunkirk, but none of the cast is able to understand it. Guy's inadequacy and escapism grate badly when he pushes Harriet away, 'gently impatient. "We must get on," he said' (254). Male heroism has already been found wanting in Harriet's critical gaze. She watches Guy posing in front of the mirror, 'distorting his face into the likeness of one famous film-star and another' (49), and observes Commander Sheppy clanking into the Athénée Palace Hotel, caricature man of action complete with artificial hand, black eye patch and 'a rattle of chains'. His manner reminds Harriet 'of someone who has taken a correspondence course in leadership' (146). Sheppy's commando tactics are comical, Guy offers no security at all, and Harriet 'shivered, feeling isolated in a country that was to her not only foreign but alien' (124). In Bucharest even the ordinary streets are a battlefield for her. She is jostled off the pavements, and becomes 'absorbed in warfare with the crowd' (27). But through a series of engagements and trials of strength Harriet establishes her front line of one, in an unstable world which she finds frightening but also exhilarating.

As Europe falls to German invasion in the summer of 1940, fear proves a not entirely negative gift. In the park Harriet sees and smells the flowers, 'these enchantments that gave so keen an edge to suspense' (267). Her life takes on an extra savour: fear intensifies awareness. Isolated from Guy, Harriet builds a new community for herself among the journalists and elderly ex-governesses who congregate in the garden of the Athénée Palace Hotel (its English bar has been overrun by Germans). The garden gives Harriet the home she needs, and

> It occurred to her that it was only during these last weeks she had become reconciled to the place. She had faced uncertainty without Guy. Those who faced it with her had become, through the exalted concord of their common fears, old friends. (274)

Thus Manning ends the first volume of *The Balkan Trilogy*, with Harriet launched on her solitary odyssey.

The Spoilt City, the second novel in *The Balkan Trilogy*, begins with a jolt:

> The map of France had gone from the window of the German Propaganda Bureau and a map of the British Isles had taken its place. People relaxed. There was regret that the next victim was to be their old ally, but it might, after all, have been Rumania herself. (9)

This is the summer of 1940, and a timely reminder of the importance of standpoint. Britain is not the only country in danger, and one's own self-interest is never so visible as someone else's. Throughout *The Spoilt City* invasion approaches inexorably; Romania is a world of rumours, ultimatums and panic in the streets. The Romanian fascists are tightening their grip and the tension invades Harriet's body. Responsive to the political climate, she has grown 'thinner during their months in this disintegrating society' (10). In vivid contrast, the blindness of those in England is marked by the arrival of the distinguished Lord Pinkrose to give a public lecture. He is pompous, self-regarding and ludicrous: ' "I plan to range over the development of our poetry from Chaucer to Tennyson. Central Office was of the opinion it would have considerable influence on Rumanian policy" ' (241). The British community in Bucharest marvel at the level of ignorance in England: ' "What were the London officials thinking about? Are they so wrapped up in the piddling chit-chat of administration that they are totally unaware of conditions in Eastern Europe?" ' (210) In comparison with the insular British in London, the British in Bucharest are deeply interested – as Manning assumes her readers to be – in the politics of the international situation. Her characters, many of them journalists, discuss events with an absorption and knowledge inevitably absent from many novels set in Britain.

Manning's way with history is illustrated by the episode of the reception for the fascist Iron Guard at the Athénée Palace Hotel.[10] She follows a public incident closely, so that it illuminates this particular moment in history at the same time as giving us an insight into how invasions happen. Her established cast play out their personal dramas in their customary settings (there are cross-currents of interpersonal wars), but also participate in and express a wider international drama. The chapter starts with Yakimov, the man most oblivious of politics, a position subsequently shown to be a dangerous liability. Yakimov has finally managed to get his beloved car out of Yugoslavia:

> His eyes filled with tears. 'The old girl herself,' he said. As he added: 'I love her,' he scarcely knew whether he referred to the Hispano-Suiza or to Dollie, who had given it to him. (80)

Yakimov's simple pleasure may be endearing; less attractive is his intention to attend the Iron Guard reception in an amoral quest for good food and drink. He is accosted by an elderly Romanian Princess wanting tickets for the Drucker trial. We have already met the hospitable Jewish Drucker family through the Pringles (young Sasha Drucker has deserted from the army and is hiding in their flat), and it is distasteful to see their persecution made a spectacle for the indifferent Romanian aristocracy. The question of allegiance for Yakimov is a meat and drink one, and he is deterred from gatecrashing the fascist reception only because the pickings don't tempt him:

> There was no sign of a buffet inside and the guests were drinking wine. Deciding the 'do' looked a pretty poor one, Yakimov went into the English Bar. (84)

At the English Bar Manning has propped an assorted flotsam of English ex-patriates, embarked on individual campaigns of self-interest. Journalists assemble here too, and in their well-informed analysis the balance of power swirls round Europe, feeding and fed by anxieties about the German invasion. Political analysis is annotated from the next room: the Iron Guard and their guests begin singing the *Horst Wessel*. The British try to leave – ' "it is a bit sinister" ' (93) – but find their way out of the bar deliberately blocked by those attending the reception. ' "When I say 'Shove', let's all shove" ' suggests one of the beleaguered British. Whereupon Harriet steps forward and earns her spurs as a sly version of England's national saviour:

> She unclasped a large brooch of Indian silver and held the pin at the ready. Before anyone could intervene – Clarence breathed '*Harry!*' in horror – she thrust the pin into the central backside. Its owner skipped forward with a yelp, leaving a space through which she led her party. (94)

But the emboldened warrior's sense of triumph is short-lived. On her way out of the hotel Harriet recognises the wife of a former pro-British Minister of Information: 'Her flat, faded, colourless face seemed to have on it the imprint of a heel. About her was an atmosphere of such unhappiness, it affected the air like a miasma' (95). The English flotsam end the chapter in ignominious flight:

> Half-way across the square Dubedat could be seen strutting at an indecorous speed while Toby, shoulders up, head down, hands in pockets, pinching himself with his own elbows, was scurrying like a man under fire. (95)

The rest of the book keeps the issue of allegiance well to the fore. Yakimov hits a low point when he sponges off Count Freddi von Flugel, an old friend now turned Nazi.[11] The photographs of Hitler, Goebbels and Himmler in von Flugel's house are a matter of indifference to Yakimov: 'To him they were nothing but the stock-in-trade of someone else's way of life. If Freddi were "in with that lot", then all the better for both of them' (147). In order to ingratiate himself with von Flugel, Yakimov betrays both Guy and Sasha Drucker. He gives von Flugel the secret plans for blowing up oil wells (a mad *Boys' Own* scheme of Commander Sheppy's), which he has stolen from the Pringles' flat. The consequences are predictable: the Pringles' flat is raided and Sasha seized.

As for Guy himself, Harriet weighs the matter of his allegiance and has her doubts, she has 'almost ceased to expect it from him'. He is 'fond of too many people', too committed elsewhere to commit himself sufficiently to Sasha or to her (131). Her own loyalties are drawn towards those she wants to protect: the wild red kitten and Sasha, both of whom she regards as 'dependent innocents' (187). Harriet's 'infuriated compassion' (214) for Guy impels her into the streets, to safeguard him among the 'utter confusion' of daily processions and empty shops. Baptising him with cold tea, she even tries to extend her watch over him into the life to come.

The first two volumes of *The Balkan Trilogy* end outside in the streets, in atmospheres of public and private uncertainty. *The Great Fortune* draws to a close with the fall of France and defeat, but with a small gesture of assertion as Harriet adopts Guy's philosophy:

> 'We'll get away because we must. The great fortune is life. We must preserve it.'
>
> They turned from the map of France with the swastika at its centre and walked home through the empty streets. (287)

By the end of *The Spoilt City* the Germans are about to occupy Bucharest, and the British are all dead, fled or disappeared. Arriving by herself in Athens, 'where even the alphabet was unknown to her' (299), Harriet has become so accustomed to strangeness that a new city can be a haven. She wanders 'about the unfamiliar streets in a transport of release from all she had left behind' (298). This time, though, Harriet ends the novel in the streets with Yakimov instead of Guy. In Bucharest she disliked Yakimov and resented his scrounging, and he feared her sharp tongue. In Athens, while she waits anxiously for news of Guy, Yakimov proves a sympathetic friend. Still a scrounger, ' "your poor old Yak" ' restores Harriet with his kindness; and in return she admires the now thread-bare famous coat:

> She said: 'I see you still have your wonderful coat.'
>
> He eagerly agreed, 'Yes,' and, turning the front hem, revealed by the light from the hotel door the shabby sable inside. 'Did I ever tell you the Czar gave it to m'poor old dad?'
>
> 'I think you did tell me once.'
>
> He lifted her hand and put his lips to it. 'If you need me, you'll always find me at Zonar's.' Patting her hand before dropping it he said,

'Good-night, dear girl.'

'Good-night.'

He waved before turning away. As he went, the fallen hem of his greatcoat trailed after him along the pavement. (303)

Friends and Heroes (1965), the last volume of *The Balkan Trilogy*, starts with fear receding. As Harriet goes to meet Guy, 'It seemed to her that when the plane arrived she would have conquered anxiety altogether' (14). Later, sitting with him in an Athenian cafe she even manages to let go for a moment:

Relaxed in her chair, she felt a subsidence of tension as though some burden, carried for too long a time, was gradually losing weight. (24)

Harriet welcomes the blessed relief from tension: ' "To feel safe!" she said. "Simply to feel safe! It's marvellous to be among people who are on your side" ' (25). But four pages later, anxiety descends again. Harriet's fantasy of escape by sea (she likes to devise escape routes for herself from war and marriage) collapses when she discovers that Guy cannot swim: 'There was no safety in the world. Here, on the summit of the Acropolis, she saw them shipwrecked in the Mediterranean and pondered the problem of keeping Guy afloat' (29). But just keeping afloat has never been Harriet's goal; after all she 'married for adventure' and revels in being unconventional (90). She is now a creature of war and confesses, ' "I couldn't believe in the peace-time society here. It was almost a relief when the air-raid siren sounded. I felt at once that I knew my way around" ' (99). ' "War is real and life is not" ' (99), and Harriet acclimatises to reality. More assured and independent than before, she asserts herself in the in-fighting at the English School, finds herself a job and embarks on relationships independent of Guy.

The sustenance of friendship in war runs throughout the trilogy, and *Friends and Heroes* brings Harriet her first friend who is also a man at war, the liaison officer Charles Warden. In their relationship Manning doubles the illicit lures of romantic battle and adulterous sex. This is the one moment in the trilogy when Harriet succumbs to the glorification of war:

lifted into a realm of poetic concepts, she saw Charles not as an ordinary young man . . . but a man-at-arms to whom was due both deference and privilege. She was her own symbol – the girl whose presence heightened

and complimented the myth. Enchanted, she was almost immediately dis-
enchanted; was indeed amazed at finding herself dazzled by the cantrips of
war. She was against war and its trappings. She was thankful to be married
to a man who, whether he liked it or not, was exempt from service. She was
not to be taken in by the game of destruction – a game in which Charles
Warden was a very unimportant figure. Giving him a sidelong glance, she
was prepared to ridicule him; instead, as she found his eyes on her, she felt
warmed and excited, and the air about them was filled with promise. (161)

On the brink of an affair, Harriet justifies herself by telling Charles he is
' "A particular friend. You are what I need most: a companion" ' (236). But
heroes do not make good friends, and Manning devotes part of this last
volume of her trilogy to the deconstruction of the man-at-arms as hero.

Men-at-arms go about their business at a distance in *The Balkan
Trilogy*. The RAF squadrons perform in a drama played out according to
ancient rules.

Guy said: 'Where has Surprise [an RAF pilot] gone?' but no one knew.
Surprise had gone without a word to anyone. Now another man, bearded
like Ajax or Achilles, was being held aloft and, swinging the bottle round
his head, he was swept away just as Surprise had been swept away. Heroes
came and went these days. (270)

In Harriet's thoughts the warrior hero, 'valiant but insubstantial',
dissolves in death. ' "A doomed man," she thought . . . they were all upon
the brink of death' (272). Later, when the defeated British and Greek
soldiers make their way back to Athens, the book offers a more bitter
critique. Harriet watches the 'heroes of Epirus', brave, beaten and
betrayed:

She had been told that many of the men had no weapons, yet, like riderless
horses in a race, they had gone instinctively into the fight. Starving,
frost-bitten, infested with lice, stupefied by cold, they had endured and
suffered simply because their comrades endured and suffered. The enemy
had not had much hand in killing them. The dead had died mostly from
frost-bite and cold.

The men she had seen, the survivors, had undergone more than any
man should be asked to undergo. They had triumphed and at the last,
unjustly defeated, here they were wandering back, lost in their own city,
begging for bread. (329)

Scenes of suffering, defeat and retreat bring *The Balkan Trilogy* to a terrible end. Yakimov is shot in an abrupt and senseless accident. 'He said in a whisper of puzzled protest: "Dear boy!" and collapsed to the ground' (315); after three novels he has become such a familiar presence that we feel we have lost a friend.

The trilogy may be drawing to a close, but the war is not. Manning's characters now broach the fear which will recur in the next trilogy, that 'For all they knew [the war] would not end in their lifetime' (317). Hence Manning's use of repetition, which may at first look like failing invention, but which gives the impression of lives trapped in an endless war. Thus Guy wants to repeat his production of *Troilus and Cressida*, and constantly restages the revues he mounts for the troops. Harriet has one cat to protect in Bucharest and another in Athens; she loses both. Lord Pinkrose's lecture is endlessly discussed; the history of Yakimov's coat is repeated over and over – this is the world stuck in the killing grooves of war. By the end of the trilogy the whole of Europe is lost territory. Greece, 'the dark end of the lost world' (307), is raided and invaded, and the Pringles are once again in flight. As they leave on the last ship out, Manning sounds the roll-call of the men lost in war:

> Harriet thought of Charles left behind with the retreating army, of David taken by the enemy, of Sasha become a stranger, of Clarence lost in Salonika, of Alan who would share the fate of the Greeks, and of Yakimov in his grave. (343)

War in the trilogy has been a series of defeats, and more anxiety lies ahead. Looking at the North African shore, 'Disturbed by its strangeness, Harriet felt their lives now would be strange and difficult' (344). But – and there always is a but – as Harriet contemplates the heightened uncertainty, she also feels the challenge of adventure, ' "We must go and see" '. Set against the death-pull of war is the reaffirmation of life, 'a depleted fortune, but a fortune', and the marriage that has lasted in war: 'They were together and would remain together, and that was the only certainty they had'. Although the trilogy closes with the invasion of Europe, with flight and uncertainty, it also ends with hope and youth, and the spark of excitement as Harriet and Guy 'moved forward to look at the new land' (344).

Manning's second trilogy traces her own odyssey from Europe to the Middle East, and her sense of culture shock. 'Nightmare' was the word she used in 1944 to describe her first reaction on arrival in Cairo.[12] War, the destructive element, moves *The Levant Trilogy* unambiguously into tragedy.[13] Harriet describes her position on the edge of the North African battlefield as ' "strange . . . like living beside Pluto's underworld" ' (38). She retains her forward momentum but it takes on an air of compulsion rather than the zest of youth. *The Levant Trilogy* sends Harriet on many journeys and has her constantly on the move; Manning's own Cairo 'restlessness' has entered her soul.[14] Despite Harriet's efforts, her temporary job terminates abruptly, and Cairo provides 'no real home and little enough to do' (25). Fear again determines her view of the war. She predicts that the army will be surrounded (107), and 'tried to work out on the map the strategy of defeat' (80). Although she tries again to turn flight into adventure – ' "But we're seeing the world. We might as well try and enjoy it" ' (167) – her body sickens and her spirits flag. Feeling that 'the killing element was not the heat of Cairo but Guy himself' (374), Harriet is forced to reconsider the merits of the 'strong potion' of 'uncertainty' (284). 'Excitement,' thinks Harriet, listening to the beautiful and frivolous Edwina singing in the shower, 'that . . . was what women most wanted, and what risks they took to attain it' (286). Her own quest, in marrying Guy and 'travell[ing] to the other side of Europe with someone she barely knew' (286), has foundered in disappointment and illness. Suspecting Guy of infidelity and fearful that even her doctor is trying to kill her, Harriet decides to return to England. She changes her mind at the last moment, but Guy hears that her ship has been torpedoed and assumes she is dead.

Harriet spends the last volume of the trilogy, *The Sum of Things*, in restless flight through the Middle East. Her attempts to live the single life fare badly and the road runs out on her: 'Baalbek was the end of the line' (472). When she realises that Guy believes her dead she hurries back to him, to appear as a miraculous resurrection at Edwina's wedding party. ' "Isn't this marvellous!" ' cries Edwina. ' "To think it should happen at my wedding! The whole of Cairo will be talking about it" ' (537). Harriet herself is more circumspect; she 'took a step towards Guy then stopped in uncertainty: "I wasn't sure you'd want me back" ' (537).

The long trajectory of six novels ends with Harriet surviving a death and returning to Guy, although what restores her is not so much her husband as her own development. She has learnt how to live in war, a difficult achievement. Friendship is part of this process, as it offers a vital and sustaining counterbalance to war. Harriet learns to temper her moral sharpness with sympathy for self-servers such as Yakimov and Major

Cookson. Through the war her criteria have shifted: 'An admirer of wit, intelligence and looks in a man, [she] was beginning to realize that kindness, if you had the luck to find it, was an even more desirable quality' (497). Thus she makes and values friends of her own independently of Guy, 'moving out from under his influence' by telling him ' "You have your friends; let me have mine" ' (561). Towards the end of *The Levant Trilogy* Manning sets Guy and Harriet on a train, as she had at the beginning of *The Balkan Trilogy*; this time Harriet 'realized he could not see what was beyond the window . . . She saw the world as a reality and he did not' (566). Six novels earlier Guy put his hand on hers 'to keep her quiet'; now Harriet 'put her hand on his knee and he patted it and let it lie there, keeping his gaze on the lines of newsprint'. While he reads, Harriet finally answers the question that has run through the six novels, 'was she content?' Her answer is born of her hard-earned independence:

> She was free to think her own thoughts. She could develop her own mind. Could she, after all, have borne with some possessive, interfering, jealous fellow who would have wanted her to account for every breath she breathed?
>
> Not for long.
>
> In an imperfect world, marriage was a matter of making do with what one had chosen. As this thought came into her head, she pressed Guy's knee and he patted her hand again. (566)

The progress of Harriet, woman-at-war, is matched in *The Levant Trilogy* by that of Simon Boulderstone, army officer and man-at-war. His is the story of initiation into battle, a theme which shapes many war narratives. Like Harriet, Simon is another lone explorer in the hazardous terrains of war and young adulthood, but his war takes him in the opposite direction from Harriet's, away from community and friendship, towards isolation and loss. War fosters friendships with great urgency but it also destroys them, as Simon discovers immediately on disembarkation in North Africa:

> He had two friends on board, Trench and Codley, who had been his family, his intimates, the people nearest to him in the world. The sense of belonging together had been deeper than love – then, at Suez, a terrible thing had happened. He lost them. (9)

Like Harriet, Simon suffers from the uncertainty engendered by war. Only twenty, suburban and uncomplicated, he hopes that friendship will be the panacea. His driver Arnold 'brought a sense of continuity to a disrupted world' (87); Arnold has also been parted from his ship-board friends, and in a gesture of friendship Simon stands to drink his tea beside Arnold, 'feeling not only that their uncertainty was a bond but that there was sympathy between them' (91). When Arnold is shot Simon feels 'bereaved' (158) and grows 'wary of friendship', wanting to 'avoid any relationship that could again inflict on him the desolation of loss' (195). Then his elder brother Hugo is killed in action, and Simon is engulfed by the fatal medium of war. 'He felt death as though he and Hugo had been one flesh and he was possessed by the certainty that if he returned here, he, too, would be killed' (204). In this universe of death words can do nothing. Simon sits in the back of a truck trying to write a letter to his parents about Hugo: ' "Dear Mum and Dad, By the time you get this . . ." '. He can write no more, and the first volume of *The Levant Trilogy* closes on Simon's helpless weeping. At this point Manning herself, the chronicler of war, seems to have lost faith in the power of the written word. 'There was nothing to be said. He tore the pages into fragments and threw them to the desert wind' (205).

The Levant Trilogy begins with the fall of Tobruk and ends with the allied victories in North Africa. Simon has a part to play in the action – ' "The Alamein Line," Simon asked Hardy, "What's that, sir?" ' (128) – but there is no sense of El Alamein as a battle and little sense of victory. Manning must have read Keith Douglas's *Alamein to Zem Zem* (1946); she had praised Douglas's poetry in her wartime *Horizon* article, and Simon Boulderstone is recognisably involved in the same campaign as Keith Douglas.[15] But although Douglas is highly individualistic (his unorthodox way of getting to the front illustrates this), he usually describes action in war as action in concert: men in tanks, tanks in groups. In contrast, most of Simon Boulderstone's significant combat experiences are solitary. His job as a liaison officer sends him across dangerous battlefields alone; like Harriet, he is posted to a front line of one.

The novel in the middle of Manning's second trilogy, *The Battle Lost and Won*, concentrates mainly on battles lost: the deaths and injuries sustained by Simon and his companions, Harriet's diminishment by sickness and unhappiness. Deaths accumulate from war and other causes,[16] and the British way of mourning falls painfully short. When Simon returns to Cairo on the day of his brother's death, his friends try to console him. Unlike the Egyptians who conduct dignified ceremonies in the City of the Dead, the British have only unfocused goodwill. They end the evening in a brothel watching a couple they have paid to copulate.

The humiliation belongs to the British, ' "We Egyptians," ' explains the young man, ' "are not like you Europeans. We are liking to do such things in private" ' (232). When Simon does reach the 'field of victory' it is 'barren ground' for him, the site of his brother's death:

> Walking back among tanks as useless as the sand they stood on, stepping over the bodies of lost young men, Simon asked, 'Is this what Hugo died for? And am I to die for this?' (280)

By the last volume of *The Levant Trilogy*, *The Sum of Things*, war has confirmed its dominion as the natural state. Guy thinks of Simon who has recovered from his wounds and is about to return to 'normal life; or rather, to the killing destruction and turbulent hatred that these days passed for normal life' (494). There seems no end in sight. Harriet wants to agree with Simon that 'the war could not go on for ever but she had no certainty' (39); characters draw comparisons with the Hundred Years War (139, 516). Manning's use of repetition reinforces the pessimistic trajectory. Cairo prepares, like Bucharest and Athens, for the arrival of the Germans with the same flood of rumours and panics; once again we witness the bonfire of papers at the British Embassy. The cast of drunken journalists from Bucharest repeats itself in Jake Jackman; Simon Boulderstone feels that he is doubling his brother Hugo, and twice we hear of torpedoed ships and characters surviving in open boats. Guy repeatedly throws himself into shows for the troops, stories are told and retold. Even the usually confident Guy is sapped by bereavement and feelings of futility:

> Lecturing on English literature, teaching the English language, he had been peddling the idea of empire to a country that only wanted one thing; to be rid of the British for good and all. And, to add to the absurdity of the situation, he himself had no belief in empire. (513–514)

Manning brings her six-volume odyssey to a close on a double note. There are small flickerings of optimism after El Alamein, and Harriet says, ' "I think things will go our way in future" ' (567); this is her first positive prediction about the war in six novels. The trilogy ends with Harriet and Guy once again in the streets, this time Alexandria in the dusk. They get as close to 'happily ever after' as Manning can allow:

> Putting his arm through Harriet's, Guy said: 'You'll never leave me again, will you?'

'Don't know. Can't promise.' Harriet laughed and squeezed his arm: 'Probably not.' (568)

But the last page belongs to Simon, the fighting man. Badly wounded, he has like Harriet endured a kind of death and developed as a consequence. 'He had been a sick, despondent boy; now he was a young man conscious of his strength and his individuality in the world' (493). Recovered from his injuries, he hears that he has been posted to the Greek island of Leros. As his hopes start to rise at the prospect ('Leros might not be so bad after all'), the unspoken irony of his destination sinks home. The British were badly defeated at Leros and suffered heavy losses;[17] we realise that Simon is heading for certain death. Manning's final Coda explicates the tragic meaning of war in its ending, an after-world not of winners and losers but of survivors, 'the stray figures left on the stage at the end of a great tragedy' (571).

POST-WAR POST-SCRIPT

Oh, from the most unpromising material.
Elizabeth Taylor, 'Gravement Endommagé', 1954

In the world of publishing, timing can be all-important. *Pigeon Pie*, Nancy Mitford's frivolous tale of society types playing at war work and spies, came out in May 1940 and was, in Mitford's words, 'a flop', 'an early and unimportant casualty of the real war which was then beginning'.[1] Five and a half years later, Mitford found very much the right moment. Published in December 1945, *The Pursuit of Love* was an instant success. 'If ever', according to Mitford's biographer, Selina Hastings, 'there were a case of the right book at the right time, this book was it.'[2] After six years of hardship and the noble goals of the People's War, *The Pursuit of Love* gave unquestioned and unabashed licence to the enjoyment of light-hearted pleasure, well-heeled romance and snobbery. The first words of the book disclose Mitford's enterprise:

> There is a photograph in existence of Aunt Sadie and her six children sitting round the tea-table at Alconleigh. The table is situated, as it was, is now, and ever shall be, in the hall, in front of a huge open fire of logs. Over the chimney-piece plainly visible in the photograph hangs an entrenching tool, with which, in 1915, Uncle Matthew had whacked to death eight Germans one by one as they crawled out of a dug-out. It is still covered with blood and hairs, an object of fascination to us as children. (5)

Having gone into protective deep-freeze for the duration, the English upper class, 'as it was, is now, and ever shall be', is ready in 1945 to be brought back to life, liberty and the pursuit of self-interest. Uncle Matthew's entrenching tool has done its work well.

Although Mitford's stylish snobbery found immediate favour, VE Day does not feature in the novels of the time as the joyful occasion of popular memory. The narrator of Pamela Hansford Johnson's *An Avenue of Stone* (1947) is 'unaccountably depressed' (73), and the soldier hero of Edith Pargeter's *Warfare Accomplished* (1947) feels 'empty, drained and cold' (340). Revelations of Nazi atrocities and news of the atom bombs dropped on Hiroshima and Nagasaki oppress the spirits of war-weary characters. Hansford Johnson describes the summer of 1945 as the time when 'history had come to a stop' (130). 'How', thinks one of her characters, 'we were going on shouting about the brutality of German bombing when we did that kind of thing quite cheerfully ourselves, God alone knew' (185). Another woman kills herself: ' "She couldn't face the 'Atomic Age', she said" ' (201). By the end of the war, women's novels were creaking with battle fatigue. Their flinty titles suggest weariness and an inability to look ahead: Hansford Johnson's *An Avenue of Stone* (1947), Mary Renault's *North Face* (1949), and Norah Hoult's *There Were No Windows* (1944).

Elizabeth Taylor paints a bleak *View of the Harbour* of post-war England in 1947. This world, as she describes it, offers a poor haven to the lonely, the dying, the divorced and the widowed. After the camaraderie and purpose of the war, people have little to say to each other. The empty pub displays a soiled card with the words ' "We Do Not Recognise the Possibility of Defeat" . . . hanging crookedly over the bar' (15). Nevertheless, the work of reconstruction is taking some tentative first steps. In Taylor's story 'Gravement Endommage'[3] wartime separation has nearly wrecked Richard and Louise's marriage. The couple spend the first day of their holiday in France, where 'War had exhaled a vapour of despair over all the scene. Grass grew over grief, trying to hide collapse, to cover some of the wounds.' Hearing the 'faint sound of trowel on stone' in the small wrecked town, Richard thinks of the hard work ahead for both literal and emotional rebuilders, 'camping-out in the shadow of even greater disaster, raking ashes, the vision lost'. As the story ends the bad-tempered Louise grudgingly accepts a drink, and,

Oh, from the most unpromising material, he thought, but he did seem to see some glimmer ahead, if only of his own patience, his own perseverance, which appeared, in this frame of mind, in this place, a small demand on him. (306)

Mary Renault's *North Face* also charts the difficulty of establishing relationships in this damaged world: the main character's fondness for difficult rock-climbing gives Renault her metaphor for life in post-war England. Marghanita Laski's *Little Boy Lost* (1949) moves to mainland Europe to survey the damage, with the suggestion that ' "you English do not begin to comprehend what Europe is like today" ' (119). Laski's protagonist manages to find and rescue his son among the ruins, the lost boy is found. Although the novel is sentimental it does ask its readers to look beyond the shores of England and contemplate the wider world of loss and ruin.

Two novels of post-war London, Margery Allingham's *The Tiger in the Smoke* (1952) and Rose Macaulay's *The World My Wilderness* (1950), bear witness to the scars inflicted upon the city and its population. Allingham's London is an ailing giant beset by fog. The smouldering bombsites show London still smoking from the blitz, the war is only slowly drawing to a close.[4] The action of the novel takes place in and around Crumb Street: this is a world of left-overs and unfinished business, the shady underworld of London in the aftermath of the war. Albert Campion and Divisional Detective Chief Inspector Luke agree, ' "Oh lord, yes, there's violence about . . . You can't miss it" ' (27). War refuses to finish cleanly from one day to the next and Allingham's gang of criminals are portrayed as its direct products. The army formed to fight for the nation has been disbanded; now bereft of purpose and employment, it regroups on the streets to fight for itself. We see it first in its masquerade form as a street band. ' "Ex-Service, I suppose?" ' guesses Campion. ' "Who isn't?" Luke was irritable. "I bet you every man under sixty in this street is ex-Service, and half the women too" ' (26). Allingham's army of rejects are physically and mentally disabled. Mutilated and dispossessed by the war, they seek their revenge from their den underneath the streets of the city. The prisoner taken to their 'vast shadowy cavern' immediately identifies its particular neatness:

He had seen places like it before, when a Company on active service under a good sergeant had dug itself in in some long-held position. Everywhere there were signs of discipline and a particular kind of personality. No rubbish or odds-and-ends were in sight, but all round the walls little packages of possessions, tied up in sacking, were hung neatly on nails, very much as one finds them in old-fashioned cottages or blacksmiths' shops. It was a definite variety of bachelor establishment, in fact; primitive and wholly masculine, yet not without a trace of civilization. (77)

This mock barrack is the breeding-ground for England's other army in the years after the war, educating its men in resentment and cruelty.

Rose Macaulay's *The World My Wilderness* (1950) also takes place among the bombsites of London, the setting for thoughts about readjustment. It is 1946, and Macaulay examines the wounds the war has left on a physically whole but psychologically damaged child. Seventeen-year-old Barbary has run wild with the maquis (the guerrilla bands of the French Resistance) in the South of France; her mother decides she needs civilising and sends her to her lawyer father in London (Barbary's parents have divorced and remarried). But some scars lie too deep for easy cure, and as Macaulay's biographer Jane Emery points out, the novel 'holds no brief for the family as a dependable bulwark'.[5] Damaged by the war, Barbary has taken on the guerrilla ways of the maquis and practises them wherever she is transposed. The Highlands of Scotland and the bombsites of London become Barbary's new maquis, the 'jungle' as she sees it.[6] But what was heroic in wartime becomes anti-social and undesirable in peacetime. What Barbary admires as the 'London Resistance movement' (61) in the bombsites is a world of petty crime, whose denizens are spivs, pickpockets, deserters and black marketeers. On the run from a policeman, Barbary 'stepped forward into nothingness, plunged steeply down a chasm into the stony ruins of a deep cellar' (195) and into a coma which, as Phyllis Lassner observes, shows that her kind of 'anarchy' is 'no solution, only an escape into inertia'.[7] When Barbary recovers it is time to move on, the resistance is over. Studying art in Paris is offered as the road to readjustment. Barbary the barbarian is on her way to being civilised, but with no danger of over-doing it, which is the fate of her 'exquisite' brother Richie. He reacts against 'three years of messy, noisy and barbaric war' with a delight in luxury and a distaste for the idea of ' "the century of the common man" ' (21).

For Macaulay herself the blitz was a time of loss and near despair. She was strongly opposed to the mythic constructions of cheery cockneys appearing in print, and her journalism was censored, according to Jane Emery, 'because she had reported a demolition worker saying, in the midst of fire, smoke, explosion and ruin, "How long can people stick it? Where will it all end?" ' The apprehension of despair and damnation permeates *The World My Wilderness*. It is 1946, but the war has not finished. Macaulay describes immorality on the bombsites of London, old scores being settled in France,[8] and a vision of the barbaric everywhere beneath the surface. Richie considers the Pyrenean foothills:

> The peace that shrouded land and sea was a mask, lying thinly over terror, over hate, over cruel deeds done. Barbarism prowled and padded, lurking in the hot sunshine, in the warm scents of the maquis, in the deep shadows of the forest. Visigoths, Franks, Catalans, Spanish, French, Germans, Anglo-American armies, savageries without number, the Gestapo torturing captured French patriots, rounding up fleeing Jews, the Resistance murdering, derailing trains full of people, lurking in the shadows to kill, collaborators betraying Jews and escaped prisoners, working together with the victors, being in their turn killed and mauled, hunted down by mobs hot with rage; everywhere cruelty, everywhere vengeance, everywhere the barbarian on the march. (149)

War does not end with the war, but the historian in Macaulay contextualises. 1946 is the moment when Britain can at last open the gates of the fortress, and the geography of her novel extends to include a view of England as others see us. Barbary's step-grandmother injects a refreshing counterblast to the saviours of the free world:

> Madame Michel, a good anglophobe, disliked the British, who lacked literature, culture, language and manners, had run away from the boches in 1940 and left France to face them, and now gave themselves the airs of liberators, when any liberating that had not been done by the French themselves had been the work of the Americans . . . England, she thought, always came well out of every war, losing neither lives nor money, while France was bled white. (9, 13)

Long perspectives can heal, and Macaulay mobilises the past in the novel's work of consolation. Barbary painting 'the rambling ruins to the west, where Silver Street ran through a golden and green and purple wilderness, past S. Olave's churchyard, past the halls of Parish Clerks and Coach-makers, past the Coopers' Arms to Noble Street and tiny Monkwell Street that ran north to Cripplegate' (159) is herself painted by Macaulay into a rich context. The streets, churches, shops and people that were London in the past criss-cross the present in a positive refrain. What sometimes appears as a Waste Land (Macaulay quotes from T.S. Eliot's poem throughout the book) is humanised and ordered by the pressure of the city's benign and guiding ghosts. The cycle of life will continue, civilisation will return. The rich and colourful ghosts 'of Noble Street and Addle Street . . . the landlady of the Post Office Hotel at the corner of Lilypot Lane, the drinkers in the Coopers' Arms and in Peter Barbierie's refreshment rooms' are on the side of reconstruction, 'lending the law the silent support of some eight centuries of property and substance' (193).

Barbary's bombsite can be enjoyed as a temporary playground, and Macaulay herself liked to scramble perilously among the ruins.[9] The cockney Mavis and her creator both hum to Marie Lloyd's tune, ' "I am very, very fond of ruins, ruins I love to scan" ' (71); Macaulay's next book was *Pleasure of Ruins* (1953). But she has no illusions. Ruins must be rebuilt, civilisation reclaimed from barbarism. In the last scene of the novel Richie watches the excavators starting to identify the different strata of London: 'civilised intelligence was at work among the ruins' (252). The weeds retreat to the country as 'men's will to recovery strove against the drifting wilderness to halt and tame it'. Barbary leaves the ruins; and her stepbrother Raoul, a confederate from maquis days, agrees to compromise: ' "I shall collaborate. That is to say, I shall observe the laws, go daily to school, obey my uncle and aunt, attend mass on Sundays, keep out of the way of the police" ' (236).

Rebuilding and compromise reclaim much of Macaulay's wilderness, but some terrain is intractable. Issues of guilt, repentance and atonement hover unresolved. The words of the 'Dies Irae' thunder through the ruined churches which are haunted by deranged clergymen – ' "We are in hell now," he said, staring apprehensively about him' (166). Barbary feels guilty about her collaborator stepfather, whom she failed to save from her maquis friends. More generally the book asks and does not answer how to deal with the guilt of the war. Barbary, who suffered sexual abuse at the hands of the Germans and whose namesake is the 'forsaken' maid in *Othello*, is a damaged soul with only the fragments of religion to help her. She has a strong belief in hell and says her prayers before the 'phantom altar' of a ruined church, 'reciting lines from the torn hymn-book pages that she kept in a niche by the wall' (185). The novel was Macaulay's own 'unconscious prayer',[10] and ends in a precarious equilibrium out in the wilderness caused by the war, where 'the shells of churches gaped like lost myths, and the jungle pressed in on them, seeking to cover them up' (254).

The last word in this study belongs to Elizabeth Bowen, the novelist who has left such a subtle record of the war's shifting moods. Her story, 'I Hear

You Say So' (1945),[11] evokes the ending of the war as a moment of intensity made strange by the new conditions of peace. 'A week after VE Day, the nightingale came to London', and in the park the warm dark evening reverberates with possibility. Objects in rooms newly illuminated after years of black-out stand out 'with stereoscopic sharpness in this intensified element of life'; 'The balance of vases on brackets and pyramids of mock fruit in bowls all seemed miraculous after all that had happened.' The nightingale is, like Keats's bird, 'too happy in thine happiness', and the people in the park are not ready to understand what they are listening to. One decides that the birdsong is on the wireless, another says ' "that must be a thrush" '. ' "It's too soon," ' says a third, ' "Much too soon, after a war like this. Even Victory's nearly been too much. There ought not to have been a nightingale in the same week." ' To the young widow, who is woken by the nightingale in the room where her husband had slept as a boy, the song brings wonderful consolation. It transports her into the past which she and her husband never had time to share: 'Ursula felt in the presence of someone she had not met yet.' The nightingale brings her 'profound happiness' in its creation of 'the magic dilatory past they had not had; their, really, irreparable loss.' The listeners in the park may not be ready for the nightingale yet; the war is only ' "half" ' over, but at least they 'hear' the nightingale 'say so', and look uncertainly towards the future: ' "You begin to wonder. I don't say I know how I feel, but I seem to know how I could. I can't help thinking – suppose the world was made for happiness, after all?" '

NOTES

The place of publication is London unless otherwise stated.

Introduction (pp. 1–15)

1. J.B. Priestley, *British Women Go To War*, Collins, 1943, 56. Women who described the war as a great learning experience include Edith Summerskill, 'Conscription and Women', *The Fortnightly*, March 1942; Margaret Goldsmith, *Women at War*, Lindsay Drummond Ltd, 1943; and Peggy Scott, *British Women in War*, Hutchinson, 1940. The journalist Anne Scott-James claimed that 'women have a new independence. They are free as they never were free before', *London Calling*, November 1942. Historians debate whether the war improved the position of women in the long term, but even revisionists stress that 'participation in the war effort ... constituted an experience of major personal importance for many women, which has been largely hidden and forgotten since the war,' Penny Summerfield, 'Women, War and Social Change: Women in Britain in World War II', in *Total War and Social Change*, ed. Arthur Marwick, Macmillan, 1988, 114.

2. David Cannadine, 'War and Death, Grief and Mourning in Modern Britain', in *Mirrors of Mortality: Studies in the Social History of Death*, ed. J. Whaley, Europa Publications Ltd, 1981.

3. *The Times*, 12 November 1920, quoted in Cannadine, 224.

4. See *The Speeches of Winston Churchill*, ed. David Cannadine, Penguin, 1990.

5. Winifred Peck, *There is a Fortress*, Faber, 1945, 113.

6. Peter Hennessy, *Never Again, Britain 1945–1951*, Jonathan Cape, 1992, 4.

7. Some excellent work is now starting to appear: Gill Plain, *Women's Fiction of the Second World War, Gender, Power and Resistance*, Edinburgh University Press, Edinburgh, 1996; Phyllis Lassner, 'The Quiet Revolution: World War

II and the English Domestic Novel', *Mosaic*, 23/3, 1990; 'Reimagining the Arts of War: Language and History in Elizabeth Bowen's *The Heat of the Day* and Rose Macaulay's *The World My Wilderness*', *Perspectives on Contemporary Literature*, vol. 14, 1988, and forthcoming book.

8. Cyril Garbett, *Reading in War-Time*, The English Association Presidential Address, Oxford University Press, Oxford, 1945, 3.

9. *New Statesman and Nation*, 29 March 1941.

10. Elizabeth Bowen, Preface to the American Edition of *The Demon Lover* (1945), reprinted in *Collected Impressions*, Longmans, Green & Co., 1950, 50.

11. Elizabeth Dunn, 'Women's Minds', *Spectator*, 24 December 1943.

12. *The Times*, 27 October 1939.

13. Janet Teissier du Cros, *Divided Loyalties, A Scotswoman in Occupied France*, 1962, reprinted by Canongate Press, Edinburgh, 1992, 184. Jane Planet appreciated Austen's ability 'to restore a sense of smallness to us who are finding the world a large unwieldy mass that insists on smothering our lives', *What Should Mrs A Do?* Thacker & Co., Bombay, 1945, 93.

14. See E.M. Delafield's Introduction to Georgina Battiscombe, *Charlotte Mary Yonge, The Story of an Uneventful Life*, Constable, 1943, 11.

15. Letters of Mrs Elizabeth Belsey, Department of Documents, Imperial War Museum.

16. Rosamond Lehmann, 'Letter to a Friend', *Penguin New Writing*, vol. 5, 1941.

17. Diana Hopkinson, 'Love in War', Department of Documents Typescript, Imperial War Museum.

18. See, for example, Eunice Buckley's *Destination Unknown*, Andrew Dakers, 1942. Buckley's novels seem to be directed to a small but identifiable readership sympathetic to European refugees.

19. *Times Literary Supplement*, 29 August 1942.

20. *Times Literary Supplement*, 23 May 1942.

21. *Time and Tide*, 24 August 1940.

22. See, for example, Robert Hewison, *Under Siege, Literary Life in London 1939–1945*, Methuen, 1977, 86.

23. See Joseph McAleer, *Popular Reading and Publishing in Britain 1914–1950*, Clarendon Press, Oxford, 1992, for figures. There were: 1095 new adult fiction titles in 1944, compared to 2046 in 1936. The drop in reprints is greater: 160 in 1944 compared to 2862 in 1936 (52).

24. See Frances Spalding, *Stevie Smith, A Critical Biography*, Faber, 1988, 169.

25. Steve Chibnall, 'Pulp Versus Penguins: Paperbacks Go To War', in *War Culture: Social Change and Changing Experience in World War Two*, eds Pat Kirkham and David Thoms, Lawrence & Wishart, 1995, 135.

26. Elizabeth Dunn, 'Women's Minds', *Spectator*, 24 December 1943.

27. Agatha Christie, *An Autobiography*, Collins, 1977, 505.

28. David Mellor, ed., *A Paradise Lost: The Neo-Romantic Imagination in Britain 1935–1955*, Lund Humphries Ltd in Association with the Barbican Art

Gallery, 1987, 12.

29. Keith Williams, *British Writers and the Media, 1930–1945*, Macmillan, 1996, 217.

30. See Sue Harper: 'The Representations of Women in British Feature Films, 1939–45' in *British Cinema and the Second World War*, ed. Philip M. Taylor, Macmillan, 1988. See also Sue Aspinall, 'Women, Realism and Reality in British Films, 1943–53' in *British Cinema History*, eds James Curran and Vincent Porter, Weidenfeld & Nicolson, 1983.

31. Pat Kirkham, 'Fashioning the Feminine: dress, appearance and femininity in wartime Britain' in *Nationalising Femininity: Culture, Sexuality and British Cinema in the Second World War*, eds Christine Gledhill and Gillian Swanson, Manchester University Press, Manchester, 1996. See also Pat Kirkham, 'Beauty and Duty: Keeping Up the (Home) Front' in *War Culture*, eds Pat Kirkham and David Thoms; and Janice Winship, 'Women's Magazines: times of war and management of the self in *Woman's Own*' in *Nationalising Femininity*.

32. Angus Calder, *The People's War, Britain 1939–1945*, Jonathan Cape, 1969; Pimlico, 1992, 506. See also Hewison, *Under Siege*, 88–89.

33. E.M. Forster 'Books in 1941', *Listener*, 10 July 1941.

34. Raymond Mortimer, *New Statesman and Nation*, 30 September 1944.

35. Diana Trilling, 'What Has Happened to our Novels?', *Harper's Magazine*, New York, May 1944.

36. During the war those differences were so marked that written introductions between the two nations were considered necessary. Phyllis Bentley wrote *Here is America* for British readers when America entered the war, and when American servicemen arrived in Britain they were given a booklet called *Over There; Instructions for American Servicemen in Britain*, 1942; reprinted by The Bodleian Library, University of Oxford, 1994. The American woman's experience differed markedly from her English counterpart in that, according to Jean Bethke Elshtain and Sheila Tobias, in America 'most women were housewives during the war . . . Nine out of ten mothers with children were *not* in the labour force and most women did not sign up', *Women, Militarism and War*, Rowman & Littlefield, Maryland, 1990, 105. American women writers tended to refer to the war in Europe in very different terms from their contemporary British counterparts, as we can see from novels as diverse as Frances Parkinson Keyes's *Joy Street* (1951), and Ann Petry's *The Street* (1946).

37. Ethel Mannin, 'Contemporary British Fiction', *Modern Reading* 8, ed. R. Moore, 1943.

38. Robert Graves, 'War Poetry in this War', *Listener*, 23 November 1941.

39. Arthur Koestler, 'The Birth of a Myth', *Horizon*, April 1943.

40. See A.T. Tolley, *The Poetry of the Forties*, Manchester University Press, Manchester, 1985, 18.

41. Review of *Night Shift* reprinted on the back of *It Was Different at the Time*;

H.G. Wells and Rebecca West were also admirers. Holden's published output from the war years included *Night Shift* (1941), *It Was Different at the Time* (1943), *There's No Story There* (1944), and *To the Boating* (1945).

42. See Frances Spalding, *Stevie Smith*, 151.

43. Robert Hewison, *Under Siege*, Chapter Three; Adam Piette, *Imagination at War, British Fiction and Poetry 1939–45*, Macmillan, 1995, 5–7.

44. See, for example, The Countess of Ranfurly, *To War With Whitaker*, Heinemann, 1994; Joan Wyndham, *Love Lessons*, Harper Collins, 1986; Mary Wesley, *The Camomile Lawn*, Macmillan, 1984.

45. Frank Swinnerton, 'The Writer in Wartime', *Harper's Magazine*, August 1942. There were probably many more.

46. Agatha Christie, *An Autobiography*, Collins, 1977, 505; Janet Morgan, *Agatha Christie: A Biography*, Collins, 1984, 253. Christie's other war work in a hospital dispensary presumably bore more useful fruit.

47. See Margaret Forster, *Daphne du Maurier*, Chatto & Windus, 1993, 150–151. Women are well represented in anthologies published on behalf of wartime causes. See, for example, *Voices on the Green*, eds A.R.J. Wise and Reginald A. Smith, Michael Joseph, 1945, which has contributions by Vita Sackville-West, Vera Brittain, Ethel Mannin, Phyllis Bottome, F. Tennyson Jesse and others, and raised funds for Manchester hospitals.

48. Diary entry for 6 September 1939, *The Diary of Virginia Woolf*, vol. V (1936–1941), ed. A.O. Bell, The Hogarth Press, 1984, 235.

49. Elizabeth Bowen, Preface to the American Edition of *The Demon Lover*, Collected Impressions, Longmans, Green & Co., 1950.

50. Adam Piette, *Imagination at War*, 5.

51. Robert Hewison, *Under Siege*, xv, 211.

52. Diary entry for 28 March 1941, quoted in Angela Bull, *Noel Streatfeild*, Collins, 1984, 180.

53. Bull, 159.

54. See Bull, 172.

55. *The Winter is Past* (1940); *I Ordered a Table for Six* (1942); and *Saplings* (1945).

56. Denis Mallard, 'New Novels', *Time and Tide*, 12 June 1943.

57. See, for example, Carola Oman's 1940 novel *Nothing to Report*: the chapter titles are all dates, following the characters in their domestic rounds through the months of 1939 up to 'Midsummer 1940'.

58. 'The Duty of the Writer', *Writers in Freedom, A Symposium Based on the XVII International Congress of the PEN Club Held in London in September 1941*, ed. Hermon Ould, Hutchinson, 1942, 14.

59. Ould, 24.

60. Ould, 52.

61. 'The Leaning Tower' (1940), *The Moment and Other Essays*, The Hogarth Press, 1947. Woolf's biographer, Hermione Lee, considers that her political writing from this period 'has tended to be misunderstood and undervalued',

Virginia Woolf, Chatto & Windus, 1996, 681.

62. Virginia Woolf, *Three Guineas* (1938); The Hogarth Press, 1986, 122.

63. Not unequivocally, as Lee's biography shows.

64. See, for example, Christine Gledhill and Gillian Swanson, eds, Introduction to *Nationalising Femininity: Culture, Sexuality and British Cinema in the Second World War*, 2. Also, Penny Summerfield, ' "The girl that makes the thing that drills the hole that holds the spring . . .": discourses of women and work in the Second World War', in Gledhill and Swanson, eds, 42, 50.

65. Pat Kirkham, 'Fashioning the feminine: dress, appearance and femininity in wartime Britain' and Antonia Lant, 'Mobile Femininity' in Christine Gledhill and Gillian Swanson, eds, *Nationalising Femininity*.

66. Daphne du Maurier, *The Years Between*, ed. Fidelis Morgan, Virago, 1994.

67. Margaret Forster, *Daphne du Maurier*, 178–179, 189–190.

68. See Gellhorn's Afterword to the Virago edition, 1986.

69. Letter of 1939, quoted in Afterword, 310.

70. See, for example, Elizabeth Simpson in Barbara Noble's *The House Opposite*, Heinemann, 1943.

71. Elizabeth Bowen, Preface to the American Edition of *The Demon Lover* (1945), *Collected Impressions*.

72. E.J. Scovell, *Selected Poems*, Carcanet, Manchester, 1991, 44–45.

73. Jean Bethke Elshtain has observed, 'War retains the power to incite parts of the self that peace cannot seem to reach', *Women and War*, Harvester, Brighton, 1987, 9.

1. Blitz and the Mothers of England, pp. 16–31

1. Angus Calder, *The Myth of the Blitz*, Jonathan Cape, 1991, 148.

2. Frances Faviell, *A Chelsea Concerto*, Cassell, 1959, 115.

3. Bryher, *Beowulf*, Pantheon Books, New York, 1956, 84.

4. Inez Holden, *Night Shift*, John Lane, The Bodley Head, 1941, 49.

5. Anthony Burgess quoted in Hermione Lee, Preface to *The Mulberry Tree, Writings of Elizabeth Bowen*, Virago, 1986; Angus Wilson, Introduction to *The Collected Stories of Elizabeth Bowen*, Jonathan Cape, 1980; Penguin, 1983.

6. 'London, 1940' reprinted in *Collected Impressions*, Longmans, 1950. For a discussion of 'Mysterious Kor', 'The Demon Lover', 'In the Square' and 'The Happy Autumn Fields', see below, Chapters 3 and 8.

7. E.J. Scovell, 'Daylight Alert', written in the 1940s, reprinted in *Collected Poems*, Carcanet, Manchester, 1988.

8. For further discussion of *The Heat of the Day*, see below, Chapter 5.

9. Angus Calder's talk 'Return to Realism' at the Royal Festival Hall in March 1995 illuminated this aspect of the surreal in representations of the war.

10. Inez Holden, *To the Boating*, John Lane, The Bodley Head, 1945.

11. *Times Literary Supplement*, 7 March 1942.

12. For another novel with a bomb-damaged form, see Lettice Cooper's *Black*

Bethlehem (1947), split into three parts, with three separate sets of characters and a twisted chronology.

13. David Mellor, 'The Body and the Land' in *A Paradise Lost: The Neo-Romantic Imagination in Britain 1935–55*, ed. David Mellor, Lund Humphries Ltd, in Association with the Barbican Art Gallery, 1987, 22.

14. Melanie Klein, 'The Oedipus Complex in the Light of Early Anxieties' (1945), *Contributions to Psycho-Analysis*, The Hogarth Press, 1968, 339–390. See also Juliet Mitchell, ed., *The Selected Melanie Klein Reader*, Penguin 1986, Introduction, 20.

15. According to Raynes Minns, 'by January 1940, 88 per cent of mothers and 86 per cent of child evacuees had returned home', *Bombers and Mash, The Domestic Front 1939–45*, Virago, 1980, 24.

16. Amoral Ben and Em'ly belong to the tribe of the Artful Dodger, revitalised by Eve Garnett's award-winning classic *The Family from One End Street*, published in 1937 and reprinted almost every year over the next two decades.

17. In *The Thirties and After* (Fontana, 1978), Stephen Spender remarks on 'the religious mood of the war . . . the sense of the sacred . . . the feeling that after the war a better world must come into existence: an England like Blake's Jerusalem' (96).

2. From Class to Community in Fortress England, pp. 32–52

1. See, for example, the work of Richard Titmuss and Arthur Marwick. For a summary and critique of this view see Penny Summerfield, 'The Levelling of Class', in *War and Social Change, British Society in the Second World War*, ed. Harold Smith, Manchester University Press, Manchester, 1986.

2. Speech of 20 August 1940, *The Speeches of Winston Churchill*, ed. David Cannadine, Penguin, 1990, 181.

3. A.J.P. Taylor, *English History, 1914–1945*, Oxford, 1965, 600.

4. Paul Addison, *The Road to 1945, British Politics and the Second World War*, Jonathan Cape, 1975, 14.

5. Steven Fielding, Peter Thompson and Nick Tiratsoo, *'England arise!' The Labour Party and popular politics in 1940s Britain*, Manchester University Press, Manchester, 1995, 26.

6. Adam Piette, *Imagination at War, British Fiction and Poetry 1939–1945*, Macmillan, 1995, 4–5.

7. Addison, 23. See also Peter Hennessy on 'war socialism', *Never Again, Britain 1945–51*, Jonathan Cape, 1992, 50, 52.

8. 'London 1940', reprinted in *Collected Impressions*, Longmans, Green & Co. 1950.

9. Letter of 1945 to William Plomer, quoted in Victoria Glendinning, *Elizabeth Bowen, Portrait of a Writer*, Weidenfeld & Nicolson, 1977, 166.

10. Evadne Price, *Jane At War*, Robert Hale Ltd, n.d. 28.

11. The juvenile Jane at war probably acted out the wishes of many adults in her

successful campaigns against the surly gardener and the cockney evacuee; in 1940 *Jane the Patient* wins a ferocious class war against two elderly working-class women patients in her hospital ward.

12. *Spectator*, 17 November 1939, 22 December 1939, and 12 January 1940.
13. Dorothy L. Sayers, *Striding Folly*, 1972, Hodder & Stoughton, 1988.
14. Anne Maybury, *Arise, Oh Sun!*, Collins, 1942, 33.
15. Patricia Wentworth, *Miss Silver Intervenes*, Hodder & Stoughton, 1944, 205.
16. Quoted in D.J. Taylor, *After the War, The Novel and English Society since 1945*, Chatto & Windus, 1993, 13.
17. Diana Trilling, Review of *Marling Hall*, 1942, reprinted in *Reviewing the Forties*, Harcourt Brace Jovanovich, New York, 1978, 12.
18. Keith Douglas wrote his poem 'Aristocrats' in 1943, reprinted in *Complete Poems*, Oxford University Press, Oxford, 1978.
19. Ethel Mannin, 'Do Women Writers Lack Distinction?', *London Calling*, 261, 8 October 1944. See also Mannin on 'Contemporary British Fiction' in *Modern Reading*, 8, ed. R. Moore, 1943.
20. Reprinted in *Wave Me Goodbye, Stories of the Second World War*, ed. Anne Boston, Virago, 1988; Penguin, 1989.
21. Sylvia Townsend Warner, *The Museum of Cheats*, 1947, reprinted in *Selected Stories*, Virago, 1990.
22. Simon Featherstone, 'The Nation as Pastoral in British Literature of the Second World War', *Journal of European Studies*, vol. 16, 155–168. The tendency of blitz novels to remove London to the country (see above, Chapter One) shows a further use of pastoral in wartime, to recuperate the damaged city.
23. The phrase 'home-made socialism' comes from a Home Intelligence study of public opinion in 1942, quoted in Addison, *The Road to 1945*, 162–63.
24. Paul Fussell, *Wartime, Understanding and Behaviour in the Second World War*, Oxford University Press, Oxford, 1989, 171.
25. Review of Jacobine Menzies-Wilson's *The Eye of a Needle*, *Times Literary Supplement*, 18 July 1942.
26. Edith Pargeter's trilogy, *The Eighth Champion of Christendom* (1945, 1946 and 1947) also follows the army, but Pargeter focuses on the individual rather than the group, on action rather than lull.
27. Gillian Beer, 'Dispersed as we are', *Times Literary Supplement*, 30 June 1995.
28. Introduction to Virago edition 1988, ix.
29. Virago Introduction, v.
30. Sylvia Townsend Warner, *Letters*, ed. W. Maxwell, Chatto & Windus, 1982, 63.
31. *The Diaries of Sylvia Townsend Warner*, ed. Claire Harman, Virago, 1995, 116, 117.
32. Wendy Mulford, *This Narrow Place, Sylvia Townsend Warner and Valentine Ackland: Life, Letters and Politics 1930–1951*, Pandora Press, 1988, 199.

33. Diary entry for 14 June 1940, *Diaries*, 104.

34. Stephen Spender, *The Thirties and After*, Fontana, 1978, 96.

35. Ian McLaine, *Ministry of Morale, Home Front Morale and the Ministry of Information in World War II*, George Allen & Unwin, 1979, 29.

36. Quoted in Virago introduction, vi.

37. See Claire Harman, *Sylvia Townsend Warner, A Biography*, Chatto & Windus, 1989, 194. The woes of Gunner Brock, whose precious books are donated in his absence to a National Salvage Week book mile, are the subject of Townsend Warner's story 'English Climate', *The Museum of Cheats and Other Stories*, Chatto & Windus, 1947.

38. Claire Harman, *Sylvia Townsend Warner*, 192–193.

39. 'Sylvia Townsend Warner in Conversation', quoted in Wendy Mulford, *This Narrow Place, Sylvia Townsend Warner and Valentine Ackland*, 197.

3. Open House and Closed Doors, pp. 53–70

1. Antonia White, *BBC At War*, BBC, 1941, 3.

2. Tom Hickman, *What Did You Do in the War, Auntie?*, BBC Books, 1995, 215.

3. Barbara Pym, 'Home Front Novel' (1939), in *Civil to Strangers and Other Writings*, Macmillan, 1987, 226.

4. See, for example, G.D.H. and Margaret Cole's *Toper's End*, Collins, 1942; and Christianna Brand's *Heads You Lose*, John Lane, The Bodley Head, 1941.

5. Sylvia Townsend Warner, 'Sweethearts and Wives', *The Museum of Cheats* 1947, reprinted in *Wave Me Goodbye, Stories of the Second World War*, ed. Anne Boston, Virago 1988; Penguin, 1989.

6. Margaret Cole, 'General Effects: Billeting' in *Evacuation Survey: A Report to the Fabian Society*, eds R. Padley and M. Cole, Routledge, 1940, 72.

7. Sylvia Townsend Warner, 'The Proper Circumstances', *The New Yorker*, 1944, reprinted in *One Thing Leading to Another and Other Stories*, ed. Susanna Pinney, Chatto & Windus, The Hogarth Press, 1984.

8. Sylvia Townsend Warner, 'Noah's Ark', *A Garland of Straw and Other Stories*, Chatto & Windus, 1943.

9. In a talk on women writers and the war, Royal Festival Hall, March 1995, Gillian Beer pointed out how, for many evacuees, the accommodation to war and country life went together.

10. See, for example, Dorothy Bowers's *A Deed without a Name*, Hodder & Stoughton, 1940; G.D.H. and Margaret Cole's *Toper's End*, Collins, 1942; and Agatha Christie's *N or M?*, Collins, 1941.

11. See, for example, Stella Gibbons's *The Bachelor*, Longmans, Green & Co., 1944; and Lettice Cooper's *Black Bethlehem*, Gollancz, 1947.

12. Barbara Pym, 'So Very Secret' (1940–1941), *Civil to Strangers and Other Writings*, Macmillan, 1987, 275.

13. Benefiting from the shortage of domestic servants in England, women from continental Europe could sometimes obtain work permits more easily than

men, and 'a German Jewish newspaper pointed out as early as December 1936, women proved to be more adaptable than men.' Marion Berghahn, 'Women Emigrés in England' in *Between Sorrow and Strength, Women Refugees of the Nazi Period*, ed. Sibylle Quack, Cambridge University Press, Cambridge, 1995.

14. Sylvia Townsend Warner, 'Emil', *Winter in the Air and Other Stories*, Chatto & Windus, 1955.

15. Fiction illustrated the drastic depopulation, from the 'twenty indoors and out at Miss Brandon's place' in Angela Thirkell's *The Brandons* (1939), through Mrs Framley's maid, secretary and butler in Noel Streatfeild's *I Ordered a Table for Six* (1942), to the vanished maids of Mollie Panter-Downes's *One Fine Day* (1947): 'Like young horses intoxicated with the feel of their freedom, Ethel and Violet had disappeared squealing into the big bright world where there were no bells to run your legs off.'

16. George Begley, *Keep Mum! Advertising Goes to War*, Lemon Tree Press, 1975, 30.

17. Virginia Woolf, diary entry for 29 December 1940, *The Diaries of Virginia Woolf*, vol. V, 1936–1941, ed. A.O. Bell, The Hogarth Press, 1984, 347.

18. Daphne du Maurier, *The Years Between*, 1944, reprinted in *The Years Between*, ed. Fidelis Morgan, Virago, 1994, 347.

19. Barbara Pym, 'So Very Secret' (1940–1941), *Civil to Strangers*, 277.

20. *Fifty Facts about British Women at War*, British Information Services, New York, 1944.

21. Sylvia Townsend Warner, 'From Above', *A Garland of Straw and Other Stories*, Chatto & Windus, 1943.

22. Elizabeth Bowen, *The Heat of the Day*, Jonathan Cape, 1949; Penguin, 1962, 94–95.

23. Penny Summerfield and Nicole Crockett, ' "You weren't taught that with the welding": Lessons in Sexuality in the Second World War', *Women's History Review*, vol.1, no. 3, 1992.

24. 'The War . . . finally killed off any of the last remaining traces of the reckless spirit of E.M. Hull and E.M. Dell or Elinor Glyn,' in Rachel Anderson, *The Purple Heart Throbs, The Sub-Literature of Love*, Hodder & Stoughton, 1974, 212, 223. See also Mary Cadogan, *And Then Their Hearts Stood Still*, Macmillan, 1994, 170–178.

25. Diana Murray Hill, *Ladies May Now Leave Their Machines*, The Pilot Press, 1944, 7. See also Inez Holden, *Night Shift*, John Lane, The Bodley Head, 1941; Monica Dickens, *The Fancy*, Michael Joseph, 1943 and the wartime diaries of Kathleen Church-Bliss and Elsie Whiteman, 'We Had to Laugh', Typescript, Department of Documents, Imperial War Museum.

26. Mary Renault, Afterword to Virago edition of *The Friendly Young Ladies*, 1984.

27. Margery Sharp, 'Night Engagement', *Lilliput*, 1941, reprinted in *Wave Me Goodbye*.

28. Diana Gardner, 'The Landgirl', *Horizon*, 1940, reprinted in *Wave Me Goodbye*.

29. Julian Maclaren-Ross, himself a *Horizon* protégé, recalled that the ubiquitous poetry editor Tambimuttu 'thought it would be good for my career to marry a girl called Diana Gardner' who 'had made a big stir in *Horizon* . . . Tambi felt that as presumably kindred souls we should make it a *Horizon* wedding, with Cyril Connolly to give away the bride and famous contributors outside the church to hold copies of the magazine over us when we emerged, as Guardees form an arch with their swords over a newly-wedded comrade and his wife. The fact that I wasn't yet divorced was held to be a minor detail, but actually I never even met Diana Gardner who had the good sense to not come round the pubs.' (Julian Maclaren-Ross, *Memoirs of the Forties*, Alan Ross Ltd, 1965, 144.)

30. See Barbara Skelton, *Tears Before Bedtime*, Hamish Hamilton, 1987.

31. Joan Wyndham, *Love Lessons, A Wartime Diary*, Heinemann, 1985, 112.

32. Virginia Woolf, diary entries for 11 and 13 June 1940, *Diary*, vol. 5, 294–295.

33. Sylvia Townsend Warner, 'Rosie Flounders', *The Museum of Cheats and Other Stories*, Chatto & Windus, 1947.

34. Looking back thirty years later, Bryher begins her wartime memoirs unambiguously: 'In wartime the only things that matter are a blanket, some food and one's friends', *The Days of Mars, A Memoir 1940–1946*, Calder & Boyars, 1972, ix.

4. Work and the Recalcitrant Factory, pp. 71–87

1. Ralph Assheton, 'The Call-Up of Women', *Listener*, 10 April 1941.

2. See John Costello, *Love, Sex and War, Changing Values 1939–45*, Collins, 1985, 208.

3. Denise Riley, *War in the Nursery, Theories of the Child and Mother*, Virago, 1983, 129. See also Penny Summerfield, *Women Workers in the Second World War, Production and Patriarchy in Conflict*, Croom Helm, 1984.

4. Song quoted in Theodora Benson, *Sweethearts and Wives, Their Part in War*, Faber, 1942, 23.

5. Antonia Lant, *Blackout: Reinventing Women for Wartime British Cinema*, Princeton University Press, New Jersey, 1991, 28.

6. Each country approached the problem in its own way. Leila Rupp demonstrates the difference between German and American campaigns to persuade women into factory work. American campaigns made 'factory work seem exciting' and 'glorified work as a glamorous duty', Leila J. Rupp, *Mobilizing Women for War, German and American Propaganda 1939–1945*, Princeton University Press, New Jersey, 1978, 178.

7. See Celia Fremlin, *War Factory*, 1943; The Cresset Library, Century Hutchinson 1978, 45.

8. See the *Listener* for reports of many of these talks.

9. The Imperial War Museum holds many unpublished memoirs of women's war work. For facts, figures and details, see Jane Waller and Michael Vaughan-Rees, *Women in Uniform 1939–45*, Macmillan 1989, and Penny Summerfield, *Women Workers in the Second World War* (1984). David Morgan and Mary Evans note that 'one of the features of wartime culture and ideology in Britain was an emphasis on documenting the lives of ordinary citizens', *The Battle for Britain: Citizenship and Ideology in the Second World War*, Routledge, 1993, 104. Perhaps this was partly because these 'ordinary' lives were changing in ways which were perceived to be significant.

10. Anne Boston makes a similar point about the short stories of the period in the Introduction to her anthology *Wave Me Goodbye, Stories of the Second World War*, Virago, 1988; Penguin, 1989, 19.

11. See Patricia Wentworth, *The Chinese Shawl*, Hodder & Stoughton, 1943, and *Miss Silver Intervenes*, Hodder & Stoughton, 1944.

12. Anne Maybury, *Arise Oh Sun!*, Collins, 1942, 31.

13. Jane Waller and Michael Vaughan-Rees, *Women in Wartime: The Role of Women's Magazines 1939–1945*, Optima MacDonald, 1987, 6.

14. Rosamond Oppersdorff, 'I Was Too Ignorant' (1942), reprinted in *Wave Me Goodbye*.

15. Mary Renault, Afterword to *The Friendly Young Ladies*, Virago, 1984.

16. Sylvia Townsend Warner, 'Poor Mary' (1947), reprinted in *Wave Me Goodbye*.

17. Barbara Pym, who worked for the Censorship in Bristol, was reading 'a novel all about Censors' in April 1943; perhaps it was Wilenski's. See Barbara Pym, *A Very Private Eye, An Autobiography in Letters and Diaries*, eds Hazel Holt and Hilary Pym, Macmillan 1984, 120.

18. Amabel Williams-Ellis's *Women in War Factories*, Gollancz, 1943, was used by the MOI. For magazine articles about work in war factories see E.C., 'A Worker's Point of View, *New Statesman and Nation*, 12 July 1941; Betty Askwith, 'Part-time Worker', *Spectator*, 29 May 1942; Constance Reaveley, 'The Machine and the Mind', *Spectator*, 7 April 1944.

19. Celia Fremlin, *War Factory*, 1987, 49.

20. Inez Holden, 'Fellow Travellers in Factory', *Horizon*, 1941.

21. This is Vera Douie's figure, *Daughters of Britain, An Account of the Work of British Women during the Second World War*, George Ronald, Oxford, 1950, 93.

22. See Diary of Miss McMurray, Department of Documents, Imperial War Museum, and Diary of Rose Uttin, Department of Documents, Imperial War Museum.

23. Miss Kathleen Church-Bliss and Miss Elsie Whiteman, 'We Had To Laugh', Typescript of War Diary 1942–45, Department of Documents, Imperial War Museum. Diary entries for September 1942 and May 1944.

5. Surveillance, Allegiance, Complicity, pp. 88–105

1. Women novelists who worked in intelligence included Elizabeth Bowen, Muriel Spark, Christine Brooke-Rose, Barbara Pym and Mary Wesley.

2. See Ian McLaine, *Ministry of Morale, Home Front Morale and the Ministry of Information in World War II*, George Allen & Unwin, 1979, 50–51.

3. Olive Renier and Vladimir Rubinstein, *Assigned to Listen, The Evesham Experience 1939–1943*, BBC, 1986, 10, 43.

4. See newspaper articles collected by Miss V.C.A. Waley, Department of Documents, Imperial War Museum.

5. Duff Cooper, 'Join the Ranks of the Silent Column', *Listener*, 18 July 1940.

6. *The Speeches of Winston Churchill*, ed. David Cannadine, Penguin, 1990, 176.

7. Sarah B. Pomeroy, *Goddesses, Whores, Wives and Slaves: Women in Classical Antiquity*, Schocken Books, New York, 1975, 24.

8. For the work women did at Bletchley Park, see Diana Payne, 'The Bombes', *Codebreakers: The Inside Story of Bletchley Park*, eds F.H. Hinsley and Alan Stripp, Oxford University Press, Oxford, 1993. For a good memoir by a woman who worked at Bletchley, see Irene Young, *Enigma Variations, A Memoir of Love and War*, Mainstream Publishing, Edinburgh, 1990.

9. Interview for 'Bookmark', 1987, quoted in Sarah Birch, *Christine Brooke-Rose and Contemporary Fiction*, Clarendon Press, Oxford 1994, 2.

10. Christine Brooke-Rose, *Remake*, Carcanet, Manchester, 1996, 107.

11. Elizabeth Bowen, 'Green Holly' (1944), *The Collected Stories of Elizabeth Bowen*, Jonathan Cape, 1980; Penguin, 1983.

12. Odette Churchill and Violette Szabo both worked for the SOE in France and were honoured in Jerrard Tickell's *Odette, The Story of a British Agent*, 1949 and R.J. Minney's *Carve her Name with Pride*, 1956. About a quarter of SOE's total strength were women, according to M.R.D. Foot, *SOE, The Special Operations Executive 1940–46*, BBC, 1984, 37, 62. For an account of the women's work in the SOE see Irene Ward *F.A.N.Y. Invicta*, Hutchinson, 1955, Chapter 6. For memoirs by women involved in underground work see Anne-Marie Walters, *Moondrop in Gascony*, Macmillan, 1946, and Muriel Gardiner, *Code Name 'Mary', Memoirs of an American Woman in the Austrian Underground*, Yale University Press, New Haven, 1983.

13. See, for example, Sebastian Knowles on its 'singular and telling absence in the war years', *A Purgatorial Flame: Seven British Writers in the Second World War*, The Bristol Press, Bristol, 1990, 175.

14. 'So Very Secret', (1940–1941), *Civil to Strangers and Other Writings*, Macmillan, 1987.

15. See R.C. Minney, *Carve her Name with Pride*, xii. For Anne-Marie Walters, effective disguise was camouflage, going native: 'I emerged from the hairdresser looking like a Toulousaine: my hair was piled at vertiginous heights on top of my head and swept into two heavy rolls at the back; it was a masterpiece of execution', *Moondrop in Gascony*, 1946, 105.

16. The similarities between this novel and *Hamlet* are well documented by Barbara Bellow Watson, 'Variations on an Enigma: Elizabeth Bowen's War Novel', *Southern Humanities Review*, vol. xv, no. 2, Spring 1981.

17. Harold Pinter, *The Heat of the Day*, *Adapted from the novel by Elizabeth Bowen*, Faber, 1989.

18. See Adam Piette's chapter on 'Propaganda', *Imagination at War: British Fiction and Poetry 1939–45*, Macmillan, 1995.

19. See above, Chapter 1.

20. Autobiographical note c. 1947, quoted by Victoria Glendinning, *Elizabeth Bowen, Portrait of a Writer*, Weidenfeld & Nicolson, 1977, 127.

21. BBC interview quoted in Heather Bryant Jordan, *How Will the Heart Endure? Elizabeth Bowen and the Landscape of War*, University of Michigan Press, Ann Arbor, 1992, 93.

22. Preface to the American edition of *The Demon Lover*, *Collected Impressions*, Longmans, Green & Co., 1950.

23. 'London 1940', *Collected Impressions*.

24. Glendinning, *Elizabeth Bowen*, 141.

25. Glendinning, *Elizabeth Bowen*, 165.

26. Virginia Woolf, 4 May 1934, *The Letters of Virginia Woolf*, vol. V, 299.

27. See Glendinning, 161–164; R.F. Foster, 'The Irishness of Elizabeth Bowen' in *Paddy and Mr Punch*, Allen Lane, 1993, and Heather Bryant Jordan, *How Will the Heart Endure?* 98–103.

28. See R.F. Foster, also Bowen's article, 'Eire', the *New Statesman and Nation*, 12 April 1941.

29. R.F. Foster, *Paddy and Mr Punch*, 115.

30. It is often marriage which asks women to inhabit more than one country, and women have written of the conflict caused by divided loyalties in the war. Sybil Bannister, an Englishwoman married to a German, found that 'Since the day when England and Germany were at war an impenetrable wall had sprung up between us, not so much a barrier of enmity as of reticence'. Informers and spies beset her and her child was taken from her; Bannister survived by flight and 'going under' – pretending to be German. (See Sybil Bannister, *I Lived Under Hitler, An Englishwoman's Story of her Life in Wartime Germany*, Rockcliff Publishing Corporation, 1957; Penguin, 1995.) Janet Teissier du Cros was a Scotswoman married to a Frenchman, she spent the war in Occupied France. Her memoir is entitled *Divided Loyalties: A Scotswoman in Occupied France* (Hamish Hamilton, 1962; Canongate Press, Edinburgh, 1992); the title speaks for itself. Aileen Armellini Lee-Selwyn was an Anglo-Canadian married to an Italian General, and her memoirs testify physically to the intractability of the times: the left-hand pages are in English, the right-hand in Italian (*La Moglie Inglese*, Ibiskos Editrice, Rome, 1994). Lee-Selwyn is circumspect about her activities in Italy, which seem to have included some hard-headed bartering and callous behaviour. Again and again

she says, 'I had no other choice'. By the last year of the war Storm Jameson was turning the problem of a woman's torn allegiance into fiction: *The Other Side* (written in 1944, published by Macmillan, 1946) tells the story of Marie, a Frenchwoman married to a German soldier, widowed, then wooed by an English soldier after the German defeat. Marie stands as a victim of war, her sense of belonging and loyalty shattered. ' "I haven't a country," ' she declares. Memoirs and novels such as these bear witness to the painful pressures in many women's lives. The remark that Harrison makes in his first scene with Stella – ' "Yes, it's funny about the war – the way everybody's on one side or the other" ' (31) – seems almost laughably simple. But all these women, unlike Bowen, who offered to act as an informant, had no choice once they were married.

31. 'Pink May', *The Collected Stories of Elizabeth Bowen*, 713.
32. Elizabeth Bowen, *Why Do I Write? An Exchange of Views between Elizabeth Bowen, Graham Greene and V.S. Prichett*, Percival Marshall, 1948, 56.
33. See Hermione Lee, *Elizabeth Bowen: An Estimation*, Vision Press, 1981, 176–178; Andrew Boyle, *The Climate of Treason*, Hutchinson, 1979, 337–338.
34. See her essay 'Disloyalties' (1950), in *The Mulberry Tree*; *Why Do I Write? An Exchange of Views between Elizabeth Bowen, Graham Greene and V.S. Pritchett*, 1948, and Foster, 117.
35. Angus Calder, *The Myth of the Blitz*, Jonathan Cape, 1991; Pimlico, 1992, 259.
36. Diary entry for 29 September 1941, Charles Ritchie, *The Siren Years, Undiplomatic Diaries 1937–1945*, Macmillan, 1974, 118.
37. Diary entry for 15 September 1940, Frances Partridge, *A Pacifist's War*, The Hogarth Press, 1978, 61.
38. Vera Brittain, *Testament of Experience, An Autobiographical Story of the Years 1920–1950*, Gollancz, 1957; Virago, 1979, 276.
39. Diary entry for 2 June 1942, Ritchie, *The Siren Years*, 143.
40. Glendinning, *Elizabeth Bowen*, 151.
41. 'The Climate of Treason', *Times Literary Supplement*, 5 March 1949.
42. Glendinning, *Elizabeth Bowen*, 151.
43. Diary Entry for 16 June 1941, Ritchie, *The Siren Years*, 111–112.
44. Diary entry for 8 November 1941, *The Siren Years*, 124.
45. 'Preface to *Stories by Elizabeth Bowen*', quoted in Phyllis Lassner, *Elizabeth Bowen*, Macmillan, 1990, 16.
46. Hermione Lee, *Elizabeth Bowen: An Estimation*, 181.
47. R.F. Foster, *Paddy and Mr Punch*, 103.
48. Looking-glass reversals proliferate, sometimes in playful puns, so that Louie's secret pregnancy is accompanied by the 'pregnant secrecy' in the newspapers about the Second Front (325). This is the looking-glass world of war, where people set off to work on Sundays or at night, and where to find out that Harrison is telling the truth about his visit to Ireland is devastating

(171). It is usually catching someone out in a lie that hurts; but here the implication is that Stella must now believe that Harrison is telling the truth about Robert's treachery.

49. A further double offers itself here from life in the shape of 'Llanfoist', the large 1920s house in Camberley which Joan Miller, who did counter-espionage work for M15, rented as a 'safe house' for agents in 1940; see Joan Miller, *One Girl's War, Personal Exploits in MI5's Most Secret Station*, Brandon Book Publishers Ltd, Dingle, Co. Kerry, 1986, 39.

50. As Adam Piette suggests, 'The "hybrid" Anglo-Irish self is capable of a double allegiance, to country and to that country's "enemy" ', *Imagination at War*, 172; but I see more unease than Piette does.

51. Glendinning, *Elizabeth Bowen*, 140.

52. 'The Climate of Treason' *Times Literary Supplement*, 5 March 1949.

53. Christine Brooke-Rose, *Remake*, 107–108.

54. Glendinning, *Elizabeth Bowen*, 157.

6. Women to Blame? Adverse Images of Women in War, pp. 106–122

1. See above, Chapter 1.

2. Introduction to *Behind the Lines, Gender and the Two World Wars*, eds M.R. Higonnet, J. Jensen, S. Michel, M.C. Weitz, Yale University Press, New Haven, 1987, 4.

3. Two versions of Gubar's essay on 'World War II and the Blitz on Women' have appeared, in *Behind the Lines*, 1987, and in Sandra Gilbert and Susan Gubar, *No Man's Land, The Place of the Woman Writer in the Twentieth Century*, vol. 3, *Letters from the Front*, Yale University Press, New Haven, 1994. The later version drops some of the earlier's more extreme judgements.

4. Anthony Powell, *The Valley of Bones*, Heinemann, 1964; Fontana, 1973; *The Soldier's Art*, Heinemann, 1966; Fontana, 1968, and *The Military Philosophers*, Heinemann, 1968; Fontana, 1971, vols 7, 8 and 9 of *A Dance to the Music of Time*.

5. Anthony Powell, *The Soldier's Art*, 118.

6. Anthony Powell, *The Military Philosophers*, 130.

7. See Frances Spalding, *Stevie Smith, A Critical Biography*, Faber, 1988, 190.

8. See Julian Maclaren-Ross, *Memoirs of the Forties*, Alan Ross Ltd, 1965, 33. See also the accounts of literary London in Robert Hewison, *Under Siege, Literary Life in London 1939–1945*, Methuen, 1977, and Andrew Sinclair, *War Like a Wasp: The Lost Decade of the 1940s*, Hamish Hamilton, 1989.

9. *Spectator*, 20 November 1942.

10. Freya Stark, *Letters*, vol. 5, *New Worlds for Old, 1943–46*, ed. Lucy Moorehead, Michael Russell, 1978, 96.

11. Letter to Alec Guiness, Edith Sitwell, *Selected Letters*, eds J. Lehmann and D. Parker, Macmillan, 1970, 85.

12. Elspeth Huxley's *Atlantic Ordeal* (Chatto & Windus, 1941) celebrated the bravery of Mary Cornish, the children's escort who survived with her charges in an open boat after the sinking of the *City of Benares*. In *From the Life* (Faber, 1944) Phyllis Bottome wrote in praise of Victoria Drummond, who was decorated for her work as a ship's engineer.

13. Vita Sackville-West, *The Eagle and the Dove, A Study in Contrasts*, Michael Joseph, 1943, 132, 152.

14. The Dowager Marchioness of Reading, 'Women's Voluntary Service', *The Fortnightly*, April 1945. See also Raynes Minns, *Bombers and Mash, The Domestic Front 1939–45*, Virago, 1980, Chapter 5. The anomalous position of the WVS woman – part but not wholly of the State, able to take her own initiative and yet answerable to the local authorities – is reflected in her uniform. Unlike other voluntary women's organisations (the Women's Institute for example) the WVS did have a uniform; but unlike that of the women's services it was quite fashionable, designed by a top London couturier. Well cut in good grey-green tweed, it was a version of what many of these women would have been wearing anyway. According to the historian of the WVS, Charles Graves, 'The success of the attempt to avoid ostentation was brought home to the Chairman when King George VI said "Aren't you going to have uniforms?" The embarrassed reply was: "Yes, sir. Actually, I am wearing one" ' (*Women in Green*, Heinemann, 1948, 31). Unlike other uniforms, however, the wearer had to pay for it herself; it would be a mark of status and independence, and could be worn with an individual flourish: The first time that Mr Winston Churchill saw a march past of the WVS he said in disgust: "Look at your girls. Each hat is worn at a different angle." Lady Reading replied: "Here is a case of individuality of operation, but uniformity of pattern" ' (*Women in Green*, 30–31).

15. Elizabeth Bowen, Review of *The People's War*, 1969, reprinted in *The Mulberry Tree*, ed. H. Lee, Virago, 1986, 184.

16. A parallel phenomenon has been noted in the films of the time. E. Ann Kaplan notes that in 'thirties maternal narratives the Mother is represented as a basically "good" figure – well-meaning, competent, able to stand alone, articulate if not intelligent', whereas 'late forties and fifties films' show mothers as 'blatantly monstrous, deliberately victimising their children for sadistic and narcissistic ends'. See E. Ann Kaplan, 'Mothering, Feminism and Representation, The Maternal in Melodrama and the Woman's Film 1910–40', in ed. Christine Gledhill, *Home is Where the Heart Is*, 1987, London, BFI, 134. The evidence of *Now Voyager* (1942) suggests that the monster mother was well in place early in the war.

17. Paul Fussell, 'The Fate of Chivalry and the Assault upon Mother', *Killing in Verse and Prose and Other Essays* 1988; Bellew Publishing London 1990, 243.

18. See Leila Rupp, *Mobilizing Women For War, German and American Propaganda 1939–1945*, Princeton University Press, New Jersey, 1978, 118.

19. The destructive mother and the hateful breast (hateful because withdrawn) appear in Melanie Klein's contemporary analyses of the child's splitting of the mother into the good and the bad. See *The Selected Writings of Melanie Klein*, ed. Juliet Mitchell, Penguin, 1986, 20.

20. Rosamond Lehmann, 'A Charming Person', *Spectator*, 10 November 1939.

21. Jan Struther, Correspondence, *New Statesman and Nation*, 23 December 1939.

22. Rosamond Lehmann, 'The Red-Haired Miss Daintreys' (1941), *The Gipsy's Baby*, Virago, 1982, 62.

23. The enemy agents in Graham Greene's *The Ministry of Fear* (Heinemann, 1943) use as their cover an organisation called 'Comforts for Mothers of the Free Nations', referred to in the title of the first chapter as 'The Free Mothers' – a sinister sounding band.

24. Rosamond Lehmann's two young children lived for some of the war with Lehmann's mother in the country. Her house was turned into a Red Cross Home and Rosamond's brother John 'often got the impression that it was my Mother who was running the whole show, having for so many years been accustomed to run every show in the neighbourhood and get her own way' (*I Am My Brother*, Longmans, Green & Co., 1960, 267). See also Gillian Tindall, *Rosamond Lehmann, An Appreciation*, Chatto & Windus, 1985, 105.

25. See Judy Simons, *Rosamond Lehmann*, Macmillan, 1992; Gillian Tindall, *Rosamond Lehmann, An Appreciation*, and Sydney Janet Kaplan, 'Rosamond Lehmann's *The Ballad and the Source*: A Confrontation with "The Great Mother" ', *Twentieth Century Literature*, vol. 27, no. 2, 1981, 127–145.

26. In antiquity sibyls were the inspired prophetesses of a deity, in particular Apollo.

27. Alan Bullock, *Hitler, A Study in Tyranny*, Odhams, 1952; Penguin, 1962, 374.

28. Sir Nevile Henderson's view of Hitler in 1940, quoted in Bullock (376), and the sculptor Gil on Mrs Jardine (237).

29. See Victoria Glendinning, *Edith Sitwell, A Unicorn among Lions*, Weidenfeld & Nicolson, 1981, 219 ff.

30. Edith Sitwell, 'Harvest', *Green Song and Other Poems*, Macmillan, 1944.

7. Letters, pp. 123–139

1. Press Announcement made by Post Office, May 1943, Post Office Archive, Post 56/99.

2. Ian Hay, *The Post Office Went to War*, HMSO, 1946, 17.

3. Between March 1944 and March 1945, for example, the one-way traffic of letters despatched overseas from Britain reached 374 million. See Post Office Commercial Accounts 1944–1945, Post Office Archive.

4. Sir Thomas Gardiner, 'An Account of the Work of the Post Office during the Second World War,' Post Office Archives, Post 56/63. General Montgomery ordered mail deliveries to begin in France on D Day itself, the first day of the

Normandy landings in June 1944.

5. Post Office Archive, Post 56/28. The correspondent wrote on a form which was photographed on to a strip and reproduced at the overseas end; about 350 million airgraphs were sent before airletters came in, their privacy a welcome improvement. For details of the airgraph, see Hay, 44–45.

6. Janet Gurkin Altman, *Epistolarity, Approaches to a Form*, Ohio State University Press, Columbus, 1982, 13.

7. Papers of Margaret Harries née Rushton, Department of Documents, Imperial War Museum.

8. Jock Lewes and Mirren Barford's relationship developed rapidly on paper, see *Joy Street, A Wartime Romance in Letters 1940–1942*, Little, Brown and Company, London, 1995. 'Numerous courtships were conducted by letter', according to Vee Robinson, *On Target*, Verity Press, Wakefield, 1991, 170.

9. Letter dated 14 April 1944, Papers of Pamela Moore, Department of Documents, Imperial War Museum.

10. Letter dated 20 August 1943, Papers of Joan Kirby, Department of Documents, Imperial War Museum.

11. Papers of Donald Grist, Department of Documents, Imperial War Museum.

12. Diana Hopkinson, 'Love in War', Typescript, Department of Documents, Imperial War Museum.

13. Diana Hopkinson, in *Private Words, Letters and Diaries from the Second World War*, ed. Ronald Blythe, Viking, 1991, 26.

14. Marion Kaplan, 'Jewish Women in Nazi Germany', in *Between Sorrow and Strength, Women Refugees of the Nazi Period*, ed. Sibylle Quack, Cambridge University Press, Cambridge, 1995, 24.

15. Honor Tracy, *The Deserters*, Methuen, 1954, 28.

16. Mirren Barford and Lieutenant John Lewes, *Joy Street*, 5.

17. Papers of Mrs P.M. Higgins, Department of Documents, Imperial War Museum.

18. Papers of Fergus Anckorn, Department of Documents, Imperial War Museum. Fergus did return at the end of the war; most of his mother's letters did not get through at the time.

19. Of the millions of wartime letters, those written by mothers have lasted least well. Usually sent away from home, they were liable to be lost or jettisoned by sons and daughters on the move.

20. Letter dated 30 June 1943, Papers of Miss Joan Kirby, Department of Documents, Imperial War Museum.

21. Letter of June 1943, Papers of Stephanie Batstone, Department of Documents, Imperial War Museum.

22. Jenny Nicholson, *Kiss the Girls Good-Bye*, Hutchinson, 1944, 14.

23. Nella Last, 25 August 1942, *Nella Last's War, A Mother's Diary 1939–45*, eds Richard Broad and Suzie Fleming, Falling Wall Press, Bristol, 1981, 214. Nancy Buchanan's letters are collected in the Papers of Captain P.A.

Buchanan, Department of Documents, Imperial War Museum; a selection of them are reprinted in *Women's Letters in Wartime*, ed. Eva Figes, Pandora, 1993. The quotation in the Epigraph to this chapter comes from a letter of 31 May 1943, in the Papers of Captain P.A. Buchanan.

24. David Hopkinson in *Private Words: Letters and Diaries from the Second World War*, ed. Ronald Blythe Viking, 1991, 26.

25. Hugh and Margaret Williams, *Always and Always: The Wartime Letters of Hugh and Margaret Williams*, John Murray, 1995, 216.

26. Formal and official censorship was of course a reality of war. It was imposed on all overseas mail, and inland mail to and from ports and other sensitive areas. See the Stephenson Report on Reorganisation of Censorship, 1940, Post Office Archive, Post 56/63. Even letters confining themselves to the safe areas of England betray a constant awareness of the censor.

27. Nancy Buchanan, Letter of 17 May 1943, Papers of Captain P.A. Buchanan, Imperial War Museum.

28. Daphne du Maurier, 'Letter Writing in Wartime', *Good Housekeeping*, September 1940, reprinted in *The Home Front, The Best of Good Housekeeping 1939–1945*, compiled by Brian Braithwaite, Noelle Walsh and Glyn Davies, Ebury Press, 1987, 21.

29. Advice quoted in Jane Waller and Michael Vaughan-Rees, *The Role of Women's Magazines 1939–1945*, Macdonald, 1987, 77.

30. Lynn visited hospitals and sent messages from wives with newborn babies. This was popular not just with the lucky few she mentioned, 'it was also good,' she later wrote, 'and reassuring for those who didn't get chosen, because they'd know that the contact was there ... it had the effect of reducing distances between people'. The BBC Board of Governors was less keen; their minutes read: ' "Sincerely Yours" deplored but popularity noted', Vera Lynn, *Vocal Refrain*, W.H. Allen, 1975, 98.

31. Virginia Woolf, *Three Guineas*, 1938; The Hogarth Press, 1968, 5.

32. Mollie Panter-Downes, *London War Notes 1939–1945*, Farrar, Straus & Giroux, New York, 1971, 3. Nicola Beauman describes Panter-Downes's work for *The New Yorker* in her Introduction to the Virago edition of *One Fine Day*.

33. See Jane Brown Gillette on the importance of moral perception in Elizabeth Taylor, ' "Oh, What a Tangled Web We Weave": The Novels of Elizabeth Taylor', *Twentieth Century Literature*, vol. 35, no. 1, Spring 1989, 94–112.

34. Rose Macaulay, 'Miss Anstruther's Letters' (1942), reprinted in *Wave Me Goodbye, Stories of the Second World War*, ed. Anne Boston, Virago, 1988; Penguin, 1989.

8. The Indirect Face of War, pp. 140–160

1. In similar style, Olivia Manning's diffident young captain 'decorate[s] ... his young face with a cavalry moustache he would have shrunk from wearing

when a civilian clerk' in 'A Spot of Leave' (1946), reprinted in *A Romantic Hero and Other Stories*, Heinemann 1967, 107.

2. Monica Dickens's title looks back to Shakespeare and Tennyson's Mariana, waiting in her lonely grange.

3. C.A. Lejeune, *Chestnuts in her Lap, 1936–1946*, Phoenix House Ltd, 1947, 81.

4. Mollie Panter-Downes, 'Goodbye, My Love' (1941), reprinted in *Wave Me Goodbye, Stories of the Second World War*, Virago, 1988; Penguin, 1989.

5. Taylor's story appeared untitled, in *Modern Reading 13*, ed. Reginald Moore, 1945; reprinted in *Hester Lilly*, Virago, 1990. Taylor's run-down garden imagery recalls Tennyson's Mariana again.

6. Elizabeth Bowen, 'Pictures and Conversations', *The Mulberry Tree*, ed. H. Lee, Virago, 1986, 282.

7. Elizabeth Bowen, Preface to the American Edition of *The Demon Lover* (1945), reprinted in *Collected Impressions*, Longmans Green & Co., 1950, 48.

8. Elizabeth Bowen, 'The Happy Autumn Fields' (1944), reprinted in *The Collected Stories of Elizabeth Bowen*, Jonathan Cape, 1980; Penguin, 1983.

9. Elizabeth Bowen, Preface to *The Demon Lover*.

10. Elizabeth Bowen, Preface to *The Demon Lover*.

11. Elizabeth Bowen, Preface to *The Demon Lover*.

12. Elizabeth Bowen, 'Mysterious Kor' (1944), reprinted in *Collected Stories*.

13. 'Bomber's moon' was a common wartime expression and the title of Negley Farson's 1941 book about the blitz. In 1942 the *New York Times* carried the story of a German pilot forced down over Leningrad: 'He landed on the roof of a high apartment house and was found gazing wonderingly down onto the moonlit city. As he was brought downstairs into the tall building past apartments in which the dwellers were leading busy lives it was apparent from his expression . . . that he had never thought of Leningrad as a real live place but only as a target on the map.' Siegfried Kracauer, *From Caligari to Hitler, A Psychological History of the German Film*, Princeton University Press 1947, 296. For a full analysis of 'Mysterious Kor', see John Bayley, *The Short Story, Henry James to Elizabeth Bowen*, Harvester, Brighton, 1988, 166–178.

14. Bowen described her childhood passion for *She* as 'the first totally violent impact I ever received from print', *Seven Winters and Afterthoughts*, Longmans, Green & Co., 1962, 235.

15. Elizabeth Bowen, 'The Demon Lover' (1941), reprinted in *Collected Stories*.

16. 'It is a fact' observed Bowen, 'that in Britain, and especially in London, in wartime many people had strange deep intense dreams.' Preface to *The Demon Lover*.

17. *The Oxford Book of Ballads*, Oxford University Press, Oxford, 1927, 123–127.

18. See Robert L. Calder, ' "A More Sinister Troth": Elizabeth Bowen's "The Demon Lover" as Allegory', *Studies in Short Fiction*, Newberry College, North Carolina, vol. 31, no. 1, 1994, 91–97.

19. See Stephen Knight, 'Murder in Wartime' and Kathleen Bell,

'Cross-Dressing in Wartime: Georgette Heyer's *The Corinthian* in its 1940 Context', in *War Culture: Social Change and Changing Experience in World War Two*, eds Pat Kirkham and David Thoms, Lawrence & Wishart, 1995.

20. For a stimulating discussion of du Maurier's writing and 'the pleasure it takes in undermining its own beliefs,' see Alison Light, *Forever England: Femininity, literature and conservatism between the wars*, Routledge, 1991, 158 ff.

21. Du Maurier's husband was Lieutenant-General Sir Frederick Browning, wartime commander of Airborne Forces.

22. Her poem 'Trafalgar Day' in praise of the 'Nelson spirit' was popular during the blitz.

23. It was a great hit with servicemen; see Paul Fussell, *Wartime, Understanding and Behaviour in the Second World War*, Oxford University Press, Oxford, 1989, 107.

24. Gellhorn's Afterword to the Virago edition describes the time she spent in the Caribbean in 1942.

25. For considerations of war in *Between the Acts*, see Gillian Beer's Introduction to the 1992 Penguin edition. See also Jeremy Hawthorn, *Cunning Passages: New Historicism, Cultural Materialism and Marxism in Contemporary Literary Debate*, Arnold, 1966, 190–200; ed. Mark Hussey, *Virginia Woolf and War*, Syracuse University Press, Syracuse, 1991; Hermione Lee, *The Novels of Virginia Woolf*, Methuen 1977; Sallie Sears, 'Theater of War: Virginia Woolf's *Between the Acts*', in *Virginia Woolf, A Feminist Slant*, ed. Jane Marcus, University of Nebraska Press, London, 1983; Karen Schneider, 'Of Two Minds: Woolf, the War and *Between the Acts*', *Journal of Modern Literature*, vol. 16, no. 1, 1989.

26. Virginia Woolf, *Pointz Hall, the Earlier and Later Typescripts of Between the Acts*, ed. Mitchell Leaska, University Publications, New York, 1983.

27. See Hawthorn, *Cunning Passages*, 190–200.

28. Diary entry for 4 August 1938, *The Diary of Virginia Woolf*, vol. V, 1936–1941, ed. A.O. Bell, The Hogarth Press, 159.

29. Letter to Ethel Smyth, 9 July 1940, *Leave the Letters Till We're Dead, The Letters of Virginia Woolf* 1936–1941, ed. Nigel Nicolson, The Hogarth Press, 1980, 404.

30. Letter to Vanessa Bell, 1 October 1938, *Letters*, vol. VI, 275.

31. Letter to Vanessa Bell, 3 October 1938, *Letters*, vol. VI, 279.

32. Letter to Jaques-Emile Blanchard, 5 October 1938, *Letters*, vol. VI, 282.

33. Letter to Vanessa Bell, 3 October 1938, *Letters*, vol. VI, 279.

34. See Leaska, 'Dating the Manuscript', *Pointz Hall*, 25–29.

35. Hermione Lee, *Virginia Woolf*, Chatto & Windus, 1996, 741.

36. The fascination with words in this novel has received much critical attention. See, for example, Sallie Sears and Gillian Beer; see also Nora Eisenberg, 'Virginia Woolf's last words on Words: *Between the Acts* and "Anon" ', *New Feminist Essays on Virginia Woolf*, ed. Jane Marcus, Macmillan, 1981.

37. Brenda R. Silver, ' "Anon" and "The Reader": Virginia Woolf's Last Essays', *Twentieth Century Literature*, 25, Autumn 1979.

38. Diary entry for 26 February 1941, *Diary*, vol. V, 356.

39. See, for example, Woolf's diary entry for 15 April 1939, which records 'the community feeling: all England thinking the same thing – this horror of war – at the same moment. Never felt it so strong before.' *The Diary of Virginia Woof*, vol. V, 215.

40. Hermione Lee, *Virginia Woolf*, 722, 731.

41. Reprinted in *The Death of the Moth and Other Essays*, The Hogarth Press, 1942.

42. Virginia Woolf, *Roger Fry*, The Hogarth Press, 1940, 285.

43. See Lee, 721.

44. This compares with the 'signal-tree' in Matthew Arnold's 'Thyrsis', a poem which Woolf quotes from in her *Diary*, vol. V, 29 December 1940, 347. The search for the tree in Arnold's poem is a quest for spiritual value. Arnold's tree is an elm, as is Miss La Trobe's in the Earlier Typescript (174). The two elm trees which Woolf could see as she wrote at Monk's House were nicknamed Leonard and Virginia; 'All the birds are sitting up in L. & V.' *Diary*, vol. V, 24 March 1940, 274.

45. Diary entry for 23 November 1940, *Diary*, vol. V, 340.

9. War Wounds, pp. 161–178

1. Martha Gellhorn, *The Face of War*, Hart Davis, 1959; Granta Books, 1993, 378.

2. Joan Riviere and Melanie Klein, *Love, Hate and Reparation*, quoted in Daniel Pick's *War Machine, The Rationalisation of Slaughter in the Modern Age*, Yale University Press, New Haven, 1993, 228.

3. Pick, *War Machine*, 231.

4. Publisher's Note to Murray Constantine's *Swastika Night*, 1937, reprinted 1940. See I.F. Clarke, *Voices Prophesying War*, Oxford University Press 1966; Andy Croft, *Red Letter Days*, Lawrence & Wishart, 1990; Angela Ingram and Daphne Patai (eds), *Rediscovering Forgotten Radicals, British Women Writers 1889–1939*, University of North Carolina Press, Chapel Hill, 1993; Maroula Joannou, ' "Ladies, Please Don't Smash These Windows": Women's Writing, Feminist Consciousness and Social Change 1918–38', Berg, Oxford, 1995.

5. Murray Constantine was the pseudonym of Katharine Burdekin. See Daphne Patai, 'Imagining Reality: The Utopian Fiction of Katharine Burdekin', in *Rediscovering Forgotten Radicals*, eds Ingram and Patai.

6. Croft, *Red Letter Days*, 326; Penguin reprinted the novel three times in nine months.

7. With the declaration of war in September 1939 the flow of prophecy died down, although the 'what if' strain did not disappear altogether. In 1942, for example, Vita Sackville-West published *Grand Canyon*, a 'cautionary tale'

about the spread of fascism to America.

8. Simone Weil, 'The *Iliad* or The Poem of Force', 1940–1941, translated by Mary McCarthy and reprinted in *Simone Weil, An Anthology*, ed. Sian Miles, Virago, 1986.

9. Against this tragic male plot Weil hoped to marshal a daring new kind of female action. She came to London to work for the Resistance, with the idea of forming a front-line nursing squad which would 'capture the imagination by its great courage' and counter the romance of male brutality. She thought that 'the symbolic presence of women in the front-line would be incalculably powerful', but de Gaulle dismissed her plans as mad; see Sian Miles, Introduction to *Simone Weil, An Anthology*, 38. Already ill, Weil took the enemy occupation of France into her own body, refusing to eat when she thought her countrymen were starving. According to her biographer David McLellan, this was not so much a punishment of her body as a principled 'communion with France by natural abstention'; see David McLellan, *Simone Weil, Utopian Pessimist*, Macmillan, 1989, 263. Weil died in 1943.

10. Louise Morgan, 'When They Come Back', *Good Housekeeping*, January 1945, reprinted in *The Home Front: The Best of Good Housekeeping 1939–1945*, compiled by Brian Braithwaite, Noelle Walsh, Glyn Davies, Ebury Press, 1987, 189. Woolf uses imagery of imprisonment and slavery in 'Thoughts on Peace in an Air Raid', *The Death of the Moth and Other Essays*, The Hogarth Press, 1942. Gertrude Stein describes life in Occupied France in 1943: 'And whole countries in prison and now we have a feeling that they who put everybody in prison are now in prison they feel themselves in prison, they feel imprisoned', *Wars I Have Seen*, Batsford, 1945; Brilliance Books, 1984, 47.

11. See Pick, *War Machine*, 232–239.

12. Sylvia Townsend Warner, 'A Red Carnation', *A Garland of Straw*, Chatto & Windus, 1943, reprinted in *Selected Stories*, Chatto & Windus, 1989; Virago, 1990. Townsend Warner herself worked for the Republican cause in Spain in 1936 and 1937, see Wendy Mulford, *This Narrow Place, Sylvia Townsend Warner and Valentine Ackland: Life, Letters and Politics, 1930–1951*, Pandora Press, 1988, 87ff.

13. Monica Stirling, 'Marie Bashkirtseff and the Hitler Youth', *Transformation two*, eds Stefan Schimanski and Henry Treece, Lindsay Drummond Ltd, 1944.

14. Sylvia Townsend Warner, 'Apprentice', *A Garland of Straw and Other Stories*, Chatto & Windus, 1943, reprinted in *Selected Stories*.

15. The phrase 'holy elementalism' comes from Elizabeth Myers, *A Well Full of Leaves, A Story of Happiness* (Chapman & Hall, 1943), into its fifth edition by 1946. See also Dorothy Cowlin, *Winter Solstice* (Jonathan Cape, 1942).

16. Sylvia Townsend Warner, 'The Level Crossing', *A Garland of Straw*, 1943, reprinted in *Selected Stories*.

17. Anna Kavan, 'Face of My People', (1944), reprinted in *Wave Me Goodbye*,

Stories of the Second World War, Virago 1988; Penguin, 1989.

18. Sylvia Townsend Warner, 'The Mothers', *A Garland of Straw*, Chatto & Windus, 1943.

19. Martha Gellhorn, 'Week-end at Grimsby', *The Honeyed Peace*, Andre Deutsch, 1954; Penguin, 1958.

20. Martha Gellhorn, 'About Shorty', *The Honeyed Peace*, Andre Deutsch, 1954; Penguin, 1958.

21. Elizabeth Bowen, Preface to the American edition of *The Demon Lover*, reprinted in *Collected Impressions*, Longmans, Green & Co., 1950.

22. Agatha Christie, *An Autobiography*, Collins, 1977, 498–499. Alison Light discusses the novel in *Forever England: Femininity, Literature and Conservatism between the Wars*, Routledge, 1991, 111–112.

23. Rosamond Lehmann, 'A Dream of Winter', 1941, reprinted in *The Gipsy's Baby*, Collins, 1946; Virago, 1982.

24. Miller's husband was a physician who 'specialised in psychiatry', and Miller, according to her daughter, 'made much use of his professional knowledge in her own work', Introduction to Betty Miller, *On the Side of the Angels*, Virago, 1985, x.

25. Angus Calder, *The Myth of the Blitz*, Jonathan Cape, 1991, Pimlico, 1992, Chapter 9.

26. Virago Introduction to *On the Side of the Angels*, xiv.

27. Betty Miller, 'Notes for an Unwritten Autobiography', *Modern Reading 13*, ed. R Moore, no. 13, 1945.

28. Nancy Huston, 'The Matrix of War: Mothers and Heroes', *The Female Body in Western Culture*, ed. Susan Sulieman, Harvard University Press, 1986, 128.

29. See Chris Weedon, *Feminist Practice and Poststructuralist Theory*, Blackwell, Oxford 1987, 51ff.

10. Olivia Manning: Front Line of One, pp. 179–197

1. Walter Allen described the first two novels' 're-creation of history in fiction' as 'remarkable' and 'entirely admirable', *Tradition and Dream*, Penguin, 1964, 282.

2. Anthony Burgess, *The Novel Now*, Faber, 1967, 95.

3. Alan Munton, *English Fiction of the Second World War*, Faber, 1989, 108.

4. Barbara Pym, 'Balkan Capital' (1941), reprinted in *Wave Me Goodbye, Stories of the Second World War*, ed. Anne Boston, Virago, 1988; Penguin, 1989.

5. Olivia Manning, 'Poets in Exile', *Horizon*, vol. X, no. 58, December 1944.

6. Olivia Manning, 'Twilight of the Gods', *Growing Up, A Collection of Short Stories*, Heinemann, 1948.

7. Olivia Manning, 'A Journey', *Growing Up, A Collection of Short Stories*, 1948, reprinted in *Wave Me Goodbye*.

8. Niamh Baker discusses the book in *Happily Ever After? Women's Fiction in Postwar Britain 1945–60*, Macmillan, 1989, 102–104.

9. An interesting comparison offers itself in Edith Pargeter's war trilogy, *The Eighth Champion of Christendom* (Heinemann 1945–1947). Pargeter's soldier-hero dutifully visits every theatre of war, from Dunkirk to North Africa, the Far East and India, and back to Europe for the Second Front.
10. This is in Chapter 7 of *The Spoilt City*.
11. See Harry J. Mooney Jr, 'Olivia Manning: Witness to History' in *Twentieth Century Women Novelists*, ed. T.F. Staley, Macmillan, 1982.
12. Olivia Manning, 'Middle East Letter', *Modern Reading 9*, ed. R. Moore, 1944.
13. See Robert K. Morris, 'Olivia Manning's *Fortunes of War*: Breakdown in the Balkans, Love and Death in the Levant', *British Novelists since 1900*, ed. Jack I. Biles, AMS Press, New York, 1986. Morris acclaims Manning's 'six-volume novel sequence' as 'one of the most remarkable books published in the last twenty-five years'.
14. Olivia Manning, 'Middle East Letter'.
15. 'Among the younger men whom the army has brought out here, Keith Douglas stands alone. He has been in contact with the enemy much of the time and he is the only poet who has written poems comparable with the works of the better poets of the last war and likely to be read as war poems when the war is over' (Manning, 'Poets in Exile', *Horizon*, 1944). The differences between Boulderstone and Douglas might be traced to the gender of their authors: Manning's protagonist is a learner and a feeler, moving between euphoria and desolation. Douglas, by contrast, presents himself as an observer and a doer.
16. Rachel Trickett, an admirer of Manning's work, observes that *The Battle Lost and Won* is 'obsessed with death . . . all the civilian characters seem to have suffered from some spiritual deadening', *Times Literary Supplement*, 24 November 1978.
17. See John W. Gordon, *The Other Desert War, British Special Forces in North Africa, 1940–1943*, Greenwood Press, New York and London, 1987.

Post-War Post-script, pp. 198–204

1. Selina Hastings, *Nancy Mitford: A Biography*, Hamish Hamilton, 1985, 128, and Nancy Mitford, Prefatory Note to *Pigeon Pie*, 1951 edition.
2. Hastings, *Nancy Mitford*, 165.
3. Elizabeth Taylor, 'Gravement Endommage', *Hester Lilly and Other Stories*, Peter Davies, 1954, reprinted in *Wave Me Goodbye, Stories of the Second World War*, ed. Anne Boston, Virago, 1988; Penguin, 1989.
4. The smoke of the title also has connotations particular to London, as Allingham's prefatory note reminds us: 'In the shady ways of Britain today it is customary to refer to the Metropolis of London as the Smoke'.
5. Jane Emery, *Rose Macaulay: A Writer's Life*, John Murray, 1991, 285.
6. David Mellor has traced the neo-Romantic figure of the 'child in the ruins' in

post-war British films, books, magazines and paintings, in 'The Body and the Land', *Paradise Lost: The Neo-Romantic Imagination in Britain 1935–55*, ed. David Mellor, Lund Humphries in association with the Barbican Art Gallery, 1987.

7. Phyllis Lassner, 'Reimagining the Arts of War; Language and History in Elizabeth Bowen's *The Heat of the Day* and Rose Macaulay's *The World My Wilderness*', *Perspectives in Contemporary Literature* 14, 1988.

8. Kay Boyle's *A Frenchman Must Die* (Faber, 1946) follows this war after the war more closely; ' "Nothing, nothing is over" ' says one of the Resistance heroes locked into battle with the collaborators and the Milice, the French version of the SS.

9. See Penelope Fitzgerald's Introduction to the Virago edition of *The World My Wilderness*, 1992.

10. Macaulay agreed with this description of the book by her spiritual confidant, Father Johnson; see Emery, *Rose Macaulay*, 288.

11. Elizabeth Bowen, 'I Hear You Say So', *New Writing and Daylight*, September 1945, reprinted in *The Collected Stories of Elizabeth Bowen*, Jonathan Cape, 1980; Penguin, 1983.

BIBLIOGRAPHY

The place of publication is London unless otherwise stated.

CONTEMPORARY SOURCES

Fiction

Only works mentioned in the text are listed here, with details of the original publication and, where relevant, additional details of editions used.

Adam, Ruth, *Murder in the Home Guard*, Chapman & Hall, 1942
Allingham, Margery, *Traitor's Purse*, Heinemann, 1941; Penguin, 1950
–, *Dance of the Years*, Michael Joseph, 1943
–, *Tiger in the Smoke*, Chatto & Windus, 1952; Penguin, 1957
Ashton, Helen, *Tadpole Hall*, Collins, 1941
–, *Yeoman's Hospital*, Collins, 1944
Beauclerk, Helen, *Shadows on a Wall*, Gollancz, 1941
Bell, Josephine, *Martin Croft*, Longmans, Green & Co., 1941
Boston, Anne, ed., *Wave Me Goodbye, Stories of the Second World War*, Virago, 1988; Penguin, 1989
Bottome, Phyllis, *The Mortal Storm*, Faber, 1937
–, *London Pride*, Faber, 1941
–, *Within the Cup*, Faber, 1943
Bowen, Elizabeth, *The Heat of the Day*, Jonathan Cape, 1949; Penguin, 1962
–, *The Collected Stories of Elizabeth Bowen*, Jonathan Cape, 1980; Penguin, 1983
Bowers, Dorothy, *A Deed without a Name*, Hodder & Stoughton, 1940
Boyle, Kay, *A Frenchman Must Die*, Faber, 1946

Brand, Christianna, *Heads You Lose*, John Lane, The Bodley Head, 1941; Penguin, 1950

Brittain, Vera, *Account Rendered*, Macmillan, 1945

Brooke-Rose, Christine, *The Languages of Love*, Secker & Warburg, 1957

Bryher, *Beowulf*, Pantheon Books, New York, 1956

Buckley, Eunice, *Destination Unknown*, Andrew Dakers, 1942

Chapman, Hester, *Long Division*, Secker & Warburg, 1943

Christie, Agatha, *N or M?*, Collins, 1941

Cole, G.D.H. and Margaret, *Toper's End*, Collins, 1942

Compton-Burnett, Ivy, *Parents and Children*, Gollancz, 1941

Constantine, Murray, *Swastika Night*, Gollancz, 1937; 1940

Cooper, Lettice, *Black Bethlehem*, Gollancz, 1947

Cowlin, Dorothy, *Winter Solstice*, Jonathan Cape, 1942; Merlin Press, 1991

Crompton, Richmal, *Mrs Frensham Describes a Circle*, Macmillan, 1942

–, *Weatherley Parade*, Macmillan, 1944

Dane, Clemence, *The Arrogant History of White Ben*, Heinemann, 1939

–, *He Brings Great News*, Heinemann, 1944

Delafield, E.M., *Late and Soon*, Macmillan, 1943

Dickens, Monica, *Mariana*, Michael Joseph, 1940; Penguin, 1950

–, *The Fancy*, Michael Joseph, 1943; Penguin, 1964

–, *The Happy Prisoner*, Michael Joseph, 1946, Penguin, 1958

Douglas, Keith, *Alamein to Zem Zem*, Editions Poetry London, 1946; Faber, 1992

du Maurier, Daphne, *Come Wind, Come Weather*, Heinemann, 1940

–, *Frenchman's Creek*, Gollancz, 1941; Arrow, 1992

–, *Hungry Hill*, Gollancz, 1943

–, *The King's General*, Gollancz, 1946; Penguin, 1962

Ertz, Susan, *Anger in the Sky*, Hodder & Stoughton, 1943

Ferguson, Rachel, *A Footman for the Peacock*, Jonathan Cape, 1940

Frankau, Pamela, *The Willow Cabin*, Heinemann, 1949; Virago, 1988

Gellhorn, Martha, *A Stricken Field*, Duell, Sloan & Pearce, New York, 1940; Virago, 1986

–, *Liana*, Home & Van Thal Ltd, 1944; Virago, 1987

–, *The Wine of Astonishment*, Charles Scribner's Sons, New York, 1948

–, *The Honeyed Peace*, Andrew Deutsch, 1954; Penguin, 1958

Gibbons, Stella, *The Rich House*, Longmans, Green & Co., 1941

–, *The Bachelor*, Longmans, Green & Co., 1944

–, *Westwood*, Longmans, Green & Co., 1946

Graham, Gwethalyn, *Earth and High Heaven*, Jonathan Cape, 1944

Green, Henry, *Caught*, The Hogarth Press, 1943

Greene, Graham, *The Ministry of Fear*, Heinemann, 1943; Penguin, 1963

Hill, Diana Murray, *Ladies May Now Leave Their Machines*, The Pilot Press Ltd, 1944

Holden, Inez, *Night Shift*, John Lane, The Bodley Head, 1941

–, 'Fellow Travellers in Factory', *Horizon*, vol. 3, February 1941

–, *There's No Story There*, John Lane, The Bodley Head, 1944

–, *To The Boating and Other Stories*, John Lane, The Bodley Head, 1945

Iles, Margaret, *Nobody's Darlings*, Gollancz, 1942

Jameson, Storm, *In the Second Year*, Cassell & Co., 1936

–, *The Other Side*, Macmillan, 1946

Johnson, Pamela Hansford, *The Family Pattern*, Collins, 1942

–, *Winter Quarters*, Collins, 1943

–, *The Trojan Brothers*, Michael Joseph, 1944

–, *An Avenue of Stone*, Michael Joseph, 1947

Lane, Margaret, *Where Helen Lies*, Heinemann, 1944

Laski, Marghanita, *Little Boy Lost*, The Cresset Press, 1949

–, *The Village*, The Cresset Press, 1952

Lehmann, Rosamond, *The Ballad and the Source*, Collins, 1944; Virago, 1984

–, *The Gipsy's Baby*, Collins, 1946; Virago, 1982

–, *A Sea-Grape Tree*, Collins, 1976; Virago, 1982

Leslie, Doris, *House in the Dust*, Hutchinson & Co., 1942

–, *Polonaise, A Romance of Chopin*, Hodder & Stoughton, 1943

Lewis, Eiluned, *The Captain's Wife*, Macmillan, 1943

Lewis, Lorna, *Tea and Hot Bombs*, Oxford University Press, Oxford, 1943

Macaulay, Rose, 'Miss Anstruther's Letters' (1942), in Boston, ed., *Wave Me Goodbye*, 1988

–, *The World My Wilderness*, Collins, 1950; Virago, 1983

McKenna, Marthe, *The Spy in Khaki*, Jarrolds, 1941

Manning, Olivia, 'Twilight of the Gods', 'A Spot of Leave' and 'A Journey', in *Growing Up, A Collection of Short Stories*, Heinemann, 1948

–, *Artist Among the Missing*, Heinemann, 1949; 1975

–, *School for Love*, Heinemann, 1951; Penguin, 1982

–, *A Different Face*, Heinemann, 1953

–, *The Great Fortune*, Heinemann, 1960; Penguin, 1974

–, *The Spoilt City*, Heinemann, 1962; Penguin, 1974

–, *Friends and Heroes*, Heinemann, 1965; Penguin, 1974

–, *The Romantic Hero and Other Stories*, Heinemann, 1967

–, *The Danger Tree*, Weidenfeld & Nicolson, 1977; published as *The Levant Trilogy*, Penguin, 1982

–, *The Battle Lost and Won*, Weidenfeld & Nicolson, 1978; published as *The Levant Trilogy*, Penguin, 1982

–, *The Sum of Things*, Weidenfeld & Nicolson, 1980; published as *The Levant Trilogy*, Penguin, 1982

Marsh, Eileen, *We Lived in London*, Lutterworth Press, 1942

Maybury, Anne, *Arise, Oh Sun!*, Collins, 1942

Miller, Betty, *Farewell Leicester Square*, Robert Hale, 1941

–, *On the Side of the Angels*, Robert Hale, 1945; Virago, 1985

Mitchell, Gladys, *When Last I Died*, Michael Joseph, 1941; The Hogarth Press, 1985

–, *Laurels are Poison*, Michael Joseph, 1942

Mitford, Nancy, *The Pursuit of Love*, Hamish Hamilton, 1945; Penguin, 1949

Morrison, Margaret, and Pamela Tulk-Hart, *Paid to be Safe*, Hutchinson, 1948

Myers, Elizabeth, *A Well Full of Leaves*, Chapman & Hall, 1943

–, *The Basilisk of St James's*, Chapman & Hall, 1945

Nicholson, Jane, (pseud. of Marguerite Steen), *Shelter*, Harrap, 1941

Noble, Barbara, *The House Opposite*, Heinemann, 1943

O'Brien, Kate, *The Land of Spices*, Heinemann, 1941; Virago, 1988

–, *The Last of Summer*, Heinemann, 1943; Virago, 1990

Oliver, Jane, *The Hour of the Angel*, Collins, 1942

–, *In No Strange Land*, Collins, 1944

Oman, Carola, *Nothing To Report*, Hodder & Stoughton, 1940

Panter-Downes, Mollie, *One Fine Day*, Hamish Hamilton Ltd, 1947; Virago, 1985

Pargeter, Edith, *She Goes to War*, Heinemann, 1942; Headline Book Publishing plc, 1990

–, *The Eighth Champion of Christendom*, Heinemann, 1945; Headline Book Publishing plc, 1990

–, *Reluctant Odyssey*, Heinemann, 1946; Headline Book Publishing plc, 1990

–, *Warfare Accomplished*, Heinemann, 1947; Headline Book Publishing plc, 1990

Peck, Winifred, *House-Bound*, Faber, 1942

–, *There is a Fortress*, Faber, 1945

Powell, Anthony, *The Valley of Bones*, Heinemann, 1964; Fontana, 1973

–, *The Soldier's Art*, Heinemann, 1966; Fontana, 1968

–, *The Military Philosophers*, Heinemann, 1968; Fontana, 1971

Preedy, George (pseud. of Marjorie Bowen), *Findernes' Flowers*, Hodder & Stoughton, 1941

Price, Evadne, *Jane the Patient*, Robert Hale, 1940

–, *Jane At War*, Robert Hale, n.d.

Pym, Barbara, *Civil to Strangers and Other Writings*, Macmillan, 1987

Renault, Mary, *The Friendly Young Ladies*, Longmans, Green & Co., 1944; Virago, 1984

–, *North Face*, Longmans, Green & Co., 1949

–, *The Charioteer*, Longmans, Green & Co., 1953

Robertson, E. Arnot, *The Signpost*, Jonathan Cape, 1943

Ross, Jean, *Aunt Ailsa*, Eyre & Spottiswoode, 1944

Russell, Sarah (pseud. of Marghanita Laski), *To Bed with Grand Music*, The Pilot Press, 1946

Sackville-West, Vita, *Grant Canyon*, Michael Joseph, 1942

Sayers, Dorothy L., 'Tallboys' (1942), in *Striding Folly*, Hodder & Stoughton, 1972

Smith, Stevie, *The Holiday*, Chapman & Hall, 1949; Virago, 1979

Stern, G.B., *The Young Matriarch*, Cassell & Co., 1942; Tom Stacey Ltd, 1971

Stirling, Monica, 'Marie Bashkirtseff and the Hitler Youth', in Schimanski, Stefan and Henry Treece (eds), *Transformation two*, Lindsay Drummond Ltd, 1944

Streatfeild, Noel, *I Ordered a Table for Six*, Collins, 1942

–, *Saplings*, Collins, 1945

Talbot, Laura, *The Gentlewomen*, Macmillan, 1952; Virago, 1985

Taylor, Elizabeth, *At Mrs Lippincote's*, Peter Davies, 1945; Virago, 1988

–, *A View of the Harbour*, Peter Davies, 1947; Virago, 1987

–, *Hester Lilly*, Peter Davies, 1954; Virago, 1990

Tey, Josephine, *Miss Pym Disposes*, Peter Davies, 1946; Penguin, 1983

Thirkell, Angela, *The Brandons*, Hamish Hamilton, 1939

–, *Cheerfulness Breaks In*, Hamish Hamilton, 1940

–, *Growing Up*, Hamish Hamilton, 1943

–, *The Headmistress*, Hamish Hamilton, 1944

Tracy, Honor, *The Deserters*, Methuen, 1950

Turk, Frances, *Five Grey Geese*, Wright & Brown Ltd, 1944

Warner, Sylvia Townsend, *A Garland of Straw and Other Stories*, Chatto & Windus, 1943

–, *The Museum of Cheats and Other Stories*, Chatto & Windus, 1947

–, *The Corner That Held Them*, Chatto & Windus, 1948; Virago, 1988

–, *Winter in the Air and Other Stories*, Chatto & Windus, 1955

–, *One Thing Leading to Another and Other Stories*, S. Pinney, (ed.) Chatto & Windus, The Hogarth Press, 1984

–, *Selected Stories*, Chatto & Windus, 1989; Virago, 1990

Waugh, Evelyn, *Put Out More Flags*, Chapman & Hall, 1942; Penguin, 1943

Wentworth, Patricia, *The Chinese Shawl*, Hodder & Stoughton, 1943

–, *Miss Silver Intervenes*, Hodder & Stoughton, 1944

Westmacott, Mary, (pseud. of Agatha Christie), *Absent in the Spring*, Collins, 1944

Whipple, Dorothy, *They Were Sisters*, John Murray, 1943

Wilenski, Marjorie, *Table Two*, Faber, 1942

Winsor, Kathleen, *Forever Amber*, Macdonald & Co., 1945

Wise, A.R.J. and Reginald A. Smith (eds), *Voices on the Green*, Michael Joseph, 1945

Woolf, Virginia, *Between the Acts*, The Hogarth Press, 1941; Penguin, 1992

–, *Pointz Hall, The Earlier and Later Typescripts*, ed. M. Leaska, University Publications, New York, 1983

Non-fiction

Anckorn, Fergus, Papers, Department of Documents, Imperial War Museum

Assheton, Ralph, 'The Call-Up of Women', *Listener*, 10 April 1941

Askwith, Betty, 'Part-time Worker', *Spectator*, 29 May 1942

Barford, Mirren and Lieutenant John Lewes, *Joy Street: A Wartime Romance in*

Letters, 1940–1942, ed. M.T. Wise, Little, Brown & Co., 1995

Batstone, Stephanie, Papers, Department of Documents, Imperial War Museum

Baxter, Richard, *Guilty Women*, Quality Press Ltd, 1941

Belsey, Elizabeth, Papers, Department of Documents, Imperial War Museum

Benson, Theodora, *Sweethearts and Wives, Their Part in the War*, Faber, 1942

Bishop, Lucy, *Henfield in Battledress: Pages from a Scrap Book*, 1947; L. Bishop, Henfield, 1981

Blythe, Ronald, ed. *Private Words, Letters and Diaries from the Second World War* Viking Penguin, 1991

Bottome, Phyllis, *From the Life*, Faber, 1944

Bowen, Elizabeth, 'Eire', *New Statesman and Nation*, 12 April 1941

–, *Bowen's Court*, Longmans, Green & Co., 1942

–, *Seven Winters, Memories of a Dublin Childhood*, Longmans, Green & Co., 1943

–, *Why Do I Write? An Exchange of Views between Elizabeth Bowen, Graham Greene and V.S. Pritchett*, Percival Marshall, 1948

–, *Collected Impressions*, Longmans, Green & Co., 1950

–, *The Mulberry Tree*, ed. H. Lee, Virago, 1986

Braithwaite, Brian, Noelle Walsh and Glyn Davies, eds, *The Home Front, The Best of Good Housekeeping 1939–1945*, Ebury Press, 1987

Brittain, Vera, *England's Hour*, Macmillan, 1941

–, *Diary 1939–1945, Wartime Chronicle*, eds A. Bishop and Y.A. Bennett, Gollancz, 1989

Buchanan, Captain P.A., Papers, Department of Documents, Imperial War Museum

Church-Bliss, Kathleen and Elsie Whiteman, 'We Had To Laugh', Typescript of War Diary 1942–1945, Department of Documents, Imperial War Museum

Cole, Margaret, 'General Effects: Billeting', eds R. Padley and M. Cole, *Evacuation Survey*, Routledge, 1940

Cooper, Duff, 'Join the Ranks of the Silent Column', *Listener*, 18 July 1940

Day-Lewis, Tamasin (ed.), *Last Letters Home*, Macmillan, 1995

Dunn, Elizabeth, 'Women's Minds', *Spectator*, 14 December 1943

Figes, Eva, ed., *Women's Letters in Wartime*, Pandora Press, 1993

Forster, E.M., 'Books in 1941', *Listener*, 10 July 1941

Garbett, Cyril, *Reading in Wartime*, English Association Presidential Address, Oxford University Press, Oxford, 1945

Gellhorn, Martha, *The Face of War*, Hart Davis, 1959; revised and updated Granta Books, 1993

Goldsmith, Margaret, *Women at War*, Lindsay Drummond Ltd, 1943

Gordon, John, *The Other Desert War, British Special Forces in North Africa 1940–43*, Greenwood Press, New York and London, 1987

Graves, Charles, *Women in Green, The Story of the WVS*, Heinemann, 1948

Graves, Robert, 'War Poetry in this War', *Listener*, 23 November 1941

Grist, Donald, Papers, Department of Documents, Imperial War Museum

Harries, Margaret, née Rushton, Papers, Department of Documents, Imperial War Museum

Harrison, Tom, 'War Books', *Horizon*, vol. 4, December 1941

Hartley, Jenny, ed., *Hearts Undefeated, Women's Writing of the Second World War*, Virago, 1994

Hay, Ian, *The Post Office Went to War*, HMSO, 1946

Higgins, Mrs P.M., Papers, Department of Documents, Imperial War Museum

Holden, Inez, *It Was Different at the Time*, John Lane, The Bodley Head, 1943

Hopkinson, Diana, 'Love in War', Typescript, Department of Documents, Imperial War Museum

Kirby, Joan, Papers, Department of Documents, Imperial War Museum

Klein, Melanie, *The Selected Melanie Klein*, ed. J. Mitchell, Penguin 1986

Koestler, Arthur, 'The Birth of a Myth', *Horizon*, vol. 7, April 1943

Last, Nella, *Nella Last's War, A Mother's Diary 1939–1945*, eds R. Broad and S. Fleming, Falling Wall Press, Bristol, 1981

Lehmann, Rosamond, 'A Charming Person' (Review of *Mrs Miniver*), *Spectator*, 10 November 1939

–, 'Letter to a Friend', *Penguin New Writing*, vol. 5, 1941

Lejeune, C.A., *Chestnuts in Her Lap, 1936–1946*, Phoenix House, 1947

Litoff, Judy Barrett, and David C. Smith, *Since You Went Away, World War II Letters from American Women on the Home Front*, Oxford University Press, Oxford, 1991

Mallard, Denis, 'New Novels', *Time and Tide*, 12 June 1943

Mannin, Ethel, 'Contemporary British Fiction', *Modern Reading 8*, ed. R. Moore, Wells, Gardner, Darton & Co., 1943

–, 'Do Women Writers Lack Distinction?', *London Calling*, 261, 8 October 1944

Manning, Olivia, 'Poets in Exile', *Horizon*, vol. 10 no. 58, October 1944

–, 'Middle East Letter', *Modern Reading*, 9, ed. R. Moore, Wells, Gardner, Darton & Co., 1944

Mass-Observation, *War Factory* 1943; The Cresset Press, Century Hutchinson, 1987

Michie, Alan, and Walter Graebner, eds, *Their Finest Hour, The War in the First Person*, George Allen & Unwin, 1940

Morgan, Fidelis, ed., *The Years Between*, Virago, 1994

Moore, Henry, *A Shelter Sketchbook*, British Museum Publications, 1988

Moore, Pamela, Papers, Department of Documents, Imperial War Museum

Nicholson, Jenny, *Kiss the Girls Good-Bye*, Hutchinson, 1944

Ould, Herman, ed., *Writers in Freedom, A Symposium Based on the XVII International Congress of the P.E.N. Club Held in London in September 1941*, Hutchinson, 1942

Panter-Downes, Mollie, *London War Notes 1939–1945*, Farrar, Straus & Giroux, New York, 1971

Partridge, Frances, *A Pacifist's War*, The Hogarth Press, 1978

Planet, Jane, *What Should Mrs A Do?*, Thacker & Co., Bombay, 1945

Priestley, J.B., *British Women Go To War*, Collins, 1943

Pym, Barbara, *A Very Private Eye, An Autobiography in Letters and Diaries*, eds H. Holt and H. Pym, Macmillan, 1984

Ranfurly, Countess of, *To War with Whitaker: The Wartime Diaries of the Countess of Ranfurly 1939–45*, Heinemann, 1994

Reading, The Dowager Marchioness of, 'Women's Voluntary Service', *The Fortnightly*, April 1945

Reaveley, Constance, 'The Machine and the Mind', *Spectator*, 7 April 1944

Reilly, Catherine, ed., *Chaos of the Night, Women's Poetry and Verse of the Second World War*, Virago, 1984

Ritchie, Charles, *The Siren Years, Undiplomatic Diaries 1937–1945*, Macmillan, 1974

Sackville-West, Vita, *The Eagle and the Dove: A Study in Contrasts*, Michael Joseph, 1943

Sayers, Dorothy L., 'Wimsey Papers', *Spectator*, 17 November 1939, 22 December 1939, 12 January 1940

Scott, Peggy, *British Women in War*, Hutchinson, 1940

–, *They Made Invasion Possible*, Hutchinson, 1944

Scott-James, Anne, 'More and More Nursery Schools', *London Calling*, 125, March 1942

Scovell, E.J., *Selected Poems*, Carcanet, Manchester, 1991

Sheridan, Dorothy, *Wartime Women, An Anthology of Women's Wartime Writing for Mass Observation*, Heinemann, 1990

Sitwell, Edith, *Selected Letters*, eds J. Lehmann and D. Parker, Macmillan, 1970

Stark, Freya, *Letters*, vol. 5, *New Worlds for Old, 1943–46*, ed. L. Moorehead, Michael Russell, 1978

Stein, Gertrude, *Wars I Have Seen*, Batsford, 1945; Brilliance Books, 1984

Stephenson, 'Report on Reorganisation of Censorship, 1940', Post Office Archive, Post 56/63

Stern, G.B., *Benefits Forgot*, Cassell, 1949

Struther, Jan, ed., *Women of Britain, Letters from England*, Harcourt Brace & Co., New York, 1941

Summerskill, Edith, 'Conscription and Women', *The Fortnightly*, March 1942

Swinnerton, Frank, 'The Writer in Wartime', *Harper's Magazine*, New York, August 1942

Tapert, Annette, ed., *Despatches from the Heart, An Anthology of Letters from the Front During the First and Second World Wars*, Hamish Hamilton, 1984

Thomas, Katherine, *Women in Nazi Germany*, Gollancz, 1943

Trilling, Diana, 'What Has Happened to our Novels?' *Harper's Magazine*, New York, May 1944

–, *Reviewing the Forties*, Harcourt Brace Jovanovich, New York, 1978

Waley, V.C.A., Papers, Department of Documents, Imperial War Museum

Walters, Anne-Marie, *Moondrop to Gascony*, Macmillan, 1946

Warner, Sylvia Townsend, *Letters*, ed. W. Maxwell, Chatto & Windus, 1982

–, *The Diaries of Sylvia Townsend Warner*, ed. C. Harman, Chatto & Windus, 1994

Wedgwood, C.V., 'Good Company', the *Spectator*, 20 November, 1942

Weil, Simone, *An Anthology*, ed. S. Miles, Virago, 1986

Whipple, Dorothy, *Random Commentary*, Michael Joseph, 1966

White, Antonia, *BBC At War*, BBC, 1941

Williams, Hugh and Margaret, *Always and Always, The Wartime Letters of Hugh and Margaret Williams*, John Murray, 1995

Williams-Ellis, Amabel, *Women in War Factories*, Gollancz, 1943

Woolf, Virginia, *Three Guineas*, 1938; The Hogarth Press, 1986

–, 'The Leaning Tower' (1940), *The Moment and Other Essays*, The Hogarth Press, 1947

–, *Roger Fry*, The Hogarth Press, 1940

–, *The Death of the Moth and Other Essays*, The Hogarth Press, 1942

–, *Leave the Letters Till We're Dead, The Letters of Virginia Woolf*, vol. VI, 1936–1941, eds N. Nicolson and J. Trautmann, The Hogarth Press, 1980

–, *The Diary of Virginia Woolf*, vol. V, 1936–1941, ed. A.O. Bell, The Hogarth Press, 1984

Wyndham, Joan, *Love Lessons, A Wartime Diary*, Heinemann, 1985

POST-WAR COMMENTARIES, MEMOIRS, BIOGRAPHY, HISTORY AND CRITICISM

Addison, Paul, *The Road to 1945, British Politics and The Second World War*, Jonathan Cape, 1975

Altman, Janet Gurkin, *Epistolarity, Approaches to a Form*, Ohio State University Press, Columbus, 1982

Anderson, Rachel, *The Purple Heart Throbs, The Sub-Literature of Love*, Hodder & Stoughton, 1974

Aspinall, Sue, 'Women, Realism and Reality in British Films 1943–1953', eds J. Curran and V. Porter, *British Cinema History*, Weidenfeld & Nicolson, 1983

Baker, Niamh, *Happily Ever After? Women's Fiction in Postwar Britain, 1945–60*, Macmillan, 1989

Balfour, Michael, *Propaganda in War, 1939–1945*, Routledge & Kegan Paul, 1979

Bannister, Sybil, *I Lived Under Hitler, An Englishwoman's Story of Her Life in Wartime Germany*, Rockcliff Publishing Corporation, 1957; Penguin, 1995

Bayley, John, *The Short Story, Henry James to Elizabeth Bowen*, Harvester, Sussex, 1978

Beauman, Nicola, *A Very Great Profession, The Woman's Novel 1914–39*, Virago, 1983; 1995

Begley, George, *Keep Mum! Advertising Goes to War*, Lemon Tree Press, 1975

Bennett, Andrew and Nicholas Royle, *Elizabeth Bowen and the Dissolution of the Novel*, Macmillan, 1995

Bentley, Phyllis, *'O Dreams, O Destinations!' An Autobiography*, Gollancz, 1962

Bergonzi, Bernard, *Wartime and Aftermath, English Literature and its Background 1939–1950*, Oxford University Press, Oxford, 1993

Birch, Sarah, *Christine Brooke-Rose and Contemporary Fiction*, Clarendon Press, Oxford, 1994

Boyle, Andrew, *The Climate of Treason*, Hutchinson & Co., 1979

Braybon, Gail, and Penny Summerfield, *Out of the Cage: Women's Experiences in Two World Wars*, Pandora, 1987

Breen, Jennifer, *In Her Own Write, Twentieth Century Women's Fiction*, Macmillan, 1990

Brooke-Rose, Christine, *Remake*, Carcanet, Manchester, 1996

Bryher, *The Heart to Artemis, A Writer's Memoirs*, Collins, 1963

–, *The Days of Mars, A Memoir 1940–1946*, Calder & Boyars, 1972

Bull, Angela, *Noel Streatfeild*, Collins, 1984

Bullock, Alan, *Hitler, A Study in Tyranny*, Odhams, 1952; Penguin, 1962

Cadogan, Mary and Patricia Craig, *Women and Children First: The Fiction of Two World Wars*, Gollancz, 1978

Calder, Angus, *The People's War, Britain, 1939–1945*, Jonathan Cape, 1969; Pimlico, 1992

–, *The Myth of the Blitz*, Jonathan Cape, 1991; Pimlico, 1992

Calder, Robert L., ' "A More Sinister Troth": Elizabeth Bowen's "The Demon Lover" as Allegory', *Studies in Short Fiction*, Newberry College, North Carolina, vol. 31, no. 1, Winter 1994

Cannadine, David, 'War and Death, Grief and Mourning in Modern Britain', ed. J. Whaley, *Mirrors of Mortality: Studies in the Social History of Death*, Europa Publications Ltd, 1981

Christie, Agatha, *An Autobiography*, Collins, 1977

Clarke, I.F., *Voices Prophesying War*, Oxford University Press, Oxford, 1966

Cooke, Miriam and Angela Woollacott (eds), *Gendering War Talk*, Princeton University Press, New Jersey, 1993

Cooper, Helen, M., Adrienne Auslander Munich, and Susan Merrill Squier, eds *Arms and the Woman: War, Gender and Literary Representation*, University of North Carolina Press, Chapel Hill, 1989

Costello, John, *Love, Sex and War: Changing Values 1939–45*, Collins, 1985

Croft, Andy, *Red Letter Days, British Fiction in the 1930s*, Lawrence & Wishart, 1990

Douie, Vera, *Daughters of Britain, An Account of British Women during the Second World War*, George Ronald, Oxford, 1950

Eisenberg, Nora, 'Virginia Woolf's Last Words on Words: *Between the Acts* and "Anon" ', ed. Jane Marcus, *New Feminist Essays on Virginia Woolf*, Macmillan, 1981

Elshtain, Jean Bethke, *Women and War*, Harvester, Sussex, 1987

Emery, Jane, *Rose Macaulay: A Writer's Life*, John Murray, 1991

Faviell, Frances, *A Chelsea Concerto*, Cassell, 1959

Featherstone, Simon, 'The Nation as Pastoral in British Literature of the Second World War', *Journal of European Studies*, vol. 16, 1986

Fielding, Steven, Peter Thompson, and Nick Tiratsoo,'*England Arise!': The Labour Party and Popular Politics in 1940s Britain*, Manchester University Press, Manchester, 1995

Forster, Margaret, *Daphne du Maurier*, Chatto & Windus, 1993

Foster, R.F., 'The Irishness of Elizabeth Bowen', *Paddy and Mr Punch*, Allen Lane, The Penguin Press, 1993

Fussell, Paul, *Wartime: Understanding and Behaviour in the Second World War*, Oxford University Press, Oxford, 1981

–, 'The Fate of Chivalry and the Assault upon Mother', *Killing in Verse and Prose and Other Essays*, Bellew Publishing, 1990

Gardiner, Sir Thomas, 'An Account of the Work of the Post Office during the Second World War', Post Office Archive, Post 56/63

Gilbert, Sandra and Susan Gubar, *No Man's Land, The Place of the Woman Writer in the Twentieth Century*, vol. 3, *Letters from the Front*, Yale University Press, New Haven and London, 1994

Gillette, Jane Brown, ' "Oh, What a Something Web We Weave": The Novels of Elizabeth Taylor', *Twentieth Century Literature*, vol. 1, no. 35, Spring 1989

Giles, Judy and Tim Middleton, *Writing Englishness 1900–1950*, Routledge 1995

Gledhill, Christine and Gillian Swanson, *Nationalising Femininity: Culture, Sexuality and British Cinema in the Second World War*, Manchester University Press, Manchester, 1996

Glendinning, Victoria, *Elizabeth Bowen, Portrait of a Writer*, Weidenfeld & Nicolson, 1977

–, *Edith Sitwell, A Unicorn Among Lions*, Weidenfeld & Nicolson, 1981

–, *Rebecca West, A Life*, Weidenfeld & Nicolson, 1987

Hancock, W.K., and M.M. Gowing, *British War Economy*, HMSO, 1949

Hanley, Lynne, *Writing War: Fiction, Gender and Memory*, University of Massachusetts Press, Amherst, 1991

Harman, Claire, *Sylvia Townsend Warner, A Biography*, Chatto & Windus, 1989

Harper, Sue, 'History with Frills: "Costume" Fiction in World War II', *Red Letters*, 14, 1982–1983.

–, 'The Representation of Women in British Feature Films, 1939–45', ed. P. Taylor, *British Cinema and the Second World War*, Macmillan, 1988

Hawthorn, Jeremy, *Cunning Passages: New Historicism, Cultural Materialism and Marxism in Contemporary Literary Debate*, Arnold, Hodder Headline, 1996

Hennessy, Peter, *Never Again, Britain 1945–1951*, Jonathan Cape, 1992

Hewison, Robert, *Under Siege, Literary Life in London 1939–1945*, Methuen, 1977

Hickman, Tom, *What Did You Do in the War, Auntie?*, BBC Books, 1995

Higonnet, Margaret Randolph, Jane Jenson, Sonya Michel and Margaret Collins Weitz, eds, *Behind the Lines: Gender and the Two World Wars*, Yale University Press, New Haven and London, 1987

Hinsley, F.H. and A. Stripp (eds), *Codebreakers: The Inside Story of Bletchley Park*, Oxford University Press, Oxford, 1993

Hussey, Mark (ed.), *Virginia Woolf and War*, Syracuse University Press, Syracuse, 1991

Huston, Nancy, 'Tales of War and Tears of Women', *Women's Studies International Forum*, vol. 5, 3/4, 1982

Huston, Nancy, 'The Matrix of War: Mothers and Heroes', ed. S.R. Suleiman, *The Female Body in Western Culture*, Harvard University Press, Massachusetts, 1986

Ingram, Angela and Daphne Patai, eds, *Rediscovering Forgotten Radicals: British Women Writers 1889–1939*, University of North Carolina Press, Chapel Hill, 1993

Joannou, Maroula, *'Ladies, Please Don't Smash These Windows': Women's Writing, Feminist Consciousness and Social Change 1919–38*, Berg, Oxford, 1995

Jordan, Heather Bryant, *How Will the Heart Endure: Elizabeth Bowen and the Landscape of War*, University of Michigan Press, Ann Arbor 1992

Kaplan, E. Ann, 'Mothering, Feminism and Representation, The Maternal in Melodrama and the Woman's Film 1910–40', ed. C. Gledhill, *Home Is Where the Heart Is*, BFI, 1987

Kaplan, Janet Sidney, 'Rosamond Lehmann's *The Ballad and the Source*: A Confrontation with "The Great Mother"', *Twentieth Century Literature*, vol. 27, no. 2, Summer 1981

Kirkham, Pat and David Thoms, eds, *War Culture: Social Change and Changing Experience in World War II*, Lawrence & Wishart, 1995

Klein, Holger, ed., *The Second World War in Fiction*, Macmillan, 1984

Knowles, Sebastian, *A Purgatorial Flame: Seven British Writers in the Second World War*, The Bristol Press, Bristol, 1990

Kracauer, Siegfried, *From Caligari to Hitler: A Psychological History of the German Film*, Princeton University Press, New Jersey, 1947

Lant, Antonia, *Blackout: Reinventing Women for Wartime British Cinema*, Princeton University Press, New Jersey, 1991

Lassner, Phyllis, 'Reimagining the Arts of War: Language and History in Elizabeth Bowen's *The Heat of the Day* and Rose Macaulay's *The World My Wilderness*', *Perspectives on Contemporary Literature*, vol. 14, 1988

–, 'The Quiet Revolution: World War II and the English Domestic Novel', *Mosaic*, University of Manitoba, Winnipeg, Summer 1990

–, *Elizabeth Bowen*, Macmillan, 1990

Lee, Hermione, *Elizabeth Bowen, An Estimation*, Vision Press, 1981

–, *Virginia Woolf*, Chatto & Windus, 1996

Lee-Selwyn, Aileen Armellini, *La Moglie Inglese*, Ibiskos Editrice, Rome, 1994

Lehmann, John, *I Am My Brother*, Longmans, Green & Co., 1960

Light, Alison, *Forever England: Femininity, Literature and Conservatism Between the Wars*, Routledge, 1991

Lynn, Vera, *Vocal Refrain, An Autobiography*, W.H. Allen, 1975

McAleer, Joseph, *Popular Reading and Publishing in Britain 1914–1950*, Clarendon Press, Oxford, 1992

MacDonald, Sharon, Pat Holden and Shirley Ardener, eds, *Images of Women in Peace and War*, Macmillan, 1987

McLaine, Ian, *Ministry of Morale, Home Front Morale and the Ministry of Information in World War II*, George Allen & Unwin, 1979

Maclaren-Ross, Julian, *Memoirs of the Forties*, Alan Ross Ltd, 1965

McLellan, David, *Simone Weil, Utopian Pessimist*, Macmillan, 1989

Marcus, Jane, ed., *Virginia Woolf, A Feminist Slant*, University of Nebraska Press, 1983

–, 'The Asylums of Antaeus: Women, War and Madness – Is there a Feminist Fetishism?', ed. H. Aram Veeser, *The New Historicism*, Routledge, 1989

Marder, Herbert, 'Virginia Woolf's "Conversion": *Three Guineas*, "Pointz Hall" and *Between the Acts*', *Journal of Modern Literature*, vol. 14, no. 4, Spring 1988

Marwick, Arthur, ed., *Total War and Social Change*, Macmillan, 1986

Mellor, David, ed., *A Paradise Lost: The Neo-Romantic Imagination in Britain 1935–1955*, Lund Humphries Ltd in Association with the Barbican Art Gallery, 1987

Miller, Joan, *One Girl's War, Personal Exploits in MI5's Most Secret Station*, Brandon Book Publishers Ltd, Dingle, Co. Kerry, 1986

Minney, R.J., *Carve Her Name with Pride*, George Newnes Ltd, 1956

Minns, Raynes, *Bombers and Mash: The Home Front 1939–1945*, Virago, 1980

Mitchell, J. Lawrence, 'In Another Country: Sylvia Townsend Warner at Large', eds R. Colt and J. Rossen, *Writers of the Old School: British Novelists of the 1930s*, Macmillan, 1992

Mooney, Harry J. Jr, 'Olivia Manning: Witness to History', ed. T. Staley, *Twentieth Century Women Novelists*, Macmillan, 1982

Morgan, David and Mary Evans, *The Battle for Britain: Citizenship and Ideology in the Second World War*, Routledge, 1993

Morgan, Janet, *Agatha Christie, A Biography*, Collins, 1984

Morris, Robert K., 'Olivia Manning's *Fortunes of War*: Breakdown in the Balkans, Love and Death in the Levant', ed. J. Biles, *British Novelists Since 1900*, AMS Press, New York, 1986

Mulford, Wendy, *This Narrow Place, Sylvia Townsend Warner and Valentine Ackland: Life, Letters and Politics 1930–1951*, Pandora Press, 1988

Munton, Alan, *English Fiction of the Second World War*, Faber, 1989

Patai, Daphne, 'Orwell's Despair, Burdekin's Hope: Gender and Power in Dystopia', *Women's studies International Forum*, vol. 7, 1984

Pick, Daniel, *War Machine: The Rationalisation of Slaughter in the Modern Age*, Yale University Press, New Haven and London, 1993

Piette, Adam, *Imagination at War: British Fiction and Poetry 1939–45*, Macmillan, 1995

Pinter, Harold, *The Heat of the Day, Adapted from the Novel by Elizabeth Bowen*, Faber, 1989

Plain, Gill, *Women's Fiction of the Second World War: Gender, Power and Resistance*, Edinburgh University Press, Edinburgh, 1996

Poole, Roger, *The Unknown Virginia Woolf*, Cambridge University Press, Cambridge, 1978

Quack, Sibylle, ed., *Between Sorrow and Strength; Women Refugees of the Nazi Period*, Cambridge University Press, Cambridge, 1995

Renier, Olive and Vladimir Rubinstein, *Assigned to Listen, The Evesham Experience 1939–43*, BBC, 1986

Riley, Denise, *War in the Nursery, Theories of the Child and Mother*, Virago, 1983

Robinson, Howard, *Carrying British Mails Overseas*, George Allen & Unwin, 1964

Rose, Jacqueline, *Why War? Psychoanalysis, Politics and the Return to Melanie Klein*, Blackwell, Oxford, 1993

Rupp, Leila, *Mobilising Women for War: German and American Propaganda 1939–1945*, Princeton University Press, New Jersey, 1978

Schneider, Karen, 'Of Two Minds: Woolf, The War and *Between the Acts*', *Journal of Modern Literature*, vol. 16, no. 1, Summer 1989

Schweik, Susan, *A Gulf So Deeply Cut: American Women Poets and the Second World War*, University of Wisconsin Press, Wisconsin, 1991

Silver, Brenda, ' "Anon" and "The Reader": Virginia Woolf's Last Essays', *Twentieth Century Literature* 25, 3/4, Autumn 1979

Simon, Judy, *Rosamond Lehmann*, Macmillan, 1992

Sinclair, Andrew, *War Like a Wasp: The Lost Decade of the 1940s*, Hamish Hamilton, 1989

Skelton, Barbara, *Tears Before Bedtime*, Hamish Hamilton, 1987

Smith, Harold, ed., *War and Social Change: British Society in the Second World War*, Manchester University Press, Manchester, 1986

Spalding, Frances, *Stevie Smith, A Critical Biography*, Faber, 1988

Spark, Muriel, *Curriculum Vitae*, Constable, 1992

Spender, Stephen, *The Thirties and After*, Fontana, 1978

Summerfield, Penny, *Women Workers in the Second World War: Production and Patriarchy in Conflict*, Croom Helm, 1984

Summerfield, Penny and Nicole Crockett, ' "You Weren't Taught That with the Welding": Lessons in Sexuality in the Second World War', *Women's History Review*, vol. 1, no. 3, 1992

Sweetman, David, *Mary Renault, A Biography*, Chatto & Windus, 1993

Taylor, D.J., *After the War: The Novel and English Society since 1945*, Chatto & Windus, 1993

Teissier du Cros, Janet, *Divided Loyalties: A Scotswoman in Occupied France*,

Hamish Hamilton, 1962; Canongate Press, Edinburgh, 1992

Tickell, Jerrard, *Odette, The Story of a British Agent*, Chapman & Hall, 1949

Tindall, Gillian, *Rosamond Lehmann: An Appreciation*, Chatto & Windus, The Hogarth Press, 1985

Tolley, A.T., *The Poetry of the Forties*, Manchester University Press, Manchester, 1985

Trickett, Rachel, 'Obsessed with Death: Olivia Manning's *The Battle Lost and Won*', *Times Literary Supplement*, 24 November 1978

Waller, Jane and Michael Vaughan-Rees, *Women in Wartime: The Role of Women's Magazines 1939–1945*, Optima MacDonald, 1987

Walters, Margaret, 'Romantic Pursuits, Rosamond Lehmann', *Encounter*, vol. LXV, no. 2, July/August 1985

Ward, Irene, *F.A.N.Y. Invicta*, Hutchinson, 1955

Watson, Barbara Bellow, 'Variations on an Enigma: Elizabeth Bowen's War Novel', *Southern Humanities Review*, vol. XV, no. 2, Spring 1981

Williams, Keith, *British Writers and the Media, 1939–45*, Macmillan, 1996

Woolf, Leonard, *The Journey Not the Arrival Matters*, The Hogarth Press, 1973

Young, Irene, *Enigma Variations: A Memoir of Love and War*, Mainstream Publishing, Edinburgh, 1990

ACKNOWLEDGEMENTS

Extracts from the Papers of Fergus Anckorn, Department of Documents, the Imperial War Museum, reprinted by permission of Fergus Anckorn and the Trustees of the Imperial War Museum. Extracts from the Papers of Elizabeth Belsey, Department of Documents, the Imperial War Museum, reprinted by permission of the author and the Trustees of the Imperial War Museum. Extracts from *The Heat of the Day* (© 1949) by Elizabeth Bowen, reproduced by permission of Curtis Brown, London. Extracts from the Typescript 'We Had To Laugh' by Kathleen Church-Bliss and Elsie Whiteman, Department of Documents, the Imperial War Museum, reprinted by permission of Mrs A.M. Spiers and the Trustees of the Imperial War Museum. Extracts from the Typescript 'Love in War' by Diana Hopkinson, Department of Documents, the Imperial War Museum, reprinted by permission of the author and the Trustees of Imperial War Museum. Extracts from the Papers of Joan Kirby, Department of Documents, the Imperial War Museum, reprinted by permission of the author (now Mrs Hatfield) and the Trustees of the Imperial War Museum. Extracts from *The Ballad and the Source* by Rosamond Lehmann, reprinted by permission of The Society of Authors as the literary representative of the Estate of Rosamond Lehmann.

My thanks go to my colleagues in the English Department at Roehampton Institute who provided teaching cover so that I could have study leave, and to the courteous and helpful librarians at the Roehampton Institute, the Imperial War Museum and the London Library. I am indebted to the friends who have listened, encouraged and made invaluable suggestion: Sarah Turvey, Ian Haywood, Paul McQuail, Ben Pimlott and Jean Seaton. To Elaine Showalter in the past and Nicola Beauman in the present I am grateful for support and expert advice; to

ACKNOWLEDGEMENTS

Cathy Wells-Cole I am indebted for hours of careful reading, and years of unflagging interest and illuminating suggestions. To my husband and sons, Ned and Gabriel, I am, as ever, thankful and appreciative for their cheer, good judgement and word-processing expertise.

BIOGRAPHICAL NOTES

Ruth **ADAM** (1907–1977), novelist and broadcaster, moved to London in 1937, had three young children during the war and worked for the Ministry of Information. She collaborated with her sister on a children's book about the American allies, *They Built a Nation* (1943).

Margery **ALLINGHAM** (1901–1966), detective novelist, helped organise evacuation and billeting in her Essex village, Tolleshunt D'Arcy, where her house became the local Warden's Post. She wrote *The Oaken Heart* (1941) about her village in wartime for her American publisher, but it was more popular in England, where it sold over 13,000 copies in two months.

Helen **ASHTON** (1891–1951) served as a nurse in the First World War and later qualified as a doctor. *Yeoman's Hospital* (1944) was made into a film called *White Corridors*.

Helen **BEAUCLERK** (1892–1969) published in French and English and worked as a translator and journalist in the First World War. With the approach of war in 1939 she decided that her previous choice of historical settings for her fiction was a form of escapism, and that a novelist's job was to describe contemporary life.

Josephine **BELL** (1897–1987), prolific author of mystery, historical and domestic fiction, had four children and was widowed in 1936. She worked as a GP in Guildford from 1936 until 1954, when she took up writing full-time.

Phyllis **BOTTOME** (1882–1963) lived for many years in Austria, until the Nazi occupation forced her back to England. She was greatly influenced by the psychological theories of Alfred Adler and wrote his biography. Between 1940 and 1943 she lectured for the Ministry of Information and moved to St Ives (Cornwall) in 1944.

Elizabeth **BOWEN** (1899–1973), Anglo-Irish novelist, lived in London throughout the war. She worked as an Air Raid Warden, and also visited Ireland (where she had a house) and reported to the Ministry of Information on Irish attitudes to the war.

Kay **BOYLE** (1902–1993), American novelist, poet, editor and translator, lived in the French Alps with her family until 1941, and helped Jews needing US visas. On her return to America she worked for the war effort and wrote about conditions in Europe.

Christianna **BRAND** (Mary Milne) (1909–1988) had a variety of jobs: nursery governess, professional ballroom dancer, secretary, mannequin, market gardener, house-decorator and saleswoman, as well as running a girls' club in the slums. She also wrote as Mary Ann Ashe, Annabel Jones, Mary Roland and China Thompson, and published historical romances, detective stories and children's books.

Vera **BRITTAIN** (1893–1970), writer and pacifist, worked tirelessly for pacificism during the war, lecturing and publishing, including her *Letters to Peace-Lovers*. Her 1944 pamphlet *Seed of Chaos* was almost the only public protest against the obliteration bombing of German cities.

BRYHER (Annie Winifred Ellerman) (1894–1983), novelist, poet and publisher of the library review *Life and Letters Today*, came to London from Switzerland in 1940. She shared a flat in Lowndes Square with the Imagist poet H.D. (Hilda Doolittle). *Beowulf* appeared in France in 1948, but Bryher could not find a publisher for the English version until 1956.

Eunice **BUCKLEY** (Rose Allatini) (c. 1890–1980) published *Despised and Rejected* (1918) under the pseudonym of A.T. Fitzroy, a novel about pacifism and homosexuality in the First World War, which was banned on publication. In 1941 Allatini left her husband, the composer and fellow-occultist Cyril Scott, and settled in Rye, Sussex, with Melanie Mills. Allatini published thirty novels as Eunice Buckley.

Hester **CHAPMAN** (1899–1976) worked as a school-mistress, governess, typist and telephonist. During the war she worked for the Fighting French, the American Red Cross and as a waitress in a canteen at Combined Operations.

Agatha **CHRISTIE** (1890–1976), described as the most commercially successful woman writer of all time, lived in London during the war and worked in the Dispensary at University College Hospital for half the week; for the other half she endeavoured to write two books at once. She also published under the name of Mary Westmacott.

Margaret **COLE** (1893–1980), socialist, feminist, political analyst and lecturer, was the Honorary Secretary of the Fabian Society during the war, and directed its successful summer schools.

Ivy **COMPTON-BURNETT** (1884–1969) spent the war in Dorset and Berkshire with Margaret Jourdain, 'fleeing from the bombs', with infrequent trips to their London flat. She continued to publish a novel every two years and was popular in the 1940s.

Murray **CONSTANTINE** (Katharine Burdekin) (1896–1963), anti-fascist and feminist author, published ten novels between 1922 and 1940 under her own name and her pseudonym. She also wrote many unpublished novels; her feminist utopia, *The End of This Day's Business*, was published by The Feminist Press in 1989. During the war Burdekin worked in a shoe factory.

Lettice **COOPER** (1897–1994) was the Public Relations Officer at the Ministry of Food from 1940 to 1945, an 'exceedingly interesting post,' according to Phyllis Bentley, 'answering thousands of queries which poured in from women when food-rationing started'. A lifelong socialist, Cooper lived with her sister in Bayswater and also worked for Civil Defence.

Dorothy **COWLIN** (1911–1962) was a graduate of Manchester University and author of at least eight novels. She was married to a school-master, had one daughter and lived in Yorkshire.

Richmal **CROMPTON** (1890–1969), author of the famous William stories for children, joined the Auxiliary Fire Service and did canteen work during the war. She continued to publish William stories as well a fiction for adults.

Clemence **DANE** (Winifred Ashton) (1887–1965), playwright, novelist and journalist, lived in Covent Garden for over thirty years. She became the President of the Society of Women Journalists in 1941 and was awarded the CBE in 1953.

E.M. **DELAFIELD** (Edmee Elizabeth Monica de la Pasture) (1890–1943), novelist and short story writer, lived in Devon during the war and lectured for the Ministry of Information. She was also involved with the work of the Women's Institutes. *The Provincial Lady in Wartime* (1940) is set in London in the first three months of the war and follows the Provincial Lady's quest for war work.

Monica **DICKENS** (1915–1992) had a succession of jobs which she turned into popular autobiographical accounts: work as a cook-general led to *One Pair of Hands* (1939) and nursing to *One Pair of Feet* (1942). She was directed to work in a factory repairing Spitfires, but later returned to nursing for the rest of the war.

Daphne **DU MAURIER** (1907–1989) wrote historical fiction during the war, as well as stories for Moral Rearmament. She lived in Hertfordshire and Cornwall, looking after her young family. In 1943 she finally obtained the lease for Menabilly, the Cornish house she 'loved(d) more than people', and devoted her energies to restoring it.

Susan **ERTZ** (1887–1985), Anglo-American novelist, did canteen work for American soldiers in England in the First World War.

Rachel **FERGUSON** (1898–1957), co-founder of the Juvenile Branch of the WSPU in 1910, actress, journalist and novelist. Ferguson was the first woman to sign her articles in *Punch*, to which she contributed as 'Rachel'. During the war she lived in Kensington, where she was bombed out.

Pamela **FRANKAU** (1908–1967), novelist, journalist and reviewer, served in the ATS, rising in rank from private to major. In 1942 she was received into the Roman Catholic Church. During her lifetime her novels were widely read; *The Willow Cabin* (1949) is her most acclaimed work.

Martha **GELLHORN** (b. 1908), distinguished American war correspondent and novelist, wrote for the American magazine *Collier's* during the war. She travelled widely and reported from Finland, China, England, Italy, France and Germany.

Stella **GIBBONS** (1902–1989), novelist, journalist, poet. Her first novel, *Cold Comfort Farm* (1932) was her most popular. She lived in Highgate in the war, while her husband was away in the Army. She was elected a Fellow of the Royal Society of Literature in 1950.

Gwethalyn **GRAHAM** (1913–1965), Canadian novelist, short story writer and journalist. *Earth and High Heaven* (1944) was her second novel and her best known; highly successful, it was translated into ten languages.

Diana Murray **HILL** went into a munitions factory in 1942, persuaded by Ministry of Information propaganda. By 1944 her health had broken down, and she was released on medical grounds.

Inez **HOLDEN**, documentary journalist and writer, had a variety of wartime jobs in aircraft and Royal Ordnance factories, Civil Defence and the Red Cross. She was sent to report on the Nuremberg Trials.

Margaret **ILES** had four novels published by Victor Gollancz in the 1930s; their emphasis was on the countryside.

Storm **JAMESON** (1891–1986), novelist, essayist and fervent anti-fascist, was President of the English branch of PEN during the war, and worked vigorously on behalf of refugee writers. Her son served in the RAF.

Pamela **HANSFORD JOHNSON** (1912–1981), well-known novelist and critic; involved in left-wing politics, she edited the weekly cyclostyled *Chelsea Democrat*. She worked as an Air Raid Warden in Chelsea, but had to give up when she became pregnant in 1940. She moved out of London to live with her mother, and had a second child in 1944.

Margaret **LANE** (1906–1994), journalist, novelist and biographer, lived in Hampshire during the war.

Marghanita **LASKI** (1915–1988), novelist, journalist and broadcaster, had two children during the war. She also nursed, ran a dairy farm, worked in Intelligence and wrote her first novel, *Love on the Supertax* (1944) while she was in hospital for the birth of her second child. She also published under the name of Sarah Russell.

Rosamond **LEHMANN** (1901–1990), novelist, translator and short story writer, took her two small children to live with her mother after her marriage failed. She became a reader for her brother John Lehmann, editor of the magazine *New Writing*, and in 1941 embarked on a close relationship with the poet Cecil Day Lewis.

Doris **LESLIE** (1891–1982), novelist and historian, served in Civil Defence from 1941 to 1945 as an Air Raid Warden, and wrote *Polonaise* (1943) while working during the worst of the London blitz. It was translated into eight languages.

Eiluned **LEWIS** (1900–1979), poet, novelist, reviewer, and *Country Life's* longest standing contributor – her 'Countrywoman's Notes' appeared from 1944 to 1979. She married in 1937 and lived in Bletchingley (Surrey) and London during the war. Her first novel, *Dew on the Grass* (1934) about her childhood in Wales was much praised by the critics.

Lorna **LEWIS** drove a van for the Red Cross in France in June 1940. During the blitz she worked in London on a mobile canteen.

Rose **MACAULAY** (1881–1958), novelist, travel writer, broadcaster and critic, joined the London Auxiliary Ambulance Service as a part-time driver. Her flat was destroyed in the blitz. She spent some of the later part of the war in Portugal.

Marthe **MCKENNA** (b. c. 1896); a Belgian, McKenna spied for the British Secret Service during the First World War, was captured and condemned to death. Freed at the end of the war, she married an Englishman and published her autobiography in 1932. This launched her on a highly successful career as a writer of spy novels.

Olivia **MANNING** (1908–1980) went with her husband Reggie Smith to Bucharest in 1939, where he worked for the British Council. They went on to Greece and then to Egypt. In Jerusalem Manning worked for the Public Information Office and the British Council.

Eileen **MARSH** wrote novels for girls as well as adults, and published twenty-three novels in the 1930s and 40s.

Anne **MAYBURY** (Anne Buxton), a prolific romantic novelist, started publishing in the early 1930s. She also publishes as Katherine Troy.

Betty **MILLER** (1910–1965), novelist and biographer, moved round the country with her two young children and her husband, a major in the RAMC with a special interest in psychiatry.

Gladys **MITCHELL** (1901–1983), author of sixty-six detective novels, taught English and History in girls' boarding schools in London and Middlesex. She also wrote children's books, and published under the pseudonyms of Malcolm Torrie and Stephen Hockaby.

Nancy **MITFORD** (1904–1973) worked with evacuees and as an ARP driver; she also helped to run a canteen for French soldiers after Dunkirk. From 1942 she worked in Heywood Hill's bookshop in Curzon Street.

Margaret **MORRISON** published a steady flow of domestic fiction and books for children between the mid 1930s and the mid 1950s.

Elizabeth **MYERS** (c. 1913–1947) worked in Fleet Street but had to give up in 1943 for reasons of ill-health – she had TB. She worked for Chapman and Hall, the publishers, and married Littleton Powys in 1943. *A Well Full of Leaves* (1943), her first novel, was admired by the critics.

Jane **NICHOLSON** (Marguerite Steen) (1894–1975), novelist and playwright, had an early career in teaching and on the stage. Her best-seller *The Sun is My Undoing* (1941) took many years to write. During the war her London home was destroyed by a bomb.

Barbara **NOBLE** published six novels, mainly domestic fiction, between 1930 and 1952.

Kate **O'BRIEN** (1897–1974), Irish novelist, playwright and journalist, lived in

London and Oxford during the war and worked for the Ministry of Information.

Jane OLIVER (Helen Rees, b. 1903), author of historical and children's fiction. Her husband, Flight Lieutenant John Llewelyn Rhys, also a writer, was killed in action in 1940.

Carola OMAN (1897–1978) historical writer, nursed in both World Wars. She worked for the Red Cross, and from 1947 to 1958 served as the County President of the Hertfordshire branch.

Mollie PANTER-DOWNES (1906–1997), novelist and journalist, wrote her fortnightly 'Letter from London' for the *New Yorker*, starting in September 1939 and continuing throughout the war. She travelled up to London every week from her home in Surrey, where she lived with her two small daughters.

Edith PARGETER (1913–1995) served as Petty Officer in the WRNS, in the Signals Office of Western Approaches HQ, first in Portsmouth, then Liverpool. Part of the team which directed the Battle of the Atlantic, Pargeter was awarded the BEM 'for meritorious service'. Angered in 1938 by what she saw as Chamberlain's duplicity over Czechoslovakia, she became a fervent Czech supporter, taught herself the language and translated work by distinguished Czech writers. She also published under the name of Ellis Peters.

Winifred PECK (1882–1962), novelist and autobiographer, lived in London and Edinburgh with her husband Sir James Peck, the Scottish Education Secretary. Her brother Dilwyn Knox was one of the key cipher-breakers at Bletchley Park.

George PREEDY (Gabrielle Margaret Vere Long) (1888–1952) also published under the name of Marjorie Bowen, and at least six other pseudonyms. She published her first novel at sixteen, and was hugely productive, writing to support her family. More than a hundred and fifty books are credited to her.

Evadne PRICE (1896–1985), journalist, playwright and children's author, published *Not So Quiet* (1930) about the First World War under the name of Helen Zenna Smith. In 1943 she became the war correspondent for the *People*; she spent two years in France and Germany, where she visited Belsen soon after it was liberated. She also covered the Nuremberg Trials.

Barbara PYM (1913–1980), novelist, worked as a postal censor in Bristol; in 1943 she joined the WRNS and served in England and Italy.

Mary RENAULT (Eileen Mary Challans, 1905–1983) nursed full-time throughout the war, first in Bristol for the Emergency Medical Services, treating the wounded from Dunkirk, and then in Oxford. Her novels after *The Charioteer* (1953) are all set in classical times.

E. ARNOT ROBERTSON (1903–1961), novelist and reviewer, achieved success with her novel *Ordinary Families* (1933). During the war she worked as an adviser on films, and after the war she took a job lecturing to British forces in Central Europe and North Africa.

Jean ROSS (Irene Dale Hewson) published a steady flow of novels for adults and children between 1944 and 1966.

Sarah RUSSELL, see Marghanita LASKI.

Vita **SACKVILLE-WEST** (1892–1962), novelist, poet and gardening expert, spent the war at Sissinghurst Castle in Kent. She helped to organise the Women's Land Army in her area.

Dorothy L. **SAYERS** (1893–1957), novelist and playwright, broadcast and lectured for the war effort. Between 1940 and 1943 she worked on the controversial but successful *Man Born To Be King*, a twelve-part dramatization of the life of Christ for BBC Children's Hour.

Stevie **SMITH** (1902–1971), poet and novelist, was employed full-time as a secretary at Newnes, the publishers. She did much reviewing, as well as fire-watching.

G.B. **STERN** (Gladys Bertha Stern, 1890–1973), novelist and critic, her London flat was destroyed by an incendiary bomb in 1940. Her series of novels about the extended Rakonitz and Czelovar families are her best-known. From a Jewish family, Stern converted to Catholicism in 1947.

Monica **STIRLING** (b. c. 1920) lived in Paris before the war, and returned to England in 1940, where she worked for Charles de Gaulle in London. After the liberation she was commissioned by *The Atlantic Monthly* to report on life in France.

Noel **STREATFEILD** (1895–1986) worked as an Air Raid Warden in London, and ran a canteen service for the shelters in Deptford. She wrote novels for children and adults, and also published nine light romantic novels under the name of Susan Scarlett.

Laura **TALBOT** (Lady Ursula Chetwynd-Talbot, 1908–1966), married her second husband, Lieutenant Commander Michael Stewart, in 1942.

Elizabeth **TAYLOR** (1912–1975) looked after her two small children and described herself as 'living, during the war, a lonely life in the country,while my husband was in the RAF'.

Josephine **TEY** (Elizabeth MacKintosh, c. 1896–1952) trained and worked as a physical education teacher, before taking up writing full-time. She also wrote plays under the name of Gordon Daviot.

Angela **THIRKELL** (1890–1961) published her first 'Barsetshire' novel, *High Rising* in 1933; she published one a year from 1935 until 1960. In 1918 she married a Tasmanian and went to Australia with him, but returned to England after her marriage failed, and lived in Beaconsfield during the war. At the request of her American publisher, Alfred Knopf, she toned down what he saw as anti-semitism in *Cheerfulness Breaks In* (1940).

Honor **TRACY** (b. 1913), journalist, novelist and travel writer, worked at the Ministry of Information from 1942 to 1945, specialising in Japan.

Pamela **TULK-HART** (b. c. 1920) joined the Air Transport Auxiliary in 1942 and flew Spitfires, Hurricanes, Mustangs and Typhoons, delivering new bombers and fighters from the factories to their bases in Britain. She also had to fly damaged aircraft to repair facilities.

Frances **TURK** (b. 1915) published a steady output of domestic fiction from the 1930s to the 1960s.

Sylvia **TOWNSEND WARNER** (1913–1978), novelist, spent much of the war in Dorset with Valentine Ackland. She wrote short stories for the *New Yorker*, worked for the WVS and lectured for the WEA, the Labour Party and the forces. She also learnt rifle-shooting and grenade-throwing.

Patricia **WENTWORTH** (Dora Amy Elles, 1878–1961) had a fifty-year publishing career as the author of sixty-five detective stories. She lived in Surrey.

Dorothy **WHIPPLE** (1893–1966) lived in Northamptonshire during the war, and took in an evacuee towards the end. A successful novelist and short story writer, she was described by J.B. Priestley as having a 'kind of North Country Jane Austen quality'.

Marjorie **WILENSKI** was the wife of Reginald Wilenksi, the art historian. He worked for the foreign service of the BBC during the war, and together they bred champion English bull-dogs.

Kathleen **WINSOR** (b. 1919), American author; *Forever Amber* (1944), her first and most successful novel, was filmed in 1947. Winsor continued publishing until the late 1980s.

Virginia **WOOLF** (1882–1941), lived mainly at Rodmell near the Sussex coast, often disturbed by enemy planes and bombs. The Woolfs' London house was severely damaged by bombs.

INDEX